Brewed in Northants

A Directory of Northamptonshire Brewers 1450 to 1998
(including the Soke of Peterborough)

by
Mike Brown, with Brian Willmott

A Brewery History Society Publication

OXFORDSHIRE COUNTY COUNCIL	
3200292171	
Cypher	31.03.02
	£9.95

INTRODUCTION

Most people, if asked to associate an industry with Northamptonshire, would no doubt immediately respond with shoe-making. However, the county also has a proud history of brewing. The reason for any lack of awareness concerning this history, may be that we no longer have a regional brewer in the county. Although there is a major plant in the form of Carlsberg, the latter tends to stresses its international image. Nevertheless, the Danes have been in the county for a thousand years!

This book, as well as acting as a directory of those known to have brewed in the county, gives the story of the growth of the "common or commercial brewers". The main focus is on brewing, but some information on malting is also included, particularly where the brewer or family was involved with both, e.g. Peaches.

The scale of brewing can be summarised as follows:-

- domestic brewers e.g. the many town houses and estate houses such as Castle Ashby
- publican brewers or brewing victuallers at a retail level e.g. Scott at Aynho, also known as brew-pubs or home brew pubs
- common brewers selling to other publicans i.e. wholesale, also sometimes known as commercial brewers, and which often became incorporated as companies.

Older readers may recall some of those in the last category. The two major ones associated with the county town, Phipps and Northampton Brewing Company (NBC), amalgamated in the 1950s, to form one of the largest businesses in the region. However, they then disappeared into Watneys and were closed in the early 1970s.

Historically, NBC was well-respected for the training it provided for many brewers, but Phipps was probably better known around the county. The other two firms in town, in living memory, were the Abington Brewery Co and Mannings.

Outside of town, Kings of Syresham lasted until 1955, whilst Hopcraft and Norris of Brackley were still brewing as late as 1959. Smiths of Oundle was the last brewery in the county, outside of town, and survived until 1962, being closed because it was brewing and selling to capacity! Had the business survived into the 1970s, to see the renewed interest in "real ale" and local products, the county might have retained some of its eminence.

Wellingborough did survive as a malting town into the seventies, but was also famous for its water, most useful in producing good beer. Indeed its popularity was such that it came close to becoming a spa town. One of the town's two breweries was Dulleys, whose Redwell Stout was named after one of the famous wells. The other business was Praeds, which took over Dulleys in 1920, but were themselves taken over and closed by Phipps in 1954. The rivalry between

drinkers concerning the merits of these local brews can be summed up:

> *"Phipps's beer is very good*
> *Dulleys' ent amiss*
> *Bedford beer is damnable*
> *and Praeds' is worse than...."*

According to Michael Spencer, of the local CAMRA branch, this is written on the wall of a Northampton pub, but it also crops up elsewhere.

Unfortunately, physical evidence of the brewing sites has been reduced by the development of the county; however, Ratliffe's Albion Brewery is remarkably intact on Commercial Street, and Frog Island are based in an old malting. Oundle is well served, with both the Anchor and Union brew houses, together with various maltings and buildings from Smiths, still standing. Other good examples of brew house buildings are Easts at Milton Malsor and Warrens at Cosgrove. Sadly one of the two remaining sites in Peterborough is about to be cleared for housing and Wellingborough lost its brewery buildings for a shopping centre. However, the preservation of Dulleys' baths as the new heritage centre should provide an excellent opportunity to celebrate the town's history. Where possible, Ordnance Survey six figure grid references are given for locations.

On the positive side, we can witness the growth of the craft, or micro-breweries, such as Frog Island, Leyland, Merivale and Rockingham. Although attempts to re-establish brew-pubs in Northampton have recently closed, the Cannon in Wellingborough seems at least to be surviving.

This book takes note of boundary changes, but those areas which have been lost to neighbouring counties are covered, in order to match the older directories. Hence, there are entries for the Soke of Peterborough, the St Martins area of Stamford and Little Bowden at Market Harborough. Additionally, some information is given on links outside of the county.

The Growth of Commercial Brewing

The story of the growth of large-scale commercial brewing has echoes of some current concerns. For example, towards the end of the 16th century, "the great brewers" in Northampton were trying to obtain the trade of the smaller and publican brewers (Starmer 1971). They were worried by the growth of the smaller concerns, such as the 'tippling houses'. The chief distinction between the inns and alehouses of Northampton was that the former were permitted to brew, and Starmer lists the following as being in existence in 1585:-

Angel, Bridge Street	Hart (or Hind), Market Street
Bell, Bridge Street	Katharine Wheel, Gold Street
Bull, George's Row	Lion, Drapery
Dolphin, Gold Street	Sallet (or Helmet), Cow Lane
George, George's Row	Swan, Drapery
Green Dragon, Bearwood Street	Talbot, Market Square

The simplest form of brewing was at a domestic level and originally, most families, including farm labourers, brewed. Around 1820, this still represented half the beer brewed in England, but this rapidly decreased afterwards and some estimates were that it was down to 20% by as early as 1830. The various advertisements for the sale of equipment can be seen in terms of these national changes. Thus, the late 18th century breweries became obsolete.

"insignificant and inconvenient buildings, situated to the rear of private houses, or inns, and approached by narrow passages down which all the ale and grains had to be rolled or carried by men and women, to the carts and wagons there to placed to receive them." Pale Ale & Bitter Beer p26

Nevertheless, an 1839 valuation of property in Wellingborough listed 19 pubs which still had brew houses and 12 houses, including Hatton Hall, of wealthier inhabitants which had brew houses in situ (Palmer 1983). The text contains details of the few surviving examples in the county, e.g. Braybrooke.

The next level up from domestic brewing was the brewing victualler. He was comparable to the local baker, whose production methods remained unchanged for a lengthy period. Indeed, several of those mentioned in the text were both brewers and bakers. The 1830 Beer Act gave a temporary boost to this scale of brewing by removing the need for a lengthy licensing process.

However, one problem is that the term "brewery" is used to refer to the actual brew house and its equipment, as well as the business which operated from it. There is also a problem in that home brew pubs might brew or not as the publican/victualler changed.

Where details of publican brewers are given in the directories, these have been included e.g. Daventry, Peterborough and Towcester. In some cases, reference to existing brew houses is made in the estates of the commercial brewers, although this usually refers to the actual building, since in most cases the brewing equipment would already have been sold.

Moving to the third category, of common brewers, we begin to notice the seeds of the industrial revolution around the end of the eighteenth century. Brewing is suitable for large-scale production, even without investment in steam power.

Thus, to take advantage of larger markets, brewers could increase the size of equipment e.g. vats and coppers, which in turn gained economies of scale. Since the product was a liquid, a tower-brewery could be run very efficiently simply by gravity.

The common brewers could also benefit from their wastage allowance, by actually not losing the amount granted. The government was prepared to condone this on the grounds that concentration on large scale producers would make the work of the excise that much easier, rather than making visits to large numbers of small scale producers.

In terms of scientific development, the thermometer was in normal use by 1789, and the introduction of the saccharometer brought the possibility of exact calculation in terms of fermentation, beer strength, duty and pricing, all of which were crucial if marketing was to be serious. The period around 1800 also saw the introduction of wort coolers which aided summer brewing and "attemperating" to control fermentation. The period also saw the introduction of beer pumps.

The common brewers were initially limited by: high transport costs, the slow turn-round of casks and the impracticability of sending representatives on long distances. The changes in transport and the market were in turn to remove these limitations.

In 1800 the ideal market was normally 3 to 5 miles in radius i.e. one which could be reached by the brewer's dray. Beer being a product of low 'value density', high transport costs limited growth to the local market. See the entry on Oundle which details how Smiths initially expanded by constructing breweries in other towns. In the case of Northamptonshire, transport was a particular limitation in that, for the early years, it bordered on being non-existent, rather than simply expensive. The establishment of businesses generally tended to be in the market towns: Wellingborough not Higham Ferrers, Kettering not Rothwell.

An advertisement in the Northampton Mercury on 5th March, 1803, was for the sale of a valuable freehold estate, including a malt mill at Daventry. It goes on to suggest that it was in an excellent situation for a public brewery, "there being no establishment of this kind within 20 miles". However, the local inns in the town were still supplying themselves. For example, that at the Wheatsheaf is mentioned in 1780 when ownership was transferred from William Rose to Sarah Brooke.

In the 1830s improved rail links between urban areas exposed the publican-brewer to increased competition. Thus, home brew pubs, which in 1841-45 still accounted for 40% of production, had fallen to a share of 10% by 1886-90 and were negligible by 1914.

"His methods were archaic and his product was often inferior. Any commercial brewer was eventually able to supply him with beer more cheaply than he could brew himself"
Vaizey p16

The decline of the publican victualler, in producing his or her own beer, is also linked to the question of the tied house. In 1817 out of 48,000 licensed alehouses in the country at large, 14,200 were tied through loan arrangements and brewer-ownership (Hawkins & Pass p27). The 1830 Act meant that a beer house licence in itself was of no value. Facilitated by free licensing, and the budget removal of tax on beer, by 1869 there were 53,000 beer shops, increasing by 2,000 a year. However, the growth may have been due as much to the upsurge in demand than the freedom of licensing. The 1869 restriction changed this, in that it limited the total number of licences, but not the number held by a brewery company, unlike recent legislation.

The tie was relatively common in the industrial towns, but rare in remote rural areas. Furthermore it was normally in the form of a loan rather than direct ownership, thus the pub owner could transfer the loan elsewhere if necessary.

The 1869 Act, which brought back the local control of licensing public houses, led the common brewers to expand their purchase of properties. At the same time, the change from partnerships to joint-stock companies, not only provided the capital for growth, but removed the family links and helped the process of take-over and rationalisation. The period 1880-1900 saw a fundamental transformation, resulting in a process of forward integration such that by 1900 only 10% of trade was still free. This became the only way of increasing sales and profits in a stagnant or at best slowly growing market. However, the rise in property prices and problems of financing from own resources strengthened the need for limited liability. This in turn was linked to the growth of mergers e.g. NBC.

The Family Brewers

"The familiar structure of ownership in almost every case gave the cobweb of personal relationships from which capital was drawn into the firms; and in no industry is this familiar structure more marked or more tenacious than in brewing"
Mathias p210

Many of the nineteenth century common brewers were family businesses which had grown out of success as publican brewers eg the Phipps's origins at Towcester. Some however had earlier roots in commercial brewing e.g. Smiths at Oundle and Phillips of Stamford and Northampton. The latter family being perhaps one of the less well-known stories of brewing in the British Isles.

Many of the brewing families were also involved with banking eg Gotches, Praeds and Smiths, both as a source of capital and also somewhere to put their cash takings.

Where possible, the directory shows just how strong were the family links between the Northamptonshire brewers, e.g. Dulleys of Little Bowden and Wellingborough, but also the occasional squabble such as Phipps and Dormans in 1902. The importance of these links lies in understanding the amalgamations which led to Watney, and hence Carlsberg, becoming the remaining major brewer in the county.

This can be seen in the role of the Phillips family, technologically strong in Burton Union brewing, in the foundation of NBC, a business with clear links to companies which ended within the Watney empire. Similarly, the Hipwells from just over the county boundary (see Kettering entry) were to provide many skilled brewers within what became Watney businesses.

One might also look at Walker & Soames of Long Buckby and later Northampton. The Walkers were another family with links to the growth of Watneys and the presence of the name in the county can perhaps be understood in these terms. Some of the Soames family's breweries also later became part of the Watney empire. In turn, they were linked with Charles MacLeod of Kings Cliffe. Furthermore, the NBC directors' book mentions that in July 1943 Charles McLeod, aged 18 and the son of Lady McLeod, was a pupil brewer at NBC. The entry states that he was related to Mr Dorman and Mr Charles Phipps and the grandson of Mr Whitehead, formerly the brewer at Allen & Burnett.

There may even be an association with Praeds of Wellingborough through the name Campbell and that a General MacLeod was trustee for the Praeds debenture holders. The Soames family also had ties with the Brampton Brewery at Chesterfield which in turn had the same Chairman as Strettons of Derby, the latter being linked with Praeds! The truth is in there?

However, the dominance of family concerns was to be eroded by a combination of legal developments such as the joint stock company, new technology and changes in the demand for their product.

The Product

In the 1820s, Hodgson of London first supplied an IPA popular in the Indian climate, pale sparkling and well-hopped rather than nut-brown. In the 1840s, the Burton Union system (named after Burton on Trent where it was most used) was a technical development which aided the production of such beers. At the same time improved glass manufacturing techniques strengthened the importance of the clarity of product being consumed, leading to a demand for lighter running beers rather than sweet dark ales. Note the comparison in 1856 between Phillips' clear amber ale and that of Phipps and Hagger.

The mid-Victorian era competition between commercial brewers revolved around the flavour, strength and reliability of their brews (Hawkins & Pass p19). Indeed, in addition to their thirst quenching properties, the new ales might be seen as more of a social product in times of rising affluence rather than the traditional reliance on ale as a food. This was also the time of growing brand loyalty; hence, the importance of the trade marks dispute with Bass over the red triangle. Between 1840 and 1875 the growth of Bass and Allsopp, without tied trade, was based on the quality and consistency of the beer, backed by advertising and the use of trade marks.

As tastes changed, the demand for brighter, less heavy, beer increased so the need for modern equipment became more pressing. The fundamental problem remained the ability to produce constantly uniform beers from constantly varying raw materials, giving rise to the need for backward integration, especially into malting.

The demand was for a product which was consistent, stable and clear. Burton pale ale provided strength and flavour with a light, clear and sparkling appearance in contrast to heavy porter.

In the 1850s the industrial revolution in brewing led to the building of steam-driven tower breweries, thus gaining further economies of scale, e.g. Phillips at Northampton. In the 1860s brewing between May and September was made possible by the improved technology such as refrigeration and was matched by a growing year round demand for lighter beers. The Phipps investment in a Union system brewery in 1864 should be seen in the context of these developments.

In many companies the old plant was retained and used for porter; however, for others there was a failure to reinvest. Timing was crucial, in that late entrants could build on a "green field site" using the latest technology, particularly the Union system.

In the late nineteenth century chilling and carbonating of bottled beer meant that it no longer needed to wait to mature in the pub. At the same time the need to acquire tied houses with a consequent requirement for capital led many of the previously family owned businesses to take advantage of going public (see Gotches of Rothwell).

The staple product of the family trade remained table beer, lower gravity light beer; however, improved water supplies were to lead to declining sales with eventual problems for businesses such as Easts of Milton Malsor and Kings of Syresham.

The continued growth in the public's taste was for clear, sparkling and filtered beer, first bottled then keg. By the 1930s bottled beer accounted for 25% of the industry sales (Hawkins & Pass p49), creating a need for appropriate plant and marketing budget. The pressures for such investment in times of depression created particular difficulties, even for those brewers with excellent reputations for their product e.g. Mannings. There was a need to expand the market covered by the larger brewing plant, but the growing use of motor transport led to lowered distribution costs. The

A 2-cylinder Thurnewell & Wareham pumping engine built in Burton on Trent c.1866. Scrapped by Phipps in 1949.
Photo: Geoffrey Starmer

introduction of keg beer reinforced the case for national expansion by making bulk distribution of draught beer economic.

One interesting sideline is that the 1940 Kelly's listing marks with an asterisk those pubs which were the brewers of the beer retailed. Although some of those listed do occur elsewhere as having a brew house, the majority do not. The explanation may be that the brewers, fearful of the imposition of restrictions similar to those of the First World War, had taken out or renewed brewing licences as a precaution against any controls on output. Certainly, there seems no evidence that brewing actually took place, since the zoning scheme introduced was not as draconian as feared.

Post-War Mergers

In the 1950s bottled beer accounted for 50% of total consumption by value, of which the nationals had half the trade. Watney's had achieved 7% of the total. This growth continued to be based on the consistency of flavour, especially after the wartime experience of poor draught beer (e.g. Phipps use of Maize, malt extract and potatoes!), improved packaging, and the impact of TV and home drinking on the off-licence trade. In 1959, Phipps bought 153 pubs (140 of Chesham & Brackley) from Ind Coope for £650,000, but the important factor was that this was linked to a trade in Double Diamond and reciprocal sales of Guinness and mineral water.

The entry on Praeds also reveals how the growth of mineral waters and soft drinks was extremely important after the Second World War. The Northants Brewers Association discussed putting a tie on their houses for such products and access to such production facilities became a determining factor in take-overs.

By 1959 packaged beer (i.e. mainly bottled) accounted for 36% of total volume. However, in 1970 this had declined to 27%, primarily because of the growth of keg beer. The bulk transport of keg was less than 2/3 the cost of bottles, leading to keg sales rising from 1% of consumption in 1959 to 17% by 1970. To this one needs to add the growth of lager from 2% to 5%. This product was mainly national, 6 brands accounting for 92% of the market in 1976. For the regional companies, such as NBC, this created problems in terms of the cost of replacing plant, whether to invest in bottle, keg or more particularly lager. Hence, the pressure for merger and eventual take-over. Similar problems of financing investment faced the Abington Brewery Co and Smiths of Oundle, despite the continued success of the latter's beer in new markets.

The merger boom between 1957 and 1969 saw 59% of the 166 companies in the industry become absorbed into larger concerns, but overall concentration ratios were still below many other industries. However, there was now the additional impact of the external city investors who had other uses for property, especially city centre pubs which could be converted into shops (a trend now reversed by Wetherspoons).

Events were happening elsewhere which were to seriously affect the future of brewing in Northampton. In 1959, Charles Clore (a shoe magnate!) made an attempt to take over the London brewer Watney Mann. The bid for Watney was at 60/- compared with a pre-bid price of 51s 3d; however, share trading forced the price up until Clore regarded it as unrealistic. To defend themselves against these unwelcome advances, Watneys decided to make themselves too large to swallow and merged with Wilson's Brewery at Newton Heath, Manchester.

Soon afterwards whispers began to spread that Phipps/NBC was on Watney's shopping list. With 1,171 licensed premises, most within a 60 mile radius of Northampton, it was an obvious target for any business trying to build a national presence.

By 1965, in looking at a brewery with a capacity of some 500,000 barrels per year, production costs (31% of the total) for new plant were less than those of an existing brewery. This was mainly through the higher depreciation being offset by reductions in labour cost to a fifth of those in a traditional plant. Hence, those companies with access to capital for investment could gain distinct economies of scale and labour-saving from new plant. This helps understand the disappearance of Phipps/NBC into Watneys and the building of plant to produce Red Barrel, but also its eventual replacement by the Carlsberg brewery.

Hence, the story of brewing in Northamptonshire closely reflects the changes which took place nationally, and indeed internationally. Hopefully, this book shows the eminence of brewing in the county and places it within this historical context.

Sources

The key source of general information is the commercial directories for the county. James Pigot entered the directory publishing business in 1811 and included a section on Northamptonshire in his London & Provincial Directory of 1823. The county was covered by him again in 1830 and 1841, and by his partner Isaac Slater in 1850. At the time, these directories were more comprehensive than anything else available (reprint of 1830 available from Northampton library).

One particularly useful area of research are the Kelly's directories, which began to appear in 1847 and lasted until recent times. The other key directories include Whellan, Slater and Melville. In addition, Manfred Friedrich's gazetteer of all commercial breweries operating in the British Isles from around 1877, and those pub breweries which were still brewing in 1914, has been used. Where appropriate the Friedrich reference numbers are shown eg **Chapman, Brackley (F571)**. Friedrich's analysis of directories is available from the Brewery History Society.

A word of caution, although the authors have attempted to cross-refer where possible, the early period is often unclear and on occasions some suppositions have had to be made. There are often errors in directories, particularly regarding the spelling of names and dates when businesses were founded eg NBC. Occasionally, individuals are listed as brewers when they may have been only agents eg Knights of Chelveston. These have been included in order to clarify the record. Clearly, any further information would be gladly received.

Perhaps as befits the county's importance as a brewing centre, the Northampton Record Office has an excellent collection of documents from a variety of brewers. We are grateful that such preservation is available for research such as this.

Acknowledgements

In addition to the staffs of the Northampton Record Office and various libraries, we are particularly grateful to Geoffrey Starmer who undertook the initial research into brewing in the county and who provided much assistance in putting together this directory.

Other particular areas of help were as follows: Jon-Paul Carr Wellingborough, Mike Evans of the Malt Shovel for access to his collections, Ray Farleigh for his research in the British Library, Bob Flood guidance on Cambridgeshire links, Jack Feast on Kings Cliffe, Frog Island for their links with Mannings, Jim Irving on the Smiths of Oundle and fascinating tours around the town, Viscount Midleton for MacCleod, John M Smith on Weedon, Bill Williams for help with Phillips of Stamford and Steve Williams for access to his notes on Peterborough. Many thanks to members of the Brewery History Society for their expertise and support, especially Ken Smith for his editorial patience, Andrew Cunningham for access to his collection, Ian Mackey for keeping us up to date and Ian Peaty, Paul Travis, Michael Jones and Jeff Sechiari for their enthusiasm.

Last but never least, our families for patience, understanding and computer time.

Bibliography

Barber, Norman: A Century of British Brewers 1890-1990. BHS
Barnard, Alfred: Noted Breweries of Great Britain and Ireland 4 vols 1889-1891
Burman, Alan: Northampton in the Making. Jones Sand, Coventry 1899
Cooper, Nicholas: Aynho: a Northants village. Leopards Head, Banbury 1984
Cox, Alan: Froth & Fizz: Northants drinks bottles before 1940. Northants Museums and Gallery 1977
Evans, B.E: The story of Milton Malsor. Gardner & Darton London 1924
Federation of Women's Institutes: Northamptonshire Village Book. 1989.
Friedrich, Manfred: Gazetteer of British Breweries. London 1982
Gaskell, E: Northants leaders: Social & Political. London 1908
Greenall, R.L: History of Northamptonshire. London 1979
Hawkins, K.H. & C.L. Pass: The brewing industry. Heinemann. London 1979
Hogg, G: English Country Inn
Janes, Hurford: The Red Barrel: History of Watney Mann. London 1963
Ireson, T: Old Kettering Book 4: A view from the 30s
Jenkins, Eric: Victorian Northants: the early years 1993
Langhorn: Notes on Sheaf Street, Daventry. Daventry Library Local Studies 1972
Luckett, F: History of brewing in Warwickshire. CAMRA
Markham, F: The 1900s in Stony Stratford 1951
Mathias, P: The Transformation of England London 1979
Monckton, H.A: History of English Ale & Beer. London 1966
Osborn, Alice Parker: Oundle in the Eighteenth century 1994
Page, Ken: The Story of the Biggleswade Brewery. 1993
Palmer, J. & M: A History of Wellingborough. 1974
Peaty, Ian: Essex Brewers. BHS. 1992
Perry, Stephen: Queen Street remembered. 1995
Pettit, Philip: Syresham: a Forest village. 1996
Randall, Philip J: Eye Life. London 1971
Rotary Club of Ise Valley: Burton Latimer: Portrait of a certain place 1991
Rotary Club, Kettering: Pictorial history of Kettering. 1985
Smith, John M: The development of Roade. Northants Local History Society Vol. 3. No.7. 1995.
Staffordshire County Council Education Dept: Pale Ale & Bitter Beer 1977
Stainwright, Trevor L: Windmills of Northants. 1997.

An example of the old signs from Northamptonshire's brewing past - The Crown Inn at Grendon.
Photo: Authors' collection.

Starmer, Geoffrey H: Breweries in Northamptonshire. Bulletin of Industrial Archaeology in CBA Group 9. No .14 Oct. 1970
Sunderland, J. & Webb, M: Towcester: The Story of an English country town. Towcester LHS 1995
Vaizey, J.E: The Brewing Industry, 1886-1952. London 1960.
Victoria County History of Northamptonshire. Vol. 3.
Walker, Thomas James: Depot for PoW: Norman Cross. London 1915
Webb, P.G: Portrait of Northamptonshire. London 1977

The Old White Hart, another example of what remains to reminds us of Northamptonshire's brewing past.

CONTENTS

ASHLEY	1	LITCHBOROUGH	22
AYNHO	1	LITTLE BOWDEN	23
BLATHERWYCKE	1	LONG BUCKBY	24
BOUGHTON	1	MIDDLETON	26
BRACKLEY	1	MILTON MALSOR	26
BRAYBROOKE	7	MOULTON	29
BRIXWORTH	7	NASEBY	29
BROUGHTON	7	NORTHAMPTON	30
BYFIELD	7	OLD	90
CANONS ASHBY	7	OLD STRATFORD	91
CASTLE ASHBY	8	OUNDLE	91
CHELVESTON	8	PETERBOROUGH	100
CHIPPING WARDEN	8	PITSFORD	112
COLD ASHBY	8	POTTERSPURY	112
CORBY	8	RAUNDS	112
COSGROVE	8	ROADE	112
COTTESBROOKE	10	ROTHERSTHORPE	113
CRANFORD ST JOHN	10	ROTHWELL	113
CRICK	11	SLIPTON	114
DAVENTRY	11	ST MARTINS	114
DEANSHANGER	13	STOKE BRUERNE	118
DESBOROUGH	13	SUDBOROUGH	118
DUSTON	13	SYRESHAM	119
EASTON ON HILL	13	THORNBY	122
EYE	13	THRAPSTON	122
FARTHINGHOE	14	TITCHMARSH	123
FINEDON	14	TOWCESTER	123
FOTHERINGHAY	14	WANSFORD	125
GEDDINGTON	14	WAPPENHAM	125
HARRINGWORTH	14	WEEDON	125
HELMDON	15	WELDON	128
HELPSTON	15	WELFORD	128
HIGHAM FERRERS	15	WELLINGBOROUGH	128
IRTHLINGBOROUGH	15	WEST HADDON	147
KETTERING	16	WHITTLESEY	147
KINGS CLIFFE	19	WILBY	147
KINGS SUTTON	22	WOLLASTON	147

Glossary

Without going too far into technicalities, this glossary covers some of words used in the text in a simplified manner.

Ale - originally used to describe unhopped malt beverage, as distinct from beer, which was brewed from malt with hops as flavouring. Nowadays synonymous with beer and a traditional top-fermented (i.e. the yeast rises to the top during fermentation) product.
Barrel Sizes - Firkin 9 gallons; Barrel 36 gallons; Hogshead 54 gallons.
Beer House - as simple as the term, a house which was licensed to sell only beer. The 1830 Beer House Act made it much simpler and cheaper to set up in business, leading to a rapid expansion, some of which brewed their own beer on a small scale.
Brew House - the actual building, within which would be found the brewing equipment.
Brewery - a term used for both the physical buildings and also the business itself.
Brown Ale - beer brewed from dark malts, bottled and normally of low gravity. The bottled equivalent of mild.
Burton Union System - a particular form of fermentation which originated at Burton on Trent. It involves a series of large connected barrels which circulated then beer during the brewing process.
Burtonised - by adding gypsum to the water (or **liquor**) used for brewing, brewers can create a pale ale typical of Burton on Trent.
Cask - general term for all draught beer containers.
Copper - vessel traditionally made of such, nowadays stainless steel, where the "wort" is boiled with hops.
Dray - wagon used to carry casks and bottles from brewery to pub.
Family trade - small or table beer, usually consumed with meals instead of water which was then unsafe. Despite its name and provision for children, the beer was probably as strong as modern day beers.
Fermentation - the process in which yeast converts wort into beer. After brewing, the beer stays in the brewery where the yeast ferments, normally takes from 4 to 8 days.
India Pale Ale (IPA) - first brewed for shipping out to troops in India.
Keg Beer - conditioned at the brewery, chilled, filtered and sealed in containers and served under pressure. Despite the nostalgia for real ale, the evidence for Northamptonshire, as with the rest of the country; is that keg products such as Red Barrel were welcomed by the majority of drinkers who saw them as providing a consistent taste which did not vary from pub to pub.
Lager - bottom fermented beer initially associated with Europe, which has been available in the county for a hundred years. Local brewers attempted to brew top-fermented versions in the 1960s (see NBC) but eventually proper draught lagers were introduced. The increasing demand for this type of beer resulted in the opening of the Carlsberg brewery.
Liquor - the name given to water used in the brewing process.
Long Pull - means of serving additional beer in order to attract custom, particularly prevalent during the "Brewers Wars" at the end of the last century. In the UK it is illegal to serve too much beer.
Malt Mill - a machine which crushes malt before it is used in brewing.
Malting - the initial stage in the process when the barley is partly germinated and then dried to stop further growth. The county's previous involvement is evidenced by two substantial buildings remaining in Northampton, one of which houses the Frog Island Brewery.
Maltster - the individual responsible for malting barley.
Mash Tun - vessel in which the crushed malt and hot water are mixed at precise temperatures to extract malt sugars, which will then be fermented by the yeast.
Mild - previously the main drink of the working male population, usually dark and not much hops. However, do not be misled by present day low gravity versions, since at the turn of the century it would have been 2 or 3 times stronger.
Original Gravity - a measure of the strength of beer used in the UK before European Union. This is now measured as alcohol by volume (ABV). Present day bitter beers are in the region 1036° to 1045° OG compared to some of those mentioned in the text.
Pale Ale - clear, sparkling and well-hopped; see NBC for the Phillips family strength in its production.
Porter - strong well-hopped dark almost black beer which originated in London. The nearest modern day equivalent being a stout such as Guinness.
Quarter - a measure of the capacity of a brew house, based on the "quarters" of malt which could be brewed.
Stout - dark beer of medium to high gravity, brewed using roasted malt.
Victualler - usually associated with an inn and providing food and possibly accommodation. Only a licensed victualler could server alcoholic drinks. In the early years, this would probably including brewing beer.
Wort - the unfermented beer at the end of the mashing stage.
Yeast - tiny micro-organism which ferments wort into beer and carbon dioxide.

ASHLEY   **Harroll, Samuel.**

In the 1762 militia list, Harroll is described as a brewer and victualler.

Wignall, George.

The militia list shows Wignall as a weaver, brewer and victualler. The only pub remaining in the village is the George.

AYNHO   **Scott, Frederick W.,** *Cartwright Arms, Croughton Road.*

The Brewers' Journal for October 1901 carried an advertisement for a working brewer for what was described as a 3 quarter country brewery and in January 1906 there was a similar request for a man to undertake the entire brewery and cellar work for a country inn with small brewery. The only brewer listed in Aynho was Frederick W.Scott in 1910, a publican brewer based at the Cartwright Arms. He continued until 1917 when the wartime sugar shortage caused him to cease brewing. Even the mighty NBC of Northampton reported an inability to obtain any sugar.

The pub, which is still trading, dates back to at least 1615, although it has been rebuilt at some stage. It was originally called the Red Lion, but the name was changed in the 1820s to that of the local family. The Cartwright family lived at Park House, which like many other large country houses brewed for the many household and estate workers. For example, a letter from Colonel William Cartwright in March 1847 states:- *"brewing will commence this week and the quantity to be brewed will be 12 hogsheads at 9 bushels of malt."* (Cooper p223).

Spiers, George, *20/24 Banbury Road.*

According to the 1854 edition of Kelly's Directory, George Spiers ran a brew house in the village. Spiers was the village grocer with an on-licensed beer house in his shop located on Banbury road, one of a terrace Numbers 20 to 24.

BLATHERWYCKE   **Bosworth, Brian,** *Rockingham Ales, c/o Wansford Road, Elton.*

Founded in July 1997 in converted farm outbuildings near Blatherwycke in the Rockingham Forest. Brian is the cellarman at the White Swan Woodnewton, where the beer is usually available. He uses a small 2 barrel plant which came from the former brewer at Yates and Jacksons. Brian only brews part time, on Sundays, producing the following beers: Forest Gold, 3.9%; Forest Amber, 3.9%; Dark Forest, 4.1%.

BOUGHTON   Boughton House is another example of a country house brewing for its workforce. The brew house is on the left of the East side opposite the unfinished "pavilion".

BRACKLEY   **Blencowe and Company (F570),** *Market Square.*

The Blencowe family originally came from Marston St Lawrence. In 1768, John Blencowe esq of Marston provided a mortgage on the Six Bells at Sulgrave, but in February 1780, Samuel Blencowe (formerly Jackson) is described as his executor. The inn was occupied by a William Rhodes, victualler. Around this time some of the Blencowe family seem to have moved to Brackley.

In 1815, the Crown Inn was for sale *"capable of carrying on malting and brewing, independent of the inn, there being no public brewery or wholesale dealer in wines and spirits in or near Brackley"*.

At the time of the above advert, William Blencowe was running a bakehouse in the Market Square and in 1824 he is also shown as a maltster. He developed the business by adding a coal yard and then around 1830, by brewing beer. At this time a John Blencowe was a maltster at High Street, Daventry, but it is not known if they were connected.

In 1834, William Blencowe purchased the Greyhound and property in Malthouse Close, for £1,570. This purchase was in conjunction with William Cave, maltster. The latter was involved with several aspects of the local trade, including the Red Lion (brewing in 1749 when owned by the Yates family), the White Lion and the Reindeer. In 1836, Blencowe is described as owning a house and brew house near the Market Place and a malthouse near Goose Green.

In 1855 William senior died and the brewery/bakery passed to the eldest son William Blencowe junior who, as a pillar of Brackley society, was secretary of both the town's cattle market and Corn Exchange. Clement Blencowe became a partner in the brewery by February 1859, when he and William purchased the Bear and its brew house in the Market Square, Banbury, for £1,085. However, the partnership was dissolved in 1869. The 1876 Harrod's Directory entry for

BRACKLEY (continued)

Brackley lists Clement as a wine and spirit and coal merchant in Banbury Road, whilst William is given as a brewer in Market Place.

In June 1880, William Blencowe bought the White Horse, at Croughton for £1,500. The pub dated back to 1638, when owned by John Heynes, blacksmith. At the time of its purchase by Blencowe it still had a brew house, although there is no mention of whether it was operating.

The business expanded to the extent of acquiring a second brewery in Cannock (F966). This was the Cannock Brewery Co registered 5th April, 1880, with a capital of £100,000, the business of George Cotterell (solicitor of Walsall) and Arthur Scattergood. The latter is listed as the brewery manager and also as a beer retailer on Hednesford Road, whilst William Scattergood is described as the working brewer.

However, a petition for bankruptcy was filed in November 1880 stating that Arthur Scattergood had debts of £56,000. The business was wound up in October 1881 and at later creditors' meetings it was stated that many of the tied houses were mortgaged. This may have been the cause of the purchase by Blencowes.

In May 1889 William Blencowe's business was registered as a limited company. In July 1890, despite the previous partnership having been dissolved, and Clement's share of the joint mortgage on the Plumber's Arms paid off, he was claiming money when the pub was sold to the company. This suggests that the previous partnership had not ended harmoniously.

William Blencowe may have died in 1894, since the purchase of the Compasses, Silverstone, mentions Clara Ann Barnes and Charles Eric Barnes as trustees for Wm Blencowe & Co Ltd. Around this time, there was an issue of £50,000 debenture stock for which the trustees were James Langton of the Marine Brewery, Radcliffe Road, London, and George Cave KC MP of Richmond, Surrey. Sir George Cave, later Solicitor General, was possibly a relation of the Brackley malting family, mentioned earlier.

The company continued to thrive into the early 20th century, owning some 33 public houses in 1912. In June 1914, they paid £1,550 for the Bear, with brew house, at Souldon Gatesend. However, in February 1922, when letting the New Inn at Shotteswell near Banbury, the business is described as William Blencowe & Co Ltd of Cannock, suggesting that the Brackley brewery may have closed. Certainly, the whole business was for sale in December 1923, when Phipps decided that the price was too high for the small trade. The company was taken over by Halls of Oxford.

The links with the Halls were somewhat tenuous, but probably go back to when Blencowe's bought the Greyhound from Isaac Shortland Bartlett, whose daughter Eliza married a Richard Shillingford. In 1852 Charles Shillingford, in a brewing partnership with Thomas Phillips (see NBC), had dealings with a John Blencowe, victualler of Oxford. Both Shillingford's Bicester and Phillips' Oxford breweries were taken over by Halls.

The Cannock brewery, complete with 32 tied pubs, was sold to William Butler's Wolverhampton Brewery in 1925. They closed the brewery and sold the equipment to a Wolverhampton firm of scrap dealers. The brewery site on Hollies Avenue was sold to Messrs A.Wootton & Son, a local firm, who used it as a timber yard until recent years, when it was cleared for development.

In October 1925, the Brackley operation was sold by auction. The brewery fetched £2,000. The premises were bought by the Hallamshire Vinegar Co Ltd of Sheffield. Blencowe's fifty tied houses were almost equally distributed amongst the counties of Northamptonshire, Warwickshire and Oxfordshire. Ownership of the pubs passed into several hands with Hopcraft and Norris and The Hook Norton Brewery the main buyers. Northampton Brewery Company bought the following:-

Crown, Napton	£3,500	*Phipps purchased:-*	
King's Head, Syresham	£2,700	Cricketers Inn, Banbury	£5,000
Six Bells, Bicester	£1,500	Greyhound, Brackley	£3,700
Three Cups, Buckingham	£2,000		

Halls retained at least the following Northamptonshire pubs: Blucher's Arms and White Horse Croughton; Compasses, Silverstone; Plumber's Arms, Brackley; and the Six Bells, Sulgrave.

The Brackley brewery was on the west side of the main street, a few yards from The Crown Hotel (SP 584 368). Admission was through an archway, which now leads to Drayman's Walk. The local band club use what look like the only remaining buildings.

BRACKLEY (continued)

Bowerman Mrs, *The Reindeer, High Street.*

Harrod's 1876 Directory lists Mrs Bowerman as a brewer in the Market Place and also as keeping the Reindeer. In 1841, Edward Bowerman had been at the Reindeer. However, Mrs Bowerman is not in Kelly's listing of 1877 and neither she nor the Reindeer are listed in 1884.

Chapman, Edward Sibbley (F571), *The Plough, High Street.*

In 1861, an Edward Chapman was at the Cross Keys, when Thomas Hutton was at the Plough. The 1869 Directory lists Edward Sibbley Chapman as a brewer and in 1876 he is shown as a builder and victualler at the Plough, but is in Kelly's 1877 listing as a small brewer. The Plough dates back to at least 1791, when kept by William Gill, a victualler. It traded as Harrows for several years but has now regained its original name.

Hopcraft and Norris (F572), *High Street.*

In 1815, Barnet John Hopcraft, described as a yeoman from Evenley, bought property in the High Street in conjunction with William Cave, maltster (see above). Hopcraft became the commissioner for the enclosure of land at Brackley in 1829, and by 1841, his own land at Halse St Peter was being farmed by his son Alfred Hopcraft. This included a maltings from 1843 and around this time Alfred began brewing in the town, near the Market House.

In 1844 Alfred Hopcraft is also listed as a brewer in Banbury. Although initially shown at High Street, this property would probably have backed on to Fish Street, where he is listed the following year. This would seem to be the start of his connection with the Crosby family of Banbury. It remains unclear whether there was a brew house in Fish Street or simply an agency and depot.

In 1847 Alfred is shown as a brewer, spirit merchant, maltster and farmer at Banbury, although he still resided at Halse. Determined to set up his brewery in a business-like manner Hopcraft employed Bevershaw Farmer a professional brewer to run the Brackley operation. Farmer was listed as a brewer at Phillips of Northampton.

In 1849, Alfred was living at Brackley Hall, Halse, where one of his three sons, Ernest, was born. He swiftly set about buying, or building, public houses and beer houses to sell his beer. In 1853, he took over supplying the Bell at Syresham from Stuchberrys of Buckingham. A lease dated 22nd November, 1855, tells how he had built the Marston Inn at Marston St Lawrence and leased it for 21 years to William Branson on the undertaking that no beer but Hopcraft's was to be sold there. In 1859 to 1863, Hopcraft is also shown as the landlord of the Wheatsheaf, 68 Fish Street, Banbury.

In 1857, George Crosby was advertising himself as an agent for Hopcraft at 63 Fish Street, whilst Hopcraft is also shown separately as trading from 63 Fish Street until 1878.

By 1871 the Brackley brewery was employing 50 men.

Upon the death of the founder the business passed to his first son, John. However, very shortly after that on 27th March, 1874, John Hopcraft died. His Will left all freehold, leasehold and copyhold property to his wife Gertrude. The joint executors of his estate were George Crosby, described as a Banbury brewer and baker, and his son George the younger. The latter had previously been a brewer's clerk, presumably Hopcrafts. However, he had then become the clerk to a Banbury attorney before becoming a solicitor, giving him knowledge of both the technical and legal aspects of the business.

The brewery, then valued at £8,000, and property were held in trust, apparently until Alfred's third son, also called Alfred, reached 21. In 1876, Hopcraft A (exors of) are listed in the High Street, Brackley and as farmers at Halse.

George Crosby junior (F122), in addition to operating as a solicitor, is shown trading as a brewer from 64 Fish Street in 1877, whilst Alfred Hopcraft (Exors of) (F126) are sometimes shown at 63 Fish Street and sometimes at 64 Fish Street. The confusion arises because George's home actually included both house numbers.

George Crosby senior died in 1879 and George junior in 1886, when he was described as a partner in Hopcraft & Norris. The deaths may have been part of the reason for the lengthy Chancery proceedings in the 1890s between John Hopcraft's children and Alfred and Ernest Hopcraft.

BRACKLEY (continued)

In September 1881, Alfred Hopcraft married a Miss E Saunders. At a celebration dinner the employees presented them with a hand-painted china dessert service. Alfred was representing the brewery at the Northants Brewers Association in 1884, suggesting that the Crosbys were no longer in sole control of the business.

However, Ernest Hopcraft in 1885 was described as the only surviving son of Alfred of Brackley Hall. This suggests that the Alfred alive at this time may have been the son of Ernest's brother Alfred.

The Brewers' Journals for July and August 1892 carry reports of an inspection of the brewery by Arthur Kinder who described it as being in a very bad state of affairs. The plant and steam engine were in a poor way, the wooden vessels unfit for use, the machinery of a very rough kind, old and generally out of repair, the cooler rotten and out of level etc. According to Ray Farleigh who provided the detail on this report, this was perhaps not uncommon when brewers were appealing against their rating assessments. The plant was described as operating on the Burton system.

The business also had a beer merchants and bottlers at Oxford Street, Daventry.

The Brackley and Banbury Brewery successfully traded as A.& E.Hopcraft for a further twenty years, suggesting that the legal proceedings had been settled in favour of the surviving brothers. In addition to both Alfred and Ernest living at Banbury Road, the latter also had a house at Rugby. Alfred then advertised for a partner to buy into the company with a view to eventual control.

In 1895, the wealthy Norris family from Bletchingley, Surrey, purchased a share in the business for their youngest son Walter (b.1863). When Walter and his wife moved up to Northamptonshire they went to live at the splendid Tudor mansion at Steane Park. It was at this Manor house that Jimmy Norris[1] the last Chairman of Hopcraft and Norris, was interviewed.

As agreed, control of the company passed to Walter H.Norris, who became a director, and the business was trading as Hopcraft & Norris Ltd from at least 1898. Ernest Hopcraft was Chairman and Managing Director in 1908. He had married in 1883, but his wife Mary died in 1900 and their only child, Edward George de Latham, does not seem to have taken any interest in the business.

Hopcraft & Norris shortly before demolition.

Photo: Authors' collection

Hopcraft and Norris retained a presence in Banbury through to at least 1906. Edwin J.Crosby continued to act as the local agent until 1896; however, he is still listed in his own right as a brewer until 1894 and as licensee of the Coach & Horses, 4 Butchers Row.

One popular memory of Edwardian Brackley was the old brewery hooter which sounded promptly at one o'clock everyday. Over half of the town took this as the signal for their dinner break. So loud was it that even farm workers in the surrounding fields used it.

---

[1] *A business called James Norris & Co brewed in Wandsworth in 1871.*

Walter's two sons were both born at Brackley. Jimmy Norris remembered being told how that old hooter was blown all day when he was born and how the whole town got drunk on free beer!

Day to day running of the brewery was left in the hands of the brewery manager and Company Secretary, Percy E.Clarkson occupying Brewery House. Walter was happy to pursue the life of a country squire and is recalled as a prominent member of both the Grafton and the Bicester Hunts.

The Anchor Brewery, Buckby Wharf, came under the control of Hopcraft and Norris in March 1910 when they bought out Walker and Soames. Forty eight tied houses were added to the Hopcraft estate as a result of this take-over. Brewing at Buckby had probably already ceased (see Walker & Soames entry) and the site became one of Hopcraft's four distribution depots (the others were in Aylesbury, Daventry and Banbury). Mr Gerald Soames became a director of the Brackley brewery.

Beer was shipped to the four distribution depots by train and it was the firm's practice to fill wagons in the brewery yard. These were then pushed down the hill to the railway sidings below the brewery. With the introduction of motorised drays the need for distribution depots declined and Hopcraft's closed them.

The Brackley Brewery was justifiably proud of the loyalty of the workforce. *"I never remember a man getting the sack"*, recalled Jimmy Norris, *"I grant they drank a lot but they worked hard and were proud of the firm and so contented. And they turned out the goods"*. Indeed the brewery won a diploma and a medal at the 1913 Brewery and Allied Trades Exhibition in London.

Hopcraft and Norris

Photo: Authors' collection

In 1914 Alfred Hopcraft was still recorded as living at Banbury Road, but it seems that he died around 1920.

On the night of 19th July, 1920, a fire was discovered at the brewery. It was spotted at the bottling stores at 9pm. The general alarm was raised with limited response. By a quirk of fate the local brigade were away taking part in a fire-fighting competition in Eastbourne. They had left just Lieutenant Green and Fireman Knibbs on duty.

The good neighbours of the brewery quickly rallied round to help this fire-fighting duo. Calls for assistance were put out to the fire services in Buckingham and Banbury. The hastily assembled crew soon had the town's appliance in operation and took water from the town main and from a brook near the gas works.

By the time the neighbouring brigades responded, the fire had been controlled. It was finally put out by 11pm but by that time it was obvious that the damage was extensive. Estimates put the cost of repair at £3,000. Most of the damage was in the bottling and cask filling areas.

In October 1926, lawyers acting on behalf of the business made an approach to Phipps of Northampton stating that one of the directors, a large shareholder of advanced years, would be interested in suitable terms for taking over the business. However, it seems that the asking price may have been too high since Phipps did not pursue the matter, although they were approached again in February 1929.

Walter Norris died in 1931 and the job of brewery chairman passed to his eldest son Robert who had served an apprenticeship at the Brighton Brewery. Bob Norris' reign was short lived for he died two years later as a result of an accident whilst horse racing. As a result NBC were approached to see if they wished to buy the business, but the negotiations did not progress.

Instead, Jimmy Norris, a professional soldier, was called upon to take charge of the brewery. He admitted that he had little knowledge of brewing and was ill-prepared for his new role. Percy Clarkson, the Company Secretary, was promoted to Managing Director so that he could run the business while Jimmy learnt the trade. To this end he went to brewing school where he first met the Nash Brothers who ran the Chesham Brewery.

In February 1943, Mr Clarkson renewed the negotiation with NBC for the sale of the brewery and 156 licensed premises. The NBC valuation was £285,500, of which the licensed premises were £229,000 and the NBC Board told Hopcraft and Norris to make an offer. Clearly, their figures did not match, since it was not accepted and in 1945 Hopcraft and Norris were in negotiations with Praeds of Wellingborough, but the latter also decided not to go ahead with the purchase of the business.

Hence, in 1946 Hopcraft's merged with the Chesham Brewery (F1043) to form the Chesham and Brackley Breweries Ltd. This merger gave the company 350 tied houses. The Nash family owned three quarters of the shares in the new firm, but Jimmy Norris became the figurehead chairman. The Head Brewer at this time was Bill McGee, although Mr C.R.Sprake (see Praeds entry) seemed to be looking after the Chesham brewery. Interestingly, an Edward Hopcraft was at the Cheltenham & Hereford Breweries at this time.

Letterhead from 1957. Note the change of directors

BHS Archives Birmingham Central Library

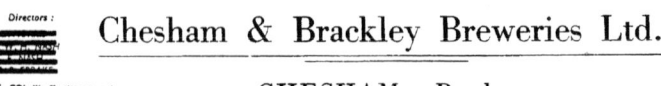

What followed was a good decade of trading, but it was becoming obvious that this could not last. The Board was composed of old men and in the words of Jimmy Norris *"they saw the light"* when Taylor Walker offered to buy them out in 1956.

Brewing ceased at Chesham in 1957 and at Brackley in 1959. The old Hopcraft and Norris brewery was sold off to Bromley's Soaps. Mr Gorman the Head Brewer at Brackley moved to Charles Wells of Bedford where he later introduced Wells Fargo, a popular strong ale. One ex-Chesham and Brackley executive said that the taste of Fargo was almost identical to Chesham's popular 4X ale.

Taylor Walker themselves were later taken over by Ind Coope and a substantial part of the old Hopcraft estate was sold to Phipps. Jimmy Norris died in 1988.

Hopcraft and Norris traded from premises which were set back from the main road on the east side of the square, overlooking what once was the site of Brackley's town railway station (SP 585 367). The entrance to the brewery site is through the archway at the side of the local advice bureau. The maltings and some of the buildings at Brackley remained until 1993, when the site was finally cleared, leaving only a few offices at the yard entrance.

BRACKLEY (continued)

Old Mill Brewery Ltd (F573), *Farm Road.*

In the 1970s a concern known as the Old Mill Brewery Ltd operated in Farm Road, intending to supply the free trade, but the affair was short lived. One of the authors recalls drinking the beer at the E.M.E.B. social club in Northampton, and that they supplied the beer in unique sealed plastic tubes, similar to childrens' ice-poles.

Taylor, Edward, *Bell Inn, High Street.*

Kelly's Directory of 1847 lists Edward Taylor as a brewer and farmer at the Bell Inn, a property which he had owned since at least 1824. However, by 1854 he is only shown as a farmer and grazier, whilst the Bell was being kept by Mrs Hannah Taylor. The pub is still standing.

BRAYBROOKE

An old farm brew house remains next to the mounds of the old fishponds on the site of old castle (Womens' Institute booklet p29). Fans of the old British comedy films of Will Hay might care to note that the actor Graham Moffat was licensee of the village pub, the Swan, for many years.

BRIXWORTH

Gauge, Samuel, *Coach & Horses, Harborough Road.*

In 1874, Gauge advertised his brewing plant for sale on his retirement from the business. The Coach and Horses is shown as being run by a Mr Gage in 1854 and a Samuel Gage in 1862, but in 1866 was kept by William Gage. The pub is still trading.

Hipwell, Richard, *Northampton Road.*

Richard Hipwell (b.1812 at Sywell) is shown as a grocer and brewer in 1847. Prior to this he may have been living in Wolverton, Buckinghamshire. When in March 1850, he tried to sell his grocer's shop he found no one interested in buying it. Soon afterwards it had become an off-licensed beer house with brew house, which was trading in 1854.

His average brew was very small, probably only a few barrels a week, and in 1861 he is listed only as a grocer. The business was located two houses up from the Red Lion. The site is now a bookmakers.

Perkins, James.

The Northampton Mercury for 7th July, 1838, carried an advertisement for *"A very commodious messuage or tenement, with bakehouse, brew house etc. now in the tenure of Mr James Perkins."* The business also included a post windmill on the Scaldwell road. The only brewer in the 1841 census is John Clark of Silver Street. However, he was aged 75 at the time so may have been too old to have been involved with this business.

BROUGHTON

Ball Mr, *The Sun, High Street.*

The pub was built in 1870 when the first landlord was a Mr Ball. In 1893, the pub was being run by his son-in-law Fred Thompson who also continued brewing. A Frederick Thompson was still at the pub in 1940, when it was included in Kelly's listing (see Introduction). The pub is still trading.

BYFIELD

Brown, Richard Guest.

Although listed as a brewer in 1877, this was probably a depot for the brewery which Brown had founded around 1874 in nearby Fenny Compton. He is listed as a coal merchant at both locations.

Frost, Samuel, *New Inn.*

According to the Brewers' Journal March 1873, Samuel Frost at the New Inn was fined £50 for failing to record in the brewing book. The pub, once one of five in the village, was bought in 1905 for £1,500 by Phipps. It ceased trading some time after 1957.

The village at one time also contained at least two malt houses. One was owned in 1768 by J.Warren of Daventry, and occupied by Robert Thornton. The other was occupied by Thomas Bromley 1746-1792.

CANONS ASHBY

At Canons Ashby House, now owned by the National Trust, the former brew house is now used as the tea-room. The 1770 inventory gives details of its contents as: Large copper with brake cock, 2 coolers lined with lead, 1 mash vat, 2 working vats, sparging tub, underback and hop sieve. In addition the brew house had a pump and spout, 2 tubs and a brewing bucket.

The inventory was undertaken by John Pratt of Helmdon who may have been the brewer, since a possible descendant of his was later brewing in Helmdon. The accounts book for 1766-70 shows that brewing was taking place every other week.

CASTLE ASHBY **Elliott, Edmund,** *Station Hotel near White Mills.*

The Mercury for 29th October, 1859 carries an advertisement for Elliott at Castle Ashby Station selling home-brewed ales. Previously he had been at the Hare & Hounds in Northampton. In 1877, the address seems to have changed to Grendon, when William Goodwood was at the Hotel. It was later a Hipwell's property, but in 1940 it was a Phipps' house, when it was closed for the duration of the war.

The Old Brew House at Castle Ashby House is now occupied by small businesses. However, it had ceased to be used for brewing by at least 1860, when it was converted to a laundry.

CHELVESTON **Knight, William Douglas.**

In August 1890, W.D.Knight, an ale and porter merchant, sold the business he had owned for 30 years to Phipps. He was offered a house at Irthlingborough, £1,200 cash and £1,000 in debenture bonds as from 1st October.

Phipps then employed his son, William Knight junior, as depot manager. An 1896 directory lists Knight as a brewer but, as mentioned, he was only an agent for Phipps' beer. The depot then moved to High Street Rushden, where William Douglas Knight kept the Station and still worked as the manager for Phipps, until he resigned in 1904. The agency closed in 1909.

CHIPPING WARDEN **Merivales Ales Ltd.,** *Warden Brewery, Manor Farm, Appletree Road.*

Originally set up just over the county border at Edgcote, and run by Ian Merivale as a small extended home brewery, the business relocated here in 1996. It is now trading under the name of Merivale Ales, on a much larger commercial scale. Partner Colin Diment provided the new premises, a large barn on the farm next to the old Chipping Warden aerodrome. The brewing capacity of 8 barrels, with two 7 barrel fermenting vessels and one 9 barrel, raises interesting questions for throughput. The plant came from a planned pub brewery in Lancashire which never actually brewed. The brewery uses a mix of pale, crystal and wheat malt in all its products. Challenger and Golding hops are used with the Hook Norton yeast strain. The beers being, Haywain abv 3.5%, CHB abv 3.9% and Twister abv 5.1% - a winter brew.

Brewing was temporarily suspended in 1996, since when the company has taken on the former brewer from the RCH Brewery. It currently supplies about 50 free trade outlets.

Sadly, as this book went to print, it was reported that Colin Diment had died at the age of 46 and the brewery was for sale.

COLD ASHBY **Neal, John,** *Old Black Horse.*

When advertised for sale in March 1860, the property in the occupation of Neal, included a brew house, pump and well of water. Neal was still at the pub in 1862. It seems to have become a Phipps' house around the turn of the century and is still trading.

CORBY **Gibson, Isaac (F1168),** *Midland Brewery, High Street.*

Prior to the development of the steel industry in the area, Corby was a small village, with addresses shown in nearby Weldon in early directories. In 1876 Isaac Gibson is listed as a baker, butcher, beer retailer and grocer. The 1901 edition of Bennett's Directory advertises:- *"J Gibson. Baker, butcher, brewer and beer retailer. The Midland Brewery, High Street, Corby. Home Brewed Ales of the best quality made from pure malt and hops only."*

The following year Kelly's Directory lists Isaac Gibson as a baker, beer retailer and butcher, but with no mention of J.Gibson nor brewing. However, the NBC property list for 1956 includes an off-licence, with brew house, bakers and butchers in Corby, suggesting the buildings survived for some time.

COSGROVE **Phipps & Company (F1195),** *The Stocks.*

Daniel Warren is shown as a coal merchant, maltster and beer retailer in 1847, and the 1851 census shows him occupying a freehold wharf, malting and land adjoining the canal. He seems to have commenced brewing around this time and opened a tied beer house in Cosgrove in the early 1850s. In 1858 he built his "New Brewery" beside the Grand Union Canal. He and his family feature in the earliest photograph taken in the village (Markham p27). They are shown outside their house near the brewery.

COSGROVE (continued)

Daniel Warren traded from the New Brewery until his death in 1874. George Cator a gentleman from Old Stratford was called upon to act for Mary Warren. In 1875 the executors put the New Brewery up for sale:-

"... an excellently arranged brewery in which is fixed a horizontal steam engine, with gearing to pumps and other machinery, ten quarter mash vat, coppers, coolers, squares, refrigeration, etc. ...." (Northampton Mercury 23rd January 1875)

The brewery passed into the hands of Francis Desvaux Bull who in the 1876 Harrod's Directory is given as a brewer and coal merchant. In some directories his name is shown as "Des Vaux", perhaps hinting at a possible connection with the Vaux family. His cards for 1883 show him selling the following beers:-

XXXX Mild	Stout	AK Bitter	Pale Ale
XXX Mild	Extra Double Stout	IPA	Old
XX Mild			
X Mild			

This shows the continuing demand for dark beers, perhaps not surprising when one notes that the 4X Mild was 45/- compared with 54/- for the IPA and AK.

On 26th November, 1888, the brewery was bought by Phipps of Northampton and Mr F.O. Bull signed an agreement to become a brewery traveller for them. The estate consisted of:-

Lamb Inn, Stoke Goldington	Bell Hotel, Apsley Guise
Prince of Wales, Staple Claydon	Horseshoe, Nash

and properties at Cosgrove, Aylesbury and Leighton Buzzard.

The brewery traveller F.O.Bull was given 3 months notice in April 1892, but F.D.Bull is still shown as the manager for Phipps & Co in 1894. In 1903, the premises were being used as store to support the agency at Wolverton.

George Linthwaite, a long-time Phipps' employee, previously based in Towcester, was the manager by 1906. The Phipps' workers ledgers show the staff being taken on to their books in that year and the following year saw staff transferring from Northampton to Cosgrove.

At this time, Francis Bull was living at Cosgrove Cottage and the Brewery House appears to have been empty. The Brewery Yard cottages were occupied by: Frank Tebbutt, Frederick Howard and William Rogers. George Linthwaite retired in 1908 and was allowed to live rent free at Brewery House, Towcester. His son, also called George, continued to run the Leighton Buzzard agency and combined it with that for Cosgrove.

In September 1911, W.H.Sampson the yard manager was reprimanded for irregular conduct and because of the failure of W.B.Key, the agent, and G.H.Linthwaite, the traveller. All three men were given 3 months notice to terminate their service agreements. The agency was then closed in February 1912. In 1932, the brewery site was sold for £1,000 to a builder, Mr R.W.Dickens.

Daniel Warren Brewery as seen in 1997

Photo: Authors' collection

The buildings on the site, a group of two and three storey adjoining red brick buildings with slate roofs, in a line at right angles to the canal, are now used for a variety of small businesses (SP 792 424). What appears to be the old brew house is occupied by Thomson Laboratories.

COTTESBROOKE   **Seamark, Thomas,** *Home Close.*

In 1816 Sir James Langham had a brew house constructed at a cost of £610. His steward described it as well laid out and a *"permanent comfort to the poor"* (NRO LC1089/91). This suggests that it was part of the charitable work which Sir James was taking on behalf of his tenants.

On 21st December, 1825, William Dean writes to Sir James in London to say that, the previous Sunday, William Hobson had died and there was a need for someone to continue brewing. He recommends one Thomas Seamark. The following May, a further letter describes Seamark as superintendent and manager of the brewery and mentions the possibility of engaging a Richard Mills as a brewer. Dean goes on to say that Seamark is managing it very well and he intends to enter his name for the common brewer licence next time.

However, the accounts for the village brew house in the NRO (LC1687) perhaps raise some question about Mr Dean's judgement. Whilst a loss might be expected with 45 persons on the entitled list, this does not excuse the error in the figures for the latter part of 1828, when he seems to have entered the same figure in different columns! There are no further mentions of Seamark, nor commercial brewing.

CRANFORD SAINT JOHN   **Battle Brothers (F1259).**

The 1831 Poll Book lists a James Battle as a farmer, occupying a bakehouse and maltings owned by a William Gent, carpenter of Little Brington. In Kelly's Directories of 1842 and 1847, James Battle (b.1800 Cranford) is listed at Burton Latimer as a baker, maltster and corn dealer.

In 1861 his son, William Battle (b.1835), in the nearby Parish of Cranford Saint John, is shown as a brewer and farmer. The following year he was trading as Wm Battle & Co. In the early 1870s he stopped farming and started a wine and spirits business which he ran in conjunction with the brewery.

In May 1879, Battle mortgaged some of his property for £1,200 to Henry Lamb and John Turner Stockburn of Kettering (see Osborn entry). The property was as follows:-

Horse and Groom, Burton Latimer ++	Leopard, Great Addington
Prince of Wales, Woodford	Red Lion, Isham (now Monk & Minstrel) ++
Royal Oak, Little Addington ++	

The pubs marked ++ are described as having brew houses attached, albeit presumably no longer being used. In addition, the purchase from Arthur Groom of Old, of the Royal Oak for £530 in 1878 mentions a malt house. This pub seems to have been built around 1842 by William Abbott, before becoming owned by Charles Groom of Irthlingborough. The malt house opposite the Horse & Groom had previously been used, from at least 1862, by William Linnell (see Northampton and Syresham), before Battle bought it to supply his brewery.

In 1885 William Battle is listed as brewer, spirit merchant and farmer. William Holland was the manager at the brewery and a beer retailer, whilst Mrs Jemima Holland kept the Red Lion.

At the turn of the century Battle had increased his small estate of tied pubs with the following:-

The Buccleuch Arms, Broughton	The Three Tuns, Broughton

The estate may also have included the Red Lion at Cranford, bought for £2,650 by Phipps in July 1925.

The brewery continued to trade as William Battle and Company until at least 1904, after which time it passed to the owner's eldest son and became Oscar Battle and Company. William Battle died aged 72 on 5th April, 1910. At the end of World War I, the business became a partnership known as Battle Brothers.

The business trademark was a five pointed star set within a circle. In addition, William Battle also used a trade mark consisting of the signature "Wm Battle" in script.

A large part of the brewery estate was sold by auction at Kettering on Friday 4th September, 1925, as follows:-

Old Red Lion, Campbell Praed £3,050	Prince of Wales, Elworthy £3,100
Buccleugh, Campbell Praed £2,700	Horse & Groom, Campbell Praed £3,700
Royal Oak, Elworthy £1,500	

NBC had looked at buying the property, but were outbid. In 1927, the Melton Arms, Kettering, was sold to Phipps and the George Hotel, Kettering to Elworthy. However, the brewery may have continued to operate until 1930. The building remained standing until the end of the Second World War, when it was levelled for an extension to a garage (SP 926 770). A housing development, Battle Close, now covers the site.

A book on the history of the nearby village of Burton Latimer, suggests that after a fire at the brewery it became a tannery belonging to the Batty family, being finally demolished in the late 1970s. Certainly the firm of W.Batty & Son traded as leather dressers in 1928 and 1936. However, this was probably the site of the maltings, opposite the Horse and Groom (now the Old Victoria), which Battle had been using in 1879.

CRICK

Goddard, Christopher, *Grand Union, Crick Wharf.*

Christopher Goddard was a brewer at Crick c.1869. In 1862 he was listed at the Grand Union pub, Crick Wharf, but by 1876 the pub was being run by Thomas Browning. The pub was part of the wharf in the 1820s, when both were owned by John Foster, a farmer and owner of a nearby brick works. In 1907, Mary Goddard sold land, which included a malting, to the nearby Elementary School.

Grove, Henry.

In 1874 Henry Grove moved his business here from Long Buckby.

DAVENTRY

Allard, Francis W and Henry, *14 High Street.*

The Allards are shown in 1881 as brewers living with their parents, but it is not known where they actually brewed. From 1898 to 1910, a Francis W.Allard was brewing at High Wycombe (F2126).

Bailey, Charles, *Dun Cow, Brook Street.*

Listed as a publican brewer in Kelly's Directory of 1877. Prior to this, in 1869, Ralph Cure Reeve seems to have been brewing at the pub, which he had been at from at least 1862. Bailey was still at the pub in 1904.

Burnham, Robert, *High Street.*

Although Burnham is listed as a small scale brewer in Kelly's Directory of 1877, most of the time he is shown only as a shopkeeper and beer retailer, including operating an agency for Ratcliff's of Coventry in 1862. However, the Royal Oak at Drayton was kept by William Burnham in 1877 and it is possible that some small scale production took place to supply it. The pub was later owned by Blencowes before being bought by Mannings in 1925.

Clarke, John, *The Peacock, Market Place.*

Clarke had taken a 7 year lease on the pub in October 1858. When advertised for sale in 1860, it was described as having a large and compact brew house, with a well-constructed pump *"of great force"* and a capacious tank for soft water, extensive wine and beer cellars capable of storing 20,000 gallons of ale. In 1862, Clarke was still at the pub, but was trading as a wine and spirit merchant.

Cox, Benjamin, *Rose & Crown, High Street, Drayton.*

Listed as a publican brewer in Kelly's Directory of 1877. The pub was a Phipps house in 1904.

Daventry & Northamptonshire Brewery Co Ltd, *10 Sheaf Street.*

The Brewers' Guardian for 18th September, 1877, shows this business was registered to purchase land and erect a brewery. Included amongst the subscribers was Jacob Ryde, described as a brewer, Daventry. The Country Brewers' Gazette stated that it had been formed to acquire the land on which a small brewery stood and build a bigger one. However, the business was wound up in 1878 with the sheriff's office in possession and it was reported that the company appeared to be a swindle.

A resource document in the town library (Langhorn 1972) mentions a contract of 4th August, 1877 to build a brewery behind No 10 and suggests that this may have been connected with the Black Boy Inn, which had been trading since at least 1772, when its brew house is mentioned.

DAVENTRY (continued)

The site is now a small shopping precinct known as Prince William Walk, presumably named after the nearby Prince Regent Inn (see below) which traded from 1847 to 1892.

Frost William, *5 Chapel Lane.*

Listed as a brewer in 1881.

Gardner, William, *The Boot, Abbey Street.*

Listed as a small scale brewer in Kelly's Directory of 1877, but the pub was owned by Walker and Soames soon afterwards.

Hollowell, Samuel, *Vicar Lane.*

Although listed in 1851 as a brewer living in Daventry, it is likely that Hollowell was actually the owner and brewer at the Melbourne Arms, Duston (see entry).

Litchborough Brewery (F2782), *21 Alvis Way, Royal Oak Industrial Estate.*

See entry on Litchborough for the background to this small company which moved to the Royal Oak Industrial Estate in 1979, when the business was sold to John Heavermann. He ran the company in conjunction with his son, with Bill Urquhart employed as a consultant. In 1984 the brewery was sold to Liddingtons of Rugby.

Messenger, William, *Coach & Horses, 23 Warwick Street.*

Listed as a small scale brewer in Kelly's Directory of 1877. At the turn of the century the pub was supplied by Lucas & Co.

North, Thomas, *Fox & Hounds, 28 London Road.*

Listed as a publican brewer in Kelly's Directory of 1877. He had been at the pub from at least 1866. Phipps bought the pub in 1887 for £1,500.

Smith, George, *Prince Regent, 20 Sheaf Street.*

Listed as a publican brewer in Kelly's Directory of 1877. A Phipps house by 1904.

Wood Brothers (F1361), *New Street Brewery, West Place, New Street.*

At the turn of the century, all but two of Daventry's pubs sold beers produced outside of the town and both Phipps and NBC had agents in the town. The two exceptions were the Albion and the Warwick House on the High Street, both of which were owned by the local firm of Wood Brothers. This small brewery serviced just four tied houses, the others being the Harrow at Braunston and the Old Crown at Barby.

The New Street Brewery had been opened by 1884 by William Roughton Henton Wood (known as Don), the landlord of the Albion, together with his brother Charles Edward. At that time the brothers lived at 3 New Street, opposite the brewery.

In 1885 C.E. was writing from the brewery to their grandfather asking for £500 to start a mineral water manufactory. They had found premises, but did not have enough money to do it themselves. Despite his statement that *"business had improved lately"*, the shortage of capital was a precursor of later events.

White's Directory for 1896 lists the Woods at 63/65 High Street and New Street. The High Street wine and spirit merchants included premises at No 63, which they had acquired from Pratt & Whitmell, who had been trading between 1847 to 1885.

C.E.Wood died suddenly of pneumonia in December 1902. Wood's Brothers were inadequately financed and they fought an endless battle to keep the four pubs up to the minimum standards required by the licensing magistrates. During the 1914-18 war the money dried up and as a result the pubs became neglected. Three of the four pubs became condemned as unfit in 1921 and without a tied estate the brewery closed in 1922.

After the collapse of the brewery, W.R.H.Wood continued to trade as a wine and spirit merchant at 63 High Street, the next door property having been sold. "Don" died aged, about 90, in the late the 1930s and the business was acquired by the Harris family (Letter Daventry Express 23 February 1989).

Thomas Harris, who had the agency for Allen & Burnett, had moved his mineral water manufactory from the Lion & Lamb to 7 Sheaf Street in 1881. The Wood's wine and spirit merchants backed onto Sheaf Street and included the Sun public house. However, the Harris family continued to trade from the site until the town development, when the High Street frontage became Barclays Bank. The letter from a member of the family suggests that the business had been mainly concerned with mineral waters.

The actual site of the brewery was probably bought by the Daventry Electric Light and Power company, indeed it now seems to be occupied by a sub-power unit. However, it is possible that the building in the yard of what is currently Fagins cafe bar is part of the original brewery site.

DEANSHANGER **Brafield, Septimus,** *Fox & Hounds, 71 High Street.*

Septimus seems to have operated as a publican brewer between 1869 and 1892. In 1872 he is shown as a coal merchant and victualler. The pub is still trading.

In 1860, household furniture, brewing plant etc was for sale on the premises of Mr Charles Brafield, Stag's Head Inn, Great Doddington. In 1847, the pub had been run by a John Cook Brafield. The Brafields seem to have been living across the road at Top Farm prior to this, and it is possible that the plant was not necessarily supplying the pubs. The Stag's Head, which dates back to 1686, is also still trading.

DESBOROUGH **Fitzhugh, J.T.,** *Angel Inn, High Street.*

The Brewers' Journal 1879 carried an advertisement for the sale of this good commercial inn, with a 3 quarter brew house. The inn was described as having a trade of some 250 quarters per year with a good spirit trade. Applications to be made to J.T.Fitzhugh at the inn. He is listed at the pub in 1876, as a butcher and victualler, and as a brewer in 1877. The pub dated back to 1750.

However, it seems that Fitzhugh may have continued in the trade since the Brewers' Journal June 1890 has a J.T.Fitzhugh selling a 3 quarter brew house with off-licence, butcher's business, large yard and outbuildings at Kettering. In 1896 Joseph Allen Dines was at the pub, but is only listed as a butcher. In 1914 the pub was occupied by a Joseph Tebbutt, and later came into the hands of Mannings and then Phipps, before ceasing trading in 1961.

Tailby, William, *Swan Inn, Lower High Street.*

The advertisement on 21st June, 1904, for the sale of this pub, on the instructions of the exors of the late W.W.Tailby, makes mention of a brew house. However, the property was leased to Phipps & Co until 1905 which suggests that the brew house was no longer in use. Prior to this the landlord was a William Woodford Tailby from 1876 and the pub had been in the family hands since at least 1854. The pub was founded in 1729, but was demolished in August 1961.

DUSTON **Wright, John.**

Only listed in Kelly 1877. In 1850 William Hollowell was a maltster at the Melbourne Arms, which he had owned from at least 1830. The brew house at the pub was still standing in the late 1950s. The pub is still trading.

EASTON ON HILL **Edwards, William,** *The Oak, 48 Stamford Road.*

William Edwards, described as a beer retailer at the Oak beer house in 1847, is also shown as a brewer in 1854 and 1861. However, he is not mentioned in 1864, and in 1884 is shown only as a publican. The pub is still trading. It was included in the 1940 Kelly's listing (see Introduction).

Woodward, Allen.

Allen Woodward is listed as a brewer and baker at an unnamed beer house in 1854. Prior to this, George Woodward had been shown as a farmer and maltster. However, by 1874 Allen Woodward is listed only as a farmer.

EYE **Cooke, William Michael,** *Eye Green.*

In 1876 and 1877, Cooke (or Cook) is shown as a brewer at Eye Green, when Edward Cook (e) was keeping an un-named beer house in the village. However, in November 1881, when described as a brewer and beer house-keeper, William was declared bankrupt.

Steels, Thomas John, *Spade & Shovel, High Street.*

Thomas Steels is listed as a brewer in 1862 when he was the publican of the Spade & Shovel (see below), where he remained until at least 1877. The same year, a George Steels was running the Red Lion in the village. By 1892, Thomas was described simply as a gentleman.

EYE (continued)

Whittle, George (F1694), *Eye Green.*

In 1842, John Whittle was the inn-keeper of the Greyhound, which brewed its own beer. John Whittle is still listed at the pub until 1869. By 1874, the Greyhound was being kept by Frederick Hunting, who is listed separately as a small scale brewer in 1877 and 1884, but only as a grocer in 1889. The Greyhound burnt down and was rebuilt in 1902.

In 1854, James George Whittle is shown separately as a brewer and is also listed in Peterborough (see entry). At this time, the Spade and Shovel (see above) was being kept by a James Whittle, presumably the same individual.

James George Whittle seems to have begun operating independently from the pub, since he is listed separately as a brewer in 1884 and 1889. He is then followed by Elizabeth Whittle in 1892 to 1898 and a George Whittle in 1910 (their son?), but entries had ceased by 1914.

FARTHINGHOE

Belcher, James, *The Fox Inn, Bakers Street.*

In 1861 Belcher (b.1813 Middleton) is shown as a licensed victualler at the Fox Inn, but with no mention of brewing. However, a John Pitts (aged 57) is listed as a brewer in the village. James Belcher is listed as a brewer in Slater's 1862 Directory. In 1877, his wife, Fanny Belcher was keeping the pub and in 1884, it was being kept by their son, James Charles Belcher (b.1857), but again there is no mention of brewing. The pub is still trading.

FINEDON

Rappitt, Alfred, *Prince of Wales, Well Street.*

The Prince of Wales was a cottage and garden in 1806, but seems to have been selling beer by 1869, when it was kept by a Jerome Coope. The first mention of its name is around 1871. Alfred Rappitt became the licensee in 1884 and he is listed as a brewer in 1892. Rappitt was at the pub until 1927, but he had probably ceased brewing well before that, since he is described only as a beer retailer in 1914. The pub is still trading.

Warner, Thomas, *Mason's Arms, 51 High Street.*

The pub was built in 1830 by Joseph Warner (b.1790), a stone mason. On his death, his wife Mary took over as the licensee. Thomas Warner (b.1827), presumably their son, was at the Masons in 1869 and was a small scale brewer to at least 1884, when he is listed as a brewer and farmer. Around 1900, Thomas "Tupney" Wilson was at the pub, which was known locally as "Tupney's". He is still listed as a brewer in 1902, but in 1914 he is shown only as a beer retailer, which may be linked to its ownership by Dulleys sometime afterwards. It closed in 1956 and is now an antiques shop.

FOTHERINGHAY

Berridge, Joseph.

In 1864 Joseph Berridge is listed as a baker, brewer and beer retailer, presumably at the Falcon Inn on Main Street, previously kept by a Charles Berridge in 1854. However, by 1874, a John Wade is shown only as a baker and victualler at the Falcon.

GEDDINGTON

Croot, Frederick James, *Star Inn, Bridge Street.*

In 1896, the Star Inn, Bridge Street, was for sale by auction on the premises, complete with 2½ quarter brew house. The pub was then in the occupation of Frederick James Croot, who had been there since 15th October, 1864.

"A large and influential company, including all the principal brewers of the county, met Messrs J Robinson & Son at the Star Inn on Wednesday, when some valuable property was put up for sale." Kettering Leader & Observer 24th July, 1896.

The pub was bought for £1,800 by Phipps.

This old establishment is still trading on the corner of Malting Lane. There had been a malt house on the lane since at least 1852 and an attached bakehouse and grocers shop had taken out a licence to sell beer in 1853. The first mention of the Star is in 1857 and it may have grown out of the first concern.

HARRINGWORTH

Barnes, George.

In 1847 George Barnes was shown only as a baker and maltster, but by 1854 he had become a brewer, maltster and beer retailer. The last mention of brewing and malting seems to be 1866. In 1874, George Harris is shown as a baker, grocer, maltster and beer retailer in the village, suggesting that he had perhaps taken over the business.

HELMDON **Pratt, John.**

John Pratt is listed in Slater's Directory for 1862 as a brewer, but by 1877 is only shown as a beer retailer at an unknown location (see also Canons Ashby entry).

HELPSTON **Bodger W.**

Mr Bodger is listed as a brewer and inn-keeper in 1876. This seems to be the only entry, although a Charles Bodger is shown as a beer retailer the following year.

Whitehead, William.

William Whitehead is listed as a brewer in 1876, but in 1884 is shown only as an agent for the Lion Brewery and was possibly the NBC Peterborough agent made redundant in 1892.

Around this time a Henry Whitehead was the Head Brewer at Allen & Burnett, Northampton. The introduction mentions his links with the Dorman and Phipps families. and that he was the grandfather of Charles McLeod. The McLeod link perhaps explains the later take-overs of local breweries at Kings Cliffe, Bourne and Spalding. Prior to that a Whitehead family owned the Two Brewers, Abington Street in 1845.

HIGHAM FERRERS **Nene Valley Brewery (F5456.1),** *Unit 1, Midland Business Centre, Midland Road.*

Opened in April 1992, before moving to this address in October of that year. In early 1996 it moved again to Wellingborough (see entry).

IRTHLINGBOROUGH Allen, John, *Minerva Brewery, Mott Street, Birmingham.*

On 15th July, 1851, Joseph Fulford a brewer and maltster of Birmingham took John Allen a farmer of Irthlingborough and William Marshall, farmer of Rushden, into a partnership to run his Birmingham brewery.

Crick, Alfred W., *High Street.*

In February 1881, Alfred, a publican in Northampton (see entry) bought the brewery of Septimus West (see below) for £1,700, but with a mortgage of £1,200 to Frederick Muscott. However, the Brewers' Journal January 1883 describes Alfred W.Crick of Irthlingborough, as bankrupt. In February his property, a brew house, with spirit and outdoor beer licence, was for sale by auction. The property became owned by Charles Crick of the Green Man at Hanslope in Buckinghamshire, where the family may have originated.

In 1847, James Crick of Hanslope had owned a property in Wellingborough. Charles later sold his property to Mannings, but the Irthlingborough site may have become a smithy at some point.

Northants & Leicester Clubs Brewery.

At some point the Northants and Leicester Clubs Brewery had a depot in the town, with beer supplied from Syston Street, Leicester. However, "Froth and Fizz" p40 has a picture of a half-pint beer bottle marked *"Northants Clubs Co Ltd, Irthlingborro"* dating from 1905. Since this pre-dates the foundation of the Northants and Leicester in 1920, they may have been bottling the product of a local producer. The brewery at Leicester closed in 1969.

Sargent, James.

Sargent is listed as a brewer between 1892 and 1895. This may be the James Sargent, officer of the Excise, painter and plumber, who was at the White Horse Inn, High Street in nearby Higham

Ferrers from 1851. In 1898, the pub was owned by Mrs Eliza Sargent, with Thomas Parker as the tenant, but with no mention of brewing.

Smith, Thomas.

The Northampton Mercury in 1801 carried an advertisement for the sale of the Red Lion at Olney. *"Interested individuals should apply for particulars to Thos Smith, brewer, Irthlingborough."* A John Smith, the father of Thomas, is also mentioned as a brewer around this time, but by 1810 he is shown at Market Harborough. The names and location suggest that this may be the Smiths of Oundle and Little Bowden (see entries).

Alternatively, in 1847, a Thomas Smith was the publican at the Railway and at Irthlingborough Wharf, the property of John Smith, Bridge Street, Northampton.

West, Septimus (F2299), *Hope Brewery, High Street.*

In 1830, James West, a baker, was buying property originally owned by the Scarboro family. However, in 1837 he was declared bankrupt and some of his property was put up for public auction at the Bull Inn. The sale produced insufficient funds and the property was bought in by the assignees John George of Bytham and Thomas Rye of Irthlingborough (the Rye family owned the King's Arms).

James Murphy of Wellingborough seems to have stood surety for West and hence he was still trading as a baker in 1847 in property shared with Robert Partridge and John Chapman. This business passed to his son Septimus. In 1849, a James West occupied the Anchor Inn, The Wharf, Higham Ferrers, on the outskirts of Irthlingborough, but it is not known if they were related.

During 1854 it seems the bakery concern was expanded to include commercial beer brewing, and in 1862 Septimus is shown as a beer retailer in addition to being a baker and flour dealer. However, Septimus, like his father, over-stretched his resources, since in September 1869 he became bankrupt, although he obtained his discharge straight away.

The 1870 edition of Mercer and Crocker's Directory lists Septimus West in bold type which singled him out from every other brewer in the county. The Irthlingborough census of 1871 gives Septimus, aged 41, as living in the High Street with the occupation of common brewer.

Septimus was able to develop the brewing side to the extent that by 1874 he passed the bakery to his son James Cornelius West.

In 1876, the Anchor was still being kept by a James West. Septimus was still brewing in 1877 when Kelly's Directory lists him at the Hope Brewery. However, in March 1879 he mortgaged the brewery, described as recently erected, for £1,200 to Frederick Muscott a tailor from Northampton. He also seems to have borrowed £850 from Joseph Gallard, of Ramsgate in 1877 and been involved with Thomas Colson a victualler in a property deal concerning Strode Road on the Victoria Estate in Wellingborough.

In 1880, when involved in a court case with Mr Lamb a corn merchant, he was described as a brewer. However, in October Muscott gave him notice to pay up or he would sell the brewery. In 1881 West sold the brewery to Alfred Crick (see above) and paid off Muscott. The site of the brewery seems to have been just to the east of the Baptist Chapel down from the Market Cross.

KETTERING

Bates, Edward, *Market Place.*

On 30th June, 1825, the sale of property owned by William Door mentions that it extended as far as the newly built brew house, late in the occupation of Edward Bates. The Golden Lion on Market Street had a brew house when mortgaged by NBC in 1887.

Bell, Charles, *Northall Street.*

Charles Bell a grocer and baker with a shop in Northall Street was listed in 1850 as a retail brewer at Freetone (or Freestone) Row. He had only just built his premises, which consisted of four properties, upon a piece of land that had previously contained slum buildings. However, in 1876 he is shown only as a baker and shopkeeper at 19 Newland Street. In 1898, Miss Bell's beer house at the top of Gas Street was tied to Phipps. The area is now covered by the Newlands shopping centre.

Elworthy, John & Company (F2333), *The Crown Brewery, 5 Gold Street.*

The original small brewery was bought by the Rose family of brushmakers, when they acquired the licence of the Crown Inn and brewery. In 1824 the inn had been kept by Mary Bailey, with an address in the High Street. By 1830, William Rose junior had taken over the Crown Inn in

KETTERING (continued)

Gold Street. Demand for his beer was such that he was able to enlarge the brew house and sell his beer to other publicans. He was also the local agent for Guinness.

However, the family also still operated as brush makers until 1840 the year in which William Rose died, leaving his wife Ann with 11 children aged between two and 21. Ann brought up the family, survived smallpox and managed the brewery for 30 years. By 1847, Rose & Co were operating on a commercial basis as brewers and brandy merchants. Of Ann's sons, William Henry, the eldest, married into a brewing family at Rayleigh, Essex (Peaty p90 in 1866). Ann was sole controller of the brewery when she died in 1871, and none of the family remained who could run it.

In 1871 the ownership of the Crown Inn and brewery was taken over by William Elworthy who also purchased other pubs in the Kettering area. From at least 1824, William Elworthy had owned the Ram Hotel in Sheep Street, Northampton, from where he ran a daily coach service to London. On taking over the Kettering brewery, he appointed his elder son William to help him, while younger son John looked after the family farm at Brixworth. The elder son died within a few years, leaving John Elworthy to take-over in 1875.

John Elworthy sold the farm and moved to Kettering to live in Brewery House. He understood the trade, as he had regularly ridden over from Brixworth to help his father and brother, and he brought trusted farm workers to staff the brewery. Available records show a Mr Baker employed as the brewery manager.

To supply beer to his growing tied estate Elworthy enlarged the capacity of the Crown Brew House. In November, 1880, Messrs Arthur Kinder of London were asked to proceed with drawings for a new brewery. The Country Brewers' Gazette January 1881 carried a list of tenders for the new 10 quarter brewery and the Brewers' Journal described it as completed and now at work in October. The importance of the brewery began to overshadow that of the inn and by 1885 it had been rechristened William Elworthy and Co, The Steam Brewery, 5 Gold Street. The Elworthy tied estate at the time was:-

Crown Inn, Gold Street, Kettering	King's Head, Kettering
King's Head, Wilbarston	Rose and Crown, Rushden
Talbot, Goose Pasture Lane, Kettering	Three Cocks Inn, Lower Street, Kettering
Three Cranes, Great Cransley	Crown, Cottingham

It seems that sales were also obtainable direct from the brewery at the Tap House, 6 Gold Street. The company also owned two unnamed beer houses, which were at Burton Latimer and Rothwell.

That the business was growing can be seen from the Brewers' Journal October 1892, when a 25 barrel steam copper for the new brewery, to Arthur Kinder & Sons design, was shown on Robert Morton's stand at the Brewers Exhibition. During this period the brewery was managed by a Mr E.D.Barber and in 1898 was trading as Elworthy Jn.

Opportunity to further develop the tied trade arose in 1899 when Frederick Tebbut put his Sudborough brewery and its tied estate up for sale. Competition for the tied pubs was fierce but Elworthy successfully bid for four of them:-

Coach and Horses, Woodford	Lord Nelson, Stanion
Mason's Arms, Twywell	Round House, Sudborough

In July 1903 William Elworthy died, aged 90. He had continued to live at Brixworth until he was 82 when he had moved to Woodwalton near Peterborough.

By 1910 the premises were described as the Crown Brewery. The brewery was registered as a limited company in 1912 adopting the title John Elworthy and Company Ltd. The company owned the George Hotel, 15 country pubs, off-licences and houses for workers.

John Elworthy died in 1924 and was succeeded as head of the business by his son William. In his mid-forties, William was well liked by the brewery employees. He had a gift for humour and at the firm's social events gave monologues as an old Devon countryman. He had for some time lived in London, looking after the firm's interests there and commuting to Kettering to help his father with the management. In 1924 he bought Beech House and came to live in Kettering.

In 1927 Elworthy's were involved with the sale of the last "free" houses in Kettering. In the space of 6 weeks, Phipps bought the Melton Arms, John Elworthy Ltd the George Hotel and T.Manning & Co Ltd the Alexander Arms.

"To toast the victors, to console the vanquished"

**KETTERING
(continued)**

Elworthy's advertisement for Kettering Choice Ales which ran along the canopy of the covered terrace on the Britannia Road side of Kettering FC's ground (Ireson Book V p92).

In 1931 William and his young wife took a short break in Paris. On returning home, William was taken ill with typhoid fever, dying shortly afterwards. This marked the end of the family connection and led to the sale of the business.

William Elworthy's nephew Gordon Thomas Seccombe Gray, later to become a Rear Admiral, recounted (Ireson Book IV p115) how after he went to Pangbourne Nautical College in 1924 his uncle made a determined effort to attract him into the business. He was shown over the brewery and at supper that night William asked him if he would like to change course and make a career in brewing. William had no children and there was no-one else in the family likely to succeed as head of the long-established and prospering business. The young man declined in order to pursue his subsequent successful career in the Navy.

In July, the Phipps' Board discussed the possibility of buying, but did not take the matter any further. Although NBC were invited to tender in August 1931, and Praeds of Wellingborough suggested putting in a joint bid, NBC went alone, but their valuation of £75,397 for the business, except the George Hotel, was not accepted. In September, Sir Sidney Herbert Evershed of Marston, Thompson and Evershed, together with Mr G.D.Langley, MD of Elworthys, C.Wesley general manager and C.H.Stringer, executor of the late C.W.Elworthy, announced the take-over of the concern, except the George Hotel.

Sir Sidney stated that brewing in Kettering was to cease; however, it seems that brewing continued at the Crown Brewery until 1940 when parts of the site were demolished. The remaining property was used by Marstons as a depot/bottle store until 27th May, 1960, when it was sold to Sainsbury Properties Ltd for £36,000. In 1964, the new owners demolished the main building and erected a row of shops on the 50 x 180 foot site.

Brewery House, which had stood at the entrance to the brewery for 200 years, as the family home of the Roses and Elworthys, had been demolished in 1933 to widen the brewery entrance.

Fortunately, the 1904 maltings and some of the old brewery yard remain on Tanner Lane/Lower Street (SP 866 789). There is an impressive four storey building, with "JE, 1904" marked on the wall. The kiln at the rear has an elaborate cowl and a slated roof, while a loading door backs on to Tanner Lane.

The Elworthy maltings

Photo: Authors' collection

Hipwell and Company (F2334), Olney and Kettering, *1 Horsemarket.*

In 1877 references are made to Hipwell and Company's Ale and Porter Stores in the Horsemarket. This site was a depot for the company's Olney brewery and supported the tied houses in the Kettering area. The Olney brewery had been built in 1853 next to the Bull Hotel.

KETTERING
(continued)

A reminder of Kettering's brewing past - Hipwells's stores in the Horse Market

Photo: Authors' collection

Hipwell's were bought out by Phipps in 1920 in an amicable agreement which put J.C.Hipwell onto the Board of the Bridge Street Brewery. The Horsemarket stores were sold for £1,250 in June 1923. It is still possible to make out an advertisement for Hipwell's Ale and Stout Store etched on the wall of the building in the Horsemarket.

Johnson, John, *Dukes Arms, Market Street.*

Johnson is listed as a brewer from 1864 to 1876, when he was keeping the Dukes Arms.

Shortland, Mirzala Mrs, *Old White Horse, 43 High Street.*

Mrs Shortland is listed as a publican brewer in 1892. James Shortland kept the pub from at least 1862. However, in 1898 the pub was being run by George Britts, with no mention of brewing.

Warner, John.

The earliest reliable record of commercial brewing in the town is for 1784, when John Warner is listed as a common brewer through to at least 1799. In 1781 he had been listed only as a farmer.

Willis, William, *The Cherry Tree Inn, Sheep Street.*

William Willis of the Cherry Tree Inn, Sheep Street was fined £5 in 1888 for concealing worts from the excise and making a false entry regarding brewing sugar (Brewers' Gazette 16 October). He was listed at the pub in 1884, prior to this Mrs Elizabeth Willis was shown as a beer retailer in the Market Place in 1876.

The pub, which was rebuilt, with a mock half-timbered look, sometime after 1905, when it is shown with three storeys, is still trading as a Charles Wells house.

Wilson, Thomas.

Holden's Directory lists Thomas Wilson as a brewer in 1811, but this is the only entry.

KINGS CLIFFE

Cunnington, John, *Eagle Brewery, West Street.*

In 1847 John Cunnington (b.1820) is shown as a maltster and brewer; however, he was one of four men with the same name living in the village! He seems to have been living in Park Street, but owning property in West Street tenanted by Thomas & Daniel Palmer.

In 1851, John, still a cooper and brewer, his wife Catherine and two daughters are shown as living in West Street. He may also have been the inn-keeper of the Eagle Tavern in West Street. At this time, he seems to have constructed a brewery at the rear of the pub. The building, which still stands, has a tablet in one of the ground floor arches marked JC 1851, suggesting the year of construction. The Eagle Tavern was kept in 1854 by James Belton. John is still listed as a cooper and brewer in the 1861; although now with four daughters.

However, Kelly's 1864 Directory lists James Low (possibly the same listed at Cambridge earlier) as the brewer and maltster at the Eagle Brewery, Park Street, which may have been his residence rather than the location of his brewery. The listing giving Low at the Eagle Brewery shows that the actual Eagle Inn was being run by Richard Skinner.

John Cunnington is only listed as a cooper in 1871, when John Chapman (b.1853 at Nassington) is shown as a brewer in West Street. The Eagle Tavern was being kept by George Saddington. This seems to be the last mention of brewing at the Eagle, although the Tavern was still in the hands of George Saddington in 1881.

On 8th September, 1891, the property of the late F.R.Dain esq was for sale by auction at the Corn Exchange, Market Harborough. Described as having a frontage of 160 ft to West Street, it included:- *"Brick built brew house, Fully licensed beer house - The Eagle, tenant George Dixon, Large substantial 3 storey maltings, stone built and slated."*

Eagle Lane is the southern boundary of what is now the Old Brewery Studio in West Street, Maltings Lane being the northern boundary. The village hall occupies the old maltings in Maltings Lane.

Cunnington, William, *West Street.*

In 1818 William Cunnington, then aged 49, advertised for mill-wrights to help in the construction of a tower mill. The mill in West Street was soon followed by a brew house and two maltings, one in 1822 and the other in 1825. The property was next to the Mill House. His brother Whittsey was a publican and farmer in Ringstead.

William's son, William II (b.1802), acquired the business in 1850 on the death of his father, In the 1851 census he is described as coal merchant, maltster and brewer employing 4 men. He was living in West Street with his wife Maria and their 4 children. In 1861 the two elder sons, William III (b.1833) and John (b.1834) are described as brewer's assistants.

In 1871, William II is shown as a brewer and maltster, but only John was still assisting at the brewery; William's elder son, William III, seems to have left the business. The brew house supplied the nearby Windmill pub, but this may have been its only outlet.

In 1874 Joseph Slingsby, a baker with a shop in Park Street, took over the mill. Brewing seems to have ceased at this time, although William continued to trade as a maltster until around 1885, when he was in his eighties. After this time, Slingsby also took over the maltings.

The windmill operated until about 1910, after which it stood derelict. The long disused brewery and maltings also stood idle until 1924 when they were demolished. The following year the old windmill followed them into oblivion.

Dixon, Reuben & Libbeus, *Golden Ball.*

The Golden Ball which closed in 1971, dated back to around 1597. In the latter part of the 19th century, it was kept by the Dixons and brewed its own ale. From 1892 to 1920, the pub was being kept by an Libbeus Dixon, whilst a G then a W.Dixon kept the Eagle.

Fane, William Henry, *Cross Keys, 2 West Street.*

The Cross Keys is a listed 17th century building which has been licensed since 1732. In 1859 it was for sale by private treaty with brew house, the tenant being Robert Holmes who had been there for many years. In 1876, John Henry Fane was the licensee of the pub. However, William "Jockey" Fane (b. 1838 Bedford), who described himself as "a family brewer" was at The Cross Keys Commercial Hotel from 1873 to at least 1894. In 1901, W.H.Fane is shown simply as a gentleman in the village.

Ketton and Kings Cliffe Brewery Company (F2406), *Malt & Hop Brewery, West Street.*

The 1896 Peterborough Directory shows the Ketton Brewery Company as operating from West Street, presumably having bought the Eagle Brewery. The Ketton brewery was founded by 1846 by Francis Whincup in the village of Geeston (F1816/ F2336 see also Stamford), who was malting at Kings Cliffe in 1862. In 1866, Whincup & Son of the Ketton Steam Brewery were also trading from Mansion House Stores in Peterborough. It was trading as the Ketton Brewery Co in 1895, when it seems to have been owned by Messrs Sealy & Wilde, with William Thompson at the Geeston Tap.

Around this time it seems to have changed its name. The Ketton & Kings Cliffe was registered as a limited company in March 1898, with a capital of £12,000. The founders seem to have been one Frederick Coutts Bourne and Julia Morley, the wife of a Samuel Morley, 19 Paulton Square Chelsea.

Courtesy of Jack Feast

Mrs Morley had apparently purchased Kings Cliffe Manor House, the Eagle Brewery and tavern, and a brewery at Ketton, including the adjoining Tap public house. The estate also included the Slater's Arms at Collyweston (now known as the Cavalier). However, in 1897, she had apparently tried to sell some of the business to a George Henry Elliss and the following year to one James Henry George.

The previous entry suggests that the Kings Cliffe plant was not operating when it had been sold in 1891. Nevertheless, Christopher Heppenstall was brought in as the Head Brewer and manager at the Company's West Street premises. The Heppenstalls owned the Albion Brewery at Newark on Trent (F3476), but this was left in the hands of Christopher's brother Harold. Christopher is listed as the manager in 1898, but does not seem to have stayed in Kings Cliffe for very long and returned to Newark.

In 1899 a firm of hop merchants brought an action against Mrs Julia Morley of the Ketton and Kings Cliffe Brewery Co. It was alleged that she was in the habit of buying breweries, not paying bills, selling out at a profit and meeting creditors with the defence that she was a married woman with no estate of her own. Any investors in the concern were soon disappointed, for the firm was dissolved on 26th October, 1900.

After the failure of the main company, the Ketton brewery appears to have been run by a Percy Crowhurst until 1908. It was then owned by a Claud Wyborn Gordon Walker possibly until as late as 1933 (Coopers Directory). Prior to this, a Mr C.W. Walker had been at Papillon Hall near Market Harborough. This was not the Ketton brewery bought by John Smith of Oundle, who actually bought Bean and Molesworths (F2335).

The now separate Kings Cliffe concern was known as the Malt & Hop Brewery, operated by Godfrey Keppel Papillon (b.1867). He was, reputedly, a county level opening batsman, whose family originally owned Papillon Hall. He is shown in the 1901-02 Bennet's Directory as the sole proprietor of the brewery and as a wine and spirit merchant and maltster. The Directory advertises *"All beers guaranteed brewed from pure malt and hops only"*. However, an E Papillon is listed in the 1901 Peterborough Directory as a *"Family Brewer"* at Kings Cliffe.

The business was now trading as the Malt and Hops Brewery Company, but also seems to have used the name the Kings Cliffe Brewery Company between 1906 and 1910. A 1909 guide to Kings Cliffe refers to the "The Eagle" or Brewery Tap as one of ten pubs in the village.

In 1910, ownership of the Malt and Hops Brewery passed to Charles Campbell MacLeod (or McLeod) who traded there until 1919. MacLeod who lived at Cawthorpe House, Cawthorpe about one mile north of Bourne, had also bought the Bourne Brewery (F557) in 1910, merging it with Soames and Company of Spalding (F4719) six years later (see also entry on Long Buckby). He went on to become the Managing Director of Soames, retiring at the time of its take-over by Steward & Patteson.

KINGS SUTTON

Blake, Fanny, *Red Lion, 17 Red Lion Street.*

In 1854, Mrs Beatea Blake is shown as a shop keeper and beer retailer, but there is no mention of the Red Lion. Fanny Blake is listed as a brewer in 1862; however, Miss Fanny Blake is shown later as a shopkeeper and beer retailer. In 1876 the Red Lion pub was being kept by a Miss Blake. The pub does not seem to have traded for very long and is thought to have been the building still standing at number 17.

Colegrove & Son (F2421), *Wales Street.*

John Colegrove owned a farm and maltings in Wales Street in 1862. In 1874, he is shown as a maltster and sometime after in partnership with his son, he began to brew beer, and in 1877 the business was known as Colegrove and Son.

In 1884, the brewery was listed as Colegrove (Mrs Hrt Ellen) and Son (Joseph White) brewers and maltsters, suggesting that the father had died.

The last reference to Colegrove and Sons Brewery is in 1903. By 1906 William Brown Colegrove is listed just as a farmer. "The Old Brewery" now a modernised house stands on the right just before the bend into the station.

LITCHBOROUGH

Jones, Thomas.

In 1847 Thomas Jones was a maltster in the village and soon after he is recorded as a small scale brewer and maltster until at least 1862.

The Litchborough Brewery (F2782), *2 Northampton Lane.*

Prior to the Watney closure of the Northampton Brewery, Bill Urquhart, who had been the Head Brewer since 1972, had been asked to produce a feasibility study which allowed for two options:-

1. Demolishing the old Phipps' brewery and erecting a new purpose built mega-brewery capable of supplying their pubs across the whole south of England
2. Selling off the Bridge Street site and establishing a small depot to serve the local monopoly in Northamptonshire and the surrounding area.

They decided on the latter!

The preparation of that feasibility study had sown an idea in Bill Urquhart's mind. If he could brew just a few barrels of beer a week to sell to local free houses then he could live reasonably well. It would be a risky business, but he was faced with unemployment anyway.

Redundant brewing equipment from Northampton was installed into an outbuilding at Bill's Litchborough home. He commenced brewing his Northamptonshire Bitter in July 1974 and launched the beer at his local - the George at Maidwell. A lager called Litchbrau followed but this was quickly scrapped.

Barrels of "Litchborough" were soon going into free houses and off-licences all across South Northamptonshire and into neighbouring counties. It even made an appearance in four Northamptonshire off-licences. Bill's experiment had paid off and he was brewing 350 barrels a year.

The Litchborough brewery, Daventry site

Photo: Authors' collection

LITCHBOROUGH (continued)

Planning to retire at 65, Bill actively sought a partner to eventually take-over from him. There was no shortage of volunteers and Frank Kenna was taken on in 1978. It became apparent that Frank did not want to take on the risk of running the brewery when Bill finally bowed out.

Premises away from Bill's house were actively sought and for a time it seemed likely that a site would be taken in the village. In October 1978 local opposition to the relocation in Litchborough thwarted Bill's plans. Eventually a year later the business was sold to John Heavermann - a former British Leyland executive - who moved the brewery to Daventry's Royal Oak Industrial Estate. He ran the company in conjunction with his son, with Bill Urquhart employed as a consultant.

In 1983 the brewery was sold to Liddingtons of Rugby. The Liddington family once brewed at Tring, Hertfordshire, but the new owners were now a firm of beer wholesalers and bottlers. With the move into Warwickshire the name Northamptonshire Bitter was killed off. Liddingtons ran the brewery for a couple of years until it closed in 1986. Bill Urquhart retired and returned to his native Scotland.

LITTLE BOWDEN

Eady and Dulley, *Northampton Road.*

Until 1888 Little Bowden was part of Northamptonshire, rather than Market Harborough, Leicestershire. The brewery was built on the Northamptonshire side of the river, around 1800. This was on land which John Smith (I), of Oundle (see entry) is thought to have bought from a Mr Hand as part of the inclosure.

John Smith bought the Butcher's Arms, Husbands Bosworth, in 1807 from John Staples, to whom he was related by marriage, he had also purchased the following:-

Fox Inn, Market Harborough, 1794
Old Crown, Market Harborough, 1805
Three Horse Shoes, East Farndon, 1802
Swan Inn, Kibworth Beauchamp, 1806

In 1804 John's son William, common brewer of Little Bowden, was involved with a property purchase involving the Green Dragon, Dagg Lane (now 14 Church Square Market Harborough). In 1813, Mr W.Smith advertised *"that old-established and extensive brewery, now in full trade"* for sale by private treaty. However, the sale seems not to have gone ahead, since in 1815, William conveyed much of the property to his own son, also called John. Meanwhile, John Smith senior (I) moved to Great Bowden where he died in 1818. The main Oundle brewery was being run by William's brothers John (II) and Thomas.

In 1819 J.T.& W.Smith, Little Bowden Brewery, were supplying the overseers of Harborough with a barrel of beer per week at 12s a barrel. The Bowden brewery was run by William, who is listed as a brewer in 1831, but by 1837 his son, John, was listed as the brewer. The business was trading as John Smith and Son in 1839 (see Weedon entry) and John took over the rest of the property, including the brewery, in 1843-4. This was part of Messrs Smith & Son, Weedon and Bowden Breweries from 1840 until around 1846.

The 1847 Poll Book describes John Smith of Little Bowden owning property on behalf of the executors of the late John Smith of Oundle. In the 1851 census, he was still living in Little Bowden with his widowed mother, wife Ellen and sons William Henry and John Percival. The last mention is in 1853, in the sale details for the Weedon brewery.

The brewery was opposite property owned by Joseph Nunnely, who bought the business from the Smiths in April 1854. His partner was J.Aggas, but the latter died the following month, although in Kelly's 1854 Directory, Nunnely & Aggas are listed as brewers and spirit merchants.

On 1st June, 1865, Nunnely formed a partnership with Joseph Chamberlain Eady (b.1838 Leicester). The brewery may have been extended around 1867 and was transferred to J.C.Eady in 1880, with the Nunnely & Eady partnership dissolved in November 1881.

In 1882, Eady formed a new partnership with James Dulley of the Wellingborough brewing family, running the business as Eady & Dulley (F3325). The brewery was rebuilt in 1893. In June 1895, the business was incorporated, with the majority of the preference and ordinary shares owned by the two partners. However, there was also a large debenture stock issue to the bank. The business owned some 36 licensed premises, 6 off-licences and the Burton Latimer Working Men's Club, as well as leasing 5 others.

New offices and stores to the design of Everard & Pick of Leicester were opened behind the Peacock Hotel. The first year as a limited company saw a dividend of 14%. However, the business could not have been that successful since in April 1900 they made an approach to Phipps of Northampton, but the latter declined to buy the business.

LITTLE BOWDEN (continued)

In 1909, Kenneth Eady and Charles Eustace Woolston, of the Wellingborough brewing/malting family, became directors. However, family did not always over-rule business, since on 18 March, 1914, J.Dulley junior was given 6 months notice to leave as brewer, in the meantime another brewer would be sought and J.D paid off with 6 months salary if one was found within the period. Unfortunately, the minutes give no indication of what had caused the decision.

J.C.Eady died on 27th May, 1920, James Dulley became the Chairman and Herbert W.Dulley and J.Toller Eady joined the Board. The brewery approached NBC, with an offer to sell the business, but NBC turned it down as being too dear. Kenneth Eady also had talks with Phipps in 1922, but the latter did not take up the offer.

In 1925, H.W.Dulley and J.T.Eady were appointed joint MDs, with respective salaries of £300 and £400 per annum. However, in 1927, James Dulley's role as Chairman began to be filled by Herbert, suggesting possible illness.

Problems with brewing clearly had not been rectified, since on 29th May, 1928, Mr Middleton the brewer was given one months notice. Mr Sprake of Wellingborough (see Praeds entry) was appointed to supervise on a salary of £150 per annum. James Dulley died in October 1928, and Kenneth Eady also seems to have died around this time. The deaths, together with the brewing problems, caused an approach to Praeds to buy them out.

However, on 6th February, 1929, Praed's turned down the offer to buy the business because of the terms and the brewery was taken over by NBC. They had offered £21 5s for the £10 Ordinary shares and £10 for the Preference, costing some £104,062 3s 3d including paying off the overdraft. Outstanding mortgage debentures meant that the business was continued as a subsidiary company.

At the time of the take-over, the business owned some 67 properties, of which 42 were on-licensed and 10 off-licensed ones. They also leased 2 fully licensed houses and were described as having a valuable wine and spirit trade with a large country connection. In October 1929, the brewery demolition was contracted and the site levelled, before being sold in 1935 to ShowFilm Ltd for £3,000. NBC bought the mash tuns at market prices and moved them to Northampton.

The registered offices were transferred to Northampton in 1933, when the £54,037 overdraft was paid off. Two years later, the private trade was transferred to the NBC subsidiary Home Butler Ltd. In 1936, the brewery offices, behind the Peacock, were considered for conversion to an office and shops. In 1938, the Eady & Dulley debenture stock was redeemed, the outstanding mortgage debenture of £54,510 paid off and the business wound up. The last remaining part of the offices were sold to the Post Office for £15,000 in October 1958.

The site of the brewery was later used as a bus-station until being cleared for a shopping development.

LONG BUCKBY (inc Buckby Wharf)

Grose, Thomas.

On 10th July, 1830, Thomas Grose a brewer and maltster was declared bankrupt (Northampton Mercury). His business stock, farm stock, and personal effects were taken by the local receivers (Messrs John Heygate of West Haddon and Henry Saunders of Harlestone).

"Lot 2, comprises of an important business, consisting of a wholesale and retail brewery, in full trade. The brewery buildings are substantially erected, and are capable of brewing 70 barrels per week, with a copper furnace containing 375 gallons, a 6 quarter mash vat, underback, three large coolers and a large square working tun, containing 22 barrels, the whole nearly new; 2 large casks containing 1,200 gallons each; and other casks of different sizes, containing 2,600 gallons and upward; one underground cellar, capable of holding 4,000 gallons, and two other cellars capable of holding 1,500 gallons, the whole well supplied with good water from two pumps; together with a new built brick and slate messuage or dwelling house adjoining the said brewery....stabling for five horses.... The whole calculated for an extensive and good business, which has been carried on upon the said premises for many years by Mr Thomas Grose." (Sale notice in the Northampton Mercury of 17th July, 1830)

The same sale included a property in Edward Street, with a brew house, the home of a butcher John Russell.

Grove, Henry.

In 1864 Henry Grove was an established maltster and brewer at Long Buckby. He brewed here for a further ten years before moving to Crick.

LONG BUCKBY (continued)

Walker and Soames (F3075), *Anchor Brewery, Buckby Wharf.*

The 1851 census shows Long Buckby as having 4 brewers and/or maltsters and 7 inn-keepers. The demand for beer from the Weedon Garrison, some 3 to 4 miles down the canal, was huge and in 1869 this helped to attract two local businessmen into commercial brewing. One was William Harris FCS a chemist from 33, Gold Street, Northampton, who had been manufacturing aerated waters and lemonade at his shop, trading as Northants Aerated Waters in 1861. He developed this sideline into the firm of Harris and Woodward (c.1863), before it became owned by Hogan & Co and then T.Dadford by 1869.

In terms of family background, in 1831, a Thomas Harris junior was a maltster at Braunston, his father Thomas senior was a victualler at Mercers Row, Northampton, whilst a William Harris owned the Harrow at Braunston. In addition, a Henry Harris and Joseph Montgomery were partners in a maltkiln at Ashby St Leger.

The other partner at Long Buckby was Francis Montgomery of the Heathencote Bone and Artificial Manure Works near Towcester. Together they founded Montgomery and Harris (Brewers) of Buckby Wharf.

In 1868, at the sale of Richard Worster's property at Buckby Wharf, Mr Montgomery, brewer, bought property to the value of £2,640. This included the Greyhound Inn, various warehouses and limekilns, and a malting being used by P.&R.Phipps. In 1869, Francis Montgomery bought the Wheatsheaf at Weedon Bec.

However, the Brewers' Journal November 1871 shows the firm of F.Montgomery, W.H.Harris & W.Montgomery junior dissolved as regarding Harris. William Harris had quit the partnership and his place was taken by William Montgomery. Hence, in 1877 the business was trading as Montgomery, Francis and William, Buckby Wharf, whilst Francis is also listed as a maltster.

In September 1878, Francis Montgomery purchased the Pomfret Arms in Northampton for £2,700, but sold the Wheatsheaf to NBC. He is also reported as owning several of the pubs in Buckby and the Anchor at Nether Heyford. The Boot at Daventry and the Crown at Staverton also seem to have been owned at this time.

The partnership of F.& W.Montgomery was dissolved in 1879, and in 1884 only F.Montgomery was listed as the brewer. The following year the brewery was being referred to as the Anchor Brewery. The concern was still fairly small, only 9 workers being employed at the brewery in 1891. The Brewers Exhibition of 1892 included an AK Light Bitter from F.Montgomery's Anchor Brewery. In 1886, the Shoulder of Mutton, Crick, was bought by Francis Montgomery, described as a brewer of Heathencote.

There is an entry in 1894 for Francis Montgomery, but shortly afterwards, the Anchor Brewery, together with the mineral water plant at Towcester, was bought by the firm of Walker and Soames. Certainly, they owned the Shoulder of Mutton in February 1897. They traded as brewers, wine and spirit merchants and maltsters at Buckby Wharf and soft drink manufacturers in Towcester. The maltings were located along the canal from the brewery. However, in 1898, the Cattle Market Restaurant at Victoria Promenade, Northampton, was shown as owned by Francis Montgomery.

The new partners, Gerald M.Soames and Gerald Walker, were committed to the local community and allowed the maltings to be used for several local functions. In 1897 a Jubilee tea was held there for 200 persons and the local church made regular use of the facilities for meetings, concerts or fetes. Mr Gerald Soames gave generous donations to the church every year and also gave money to the village cricket team.

The Weedon Garrison continued to be a valuable market; however, in 1898 Walker and Soames were fined for short measure in five barrels of mild sold to the canteen.

In 1899 the company increased their business to 48 tied pubs by taking over Edward Major-Lucas' Victoria Brewery in Northampton. The Anchor Brewery is reputed to have ceased brewing in 1903, with production concentrated at Northampton. Certainly the licensed houses, which were leased to a Mr Browning, were offered to Phipps in 1904. Walter Buchanan Browning retired officially from the business in 1905, when the brewery and houses were offered again at £30,000, but the Phipps' view was that they were not worth anything like that. When Captain Hugh E Browning died in June 1907, yet again properties were offered to Phipps, but once more declined.

During 1910, Hopcraft and Norris acquired Walker and Soames. Ownership of the Shoulder of Mutton was transferred the following year. The Long Buckby site became a distribution depot for the Brackley and Banbury concern. The brewery building was subsequently demolished in the early 1920s, although Anchor cottage is still standing near Lock No 8 (SP 607 655).

Gerald Soames was the nephew of Captain Robert Soames of Soames & Company the Spalding brewers, who were later to have connections with the Malt & Hop Brewery (see Kings Cliffe entry). Gerald Soames bought a house called Hillside at Buckby Wharf soon after the sale of the brewery and continued to live there for many years. Gerald Walker went to live in East Grinstead, Surrey.

*BHS Archive
Birmingham Central Library*

Captain Robert Soames lived in the village of Scaldwell from the late 1870s until his death in May 1923 at the age of 85. The Soames family may also have had some connection with W.& S.and A.Soames trading in Great Grimsby in 1877 and Holes of Newark.

MIDDLETON

Ashwell, Richard.

The 1762 militia listing show Ashwell's occupation as being that of ale brewer, although the pub or inn is not identified.

MILTON MALSOR

Compasses, The, *61 Green Street.*

In 1998, Nolan Inns bought the plant from the Abington Park brewery intending to supply the 6 houses in their small chain. It was to be located at the Compasses, but after a change of plan, the plant was broken up and sold.

Dunckley, Sarah.

The earliest record of a brewer at Milton is in a church register dated 1719 which refers to *"Sarah Dunckley, widow, who sold ale"*. A similar source records William Marks as a brewer here in 1824. Another claim to fame for the village is that it housed the hop gardens of Phipps' brewery as shown in an excise entry in Thomas Phipps' journal for 1852.

"I, Thomas Phipps of Bridge Street, Northampton do hereby make an entry of one kiln or oast, marked 2k, for the purpose of drying hops, the produce of my own hop ground in Milton Field in the parish of Milton".

East, W.J. & Co (F3394), *The Hope Brewery.*

The deeds of the Greyhound Inn provide the history of the Hope Brewery which grew up beside it. The earliest record is dated 3rd November, 1795, when Nathan Wilson (see Northampton) of Little Doddington (Denton) bought the Greyhound Inn and brew house.

Wilson sold the inn to the partnership of Thomas Cockerill and William Buswell on 25th September, 1812. Thomas Cockerill, related by marriage to Sarah Dunckley, immediately set about enlarging the brew house which he then christened "The Hope Brewery". The partners were then able to advertise in the Northampton Mercury *"Home brewed ale for farmers and others"*. Ownership of the Greyhound and the Hope Brewery passed to William Minards in 1825. The business was little changed when it passed to James Lilley ten years later. Thomas Cockerill was then described as a maltster at Pattishall.

It is recorded that the water from the brew house well was exceptionally pure and this made for very good beer. Seeing its potential William John East purchased the business on 28th June, 1866. The brewery was soon enlarged to considerably increase the capacity.

The original Milton brew house was demolished in 1879 and East erected a tower brewery in its place.

The following year Herbert East was taken into partnership by his father and the business traded as William J.East & Son. Over the next ten years he took on more and more responsibility, becoming the Chairman on 5th December, 1891.

MILTON MALSOR
(continued)

W.J. East and Company, the brewery buildings in 1995

Photo: Authors' collection

The Hope Brewery successfully ran a "beer at home" service which accounted for majority of its production, with over 1,300 private customers on its books.

W.J. EAST and SON HOPE BREWERY, MILTON, NORTHAMPTON STORES:-

51 WOOLMONGER STREET

ALE, STOUTS AND PORTERS ARE BREWED EXPRESSLY FOR PRIVATE FAMILIES FROM FINEST MALT AND HOPS WHICH CAN BE RECOMMENDED AS BEING AGREEABLE IN FLAVOUR, MODERATE IN PRICE AND ABSOLUTELY PURE. THE ABOVE GENUINE HOME BREWED ALES AND STOUTS ARE SUPPLIED IN 6, 9, 18 AND 36 GALLON CASKS. CARRIAGE FREE.

N.b THESE CELEBRATED HOME BREWED ALES AND STOUTS ARE STRONGLY RECOMMENDED FOR HAY AND HARVEST PURPOSES.

Northampton Guardian 13th October, 1883

MILTON MALSOR
(continued)

W.J.East's Brewery Milton Malsor - Front elevation of the brew houses

Photo: Ian P Peaty

In 1888 Herbert East built a brand new three storey brewery extension to the one built by his father nine years previously. A full description of the Hope Brewery is recorded in the book "Barnard's Noted Breweries". This source describes how the company ran the two breweries in tandem. *".... the wort gravitated into 3 coppers, one of which was in the old brewery and the other two in the new copper house...the wort passed to the fermenting rooms of which there were three. No. 1 fermenting room ...held 4 fermenting squares, each holding 35 barrels.... No. 2 fermenting room had 10 similar fermenting squares and No.3 fermenting room, situated in the adjoining old brew house, had 5 fermenting vessels of 50 barrel capacity...."*

Barnard mentions tasting their XXX, which he describes as a superior full-bodied drink of considerable strength. At the time East's price list per gallon was as follows:-

ALES		STOUTS	
K Table	10d	S Family	1/-
X Household	1/-	SS Single	1/2
XX Mild	1/2	DS Double	1/4
XXX Mild	1/4	EDS Invalid	1/6
XXXX Strong	1/6		
		PALE ALES	
		AK Light Bitter	1/-
		PA or Primrose Ale	1/2
		IPA	1/4

On 23rd January, 1897, the Hope Brewery became a limited company trading as W.J.East and Company Ltd. The widespread tied estate consisted of at least nine pubs, but the majority of the business was still *"beer at home"* with 1,300 private customers listed on the company accounts. To serve these accounts, East's had five depots/stores:-

Northampton - 51 Woolmonger Street and 5 Derngate	Poddington near Rushden
Kettering - Eden Street	Wellingborough

The licensed premises included the following:-

Barley Mow, Cosgrove	Boot Inn, Eastcote
Greyhound, Milton Malsor	Half Moon, Grendon closed 1915
Queen's Head, Astcote	Rifle Butts, New Duston
Royal Oak, Collingtree closed 1908	Royal Oak, Great Glen
World Upside Down, Raunds	

They also supplied the Refreshment Rooms at the Northampton cattle market, which were licensed to Walter Francis East. There were also 4 off-licensed premises.

Financial problems seem to have beset the Milton brewery at the end of the 19th century. In 1897 they were forced to mortgage the Hope Brewery to the Northampton Union Bank. In addition, William John East died aged 62 on 19th October, 1900.

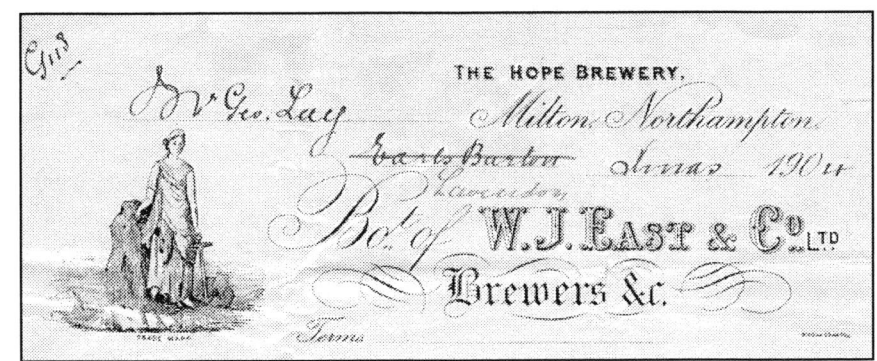

A bill from 1904 which post dates the take-over by NBC. It shows Hope, a rare motif on East's paperwork.

Furthermore, the business became caught up the arsenic scare of 1901 when supplies of malt from a Liverpool maltster were contaminated with arsenic from the malt house coal and distributed to brewers far and wide. East's were one of the firms supplied and were fined £10 for arsenic in their beer and all casks on the premises were confiscated.

In December 1904, East's were offered to the Northampton Brewery for £13,000. The take-over was completed by March 1st of the following year. The final bill to NBC was £10,376, including the book debts, stock, loose effects and valuation. The brewery plant was sold and the site made available for sale or rent. However, NBC were still trying to rent the site as late as 1920.

In 1906, Walter Francis East was shown as the licensee of the Fleece on Bridge Street, Northampton (see entry for Brown).

Both brew houses are still standing next to the Greyhound on the old Northampton to Towcester road (SP 733 556). The Hope Brewery malt house on the village green is now a terrace of 6 cottages. The Hope Brewery premises were later taken over by Persimmon Homes and are now offices.

MOULTON

Bunton, William Wallis, *Artichoke, Church Street.*

The pub dates back to 1621. In 1861 Mr Bunton is listed as a licensed brewer and inn-keeper. He is shown at the Artichoke in 1864 and 1866, although the latter date shows him as a farrier. Around this time, Thomas Checkley is shown as a licensed brewer and baker, but with no mention of location.

In 1877, the Artichoke was being kept by a Thomas Clarke, but there is no mention of brewing. It was later a Ratliffe & Jeffrey property, and is still trading.

NASEBY

Fitzgerald Arms, *Church Street..*

The shell of the old brew house at the rear of the Fitzgerald Arms is still standing, but now houses the toilets. The pub dates back to the 18th century when it replaced the Bell, and at one time was owned by Hunt, Edmunds of Banbury.

The Fitzgerald Arms brew house

Photo: Authors' collection

NORTHAMPTON

Abington Park Brewery Company, *Wellingborough Road.*

In September 1984 The Abington Park Hotel began to brew beer on the premises. Clifton Inns, part of Grand Metropolitan Hotels, had introduced this scheme into half a dozen of its houses. The brewing equipment was designed and supplied by Inn Brewing Ltd, a company set up by two ex-Whitbread brewers.

Originally called the Abington Brewery, Clifton Inns had to change the name when Charles Wells objected, since they still owned the company of this name which used to brew some 100 yards down the road. They still use the name on low-price supermarket beer sold in plastic containers.

The five-barrel brew house regularly brewed two beers called Cobblers Ale (after the town's football team) and Abington Extra. This range was extended and altered numerous times, but two new brews which became regulars were Cricketer's Ale and Lionheart Porter. The beers were stored in cellar tanks under CO^2 at atmospheric pressure.

With the further mergers in the industry, the pub is now owned by Scottish Courage. Unfortunately, it was decided to stop brewing in 1997; although there was an attempt to move the plant to Milton Malsor (see entry).

The Abington Park Brewery

Photo: Authors' collection

Allen & Burnett (F3577), *Lion Brewery, South Bridge.*

The Lion Brewery was founded by Thomas Hagger, a prominent Northampton businessman, liberal councillor and nonconformist. Hagger was born at Potton in Bedfordshire in 1795.

Until 31st May, 1833, he had been a partner in the Bridge Street based *"Barwell and Hagger, Iron and Brass Founders"*. Upon leaving the Eagle Foundry, Hagger started a liquor business. The first reference to this appears in a string of adverts in the Northampton Mercury throughout 1835.

"To Let. The Lion and Lamb situated in Bridge Street, Northampton. Now in full trade apply ... Mr Hagger maltster and spirit merchant."

In the 1836 electoral register, Thomas Hagger is shown as living in Sheep Street and also the tenant of a house, brewery and coal wharf at Cotton End, the property of George Osborn, 30 Paradise Terrace, Islington. This may have been the brewery previously used by the Thompsons (see entry). The wharf owned by George Osborn was tenanted by John & John Pettifor in 1833, which suggests that Hagger occupied it shortly afterwards.

It is possible that the Lion Brewery may have taken its name from the nearby Lion and Lamb Inn, kept by Thomas Campton in 1824. The first mention of the brewery is in the Mercury of 30th June, 1838, when the joint nonconformist Sunday schools held their celebrations for Victoria's Coronation there.

A sale notice for the Shoulder of Mutton at Crick asked those interested to contact:- *"Mr Hagger, Common Brewer, Northampton"* (Northampton Mercury 21st December, 1839). It seems that he sold the pub in 1842.

NORTHAMPTON
(continued)

```
LION BREWERY, NORTHAMPTON.
MESSRS. JOPE & JOPE
HAVING completed their NEW BREWERY, which is fitted with every modern appliance necessary to the process
of Brewing on the Steam Principle, are prepared to supply the Public, and Private Families, with a first-class
Article at the following Prices:—
              Per 9 Gals.   18 Gals.                          Per 9 Gals.   18 Gals.
    X  ALE      7s. 6d.    15s. 0d.     PORTER           9s. 0d.    19s. 6d.
    XX  "       9s. 9d.    19s. 6d.     SINGLE STOUT   12s. 0d.    24s. 0d.
    XXX "      12s. 9d.    25s. 6d.     DOUBLE STOUT   13s. 6d.    27s. 0d.
    XXXX "     13s. 6d.    27s. 0d.
STORES:—COVENTRY, TOWCESTER, WELLINGBOROUGH, AND RUGBY.
Messrs. JOPE & JOPE are appointed SOLE AGENTS in this District for the BURTON BREWERY CO.'S
ALES, at the following Prices:—
   BURTON ALES ........ 1s., 1s. 2d., 1s. 4d., 1s. 6d., and 1s. 8d. per Gallon.
   PALE ALES .......... 1s. 6d. and 1s. 8d. per Gallon.
They also beg to call the attention of Private Families to the following PRICE LIST of SPIRITS, of first-rate
quality:—
                                Per Gal.                                Per Gal.
   PALE BRANDY (Best Foreign) ... 30s.   BEST GIN ................ 14s.
   BROWN "     (Best Foreign) ... 28s.   GIN ..................... 13s.
   BROWN BRANDY .................. 24s.   BEST RUM ................ 16s.
                                  20s.   RUM ..................... 17s.
   WHISKEY (Super Scotch) ........ 21s.
N.B.—Messrs J. & J. are desirous of receiving APPLICATIONS for AGENCIES for the SALE of their ALES
and PORTER, in the following Towns, on liberal Commission:—
       LEICESTER, MARKET HARBOROUGH, KETTERING, and DAVENTRY.
```

During this period the liberals dominated the town's politics and Hagger was Mayor of the town in 1838 and again in 1851. In 1840 Thomas Hagger's address is shown as South Bridge; however, by 1850 he had acquired a new site in Cotton End, Hardingstone, which he converted into a brewery (SP 756 597). His original premises were then used as a coal yard. The maltings were nearby at Weston Wharf. He also owned the Wheat Sheaf at West Haddon. By this time, the family had business interests in London which were overseen by one of Thomas' sons, who lived in Pimlico.

The Lion and Lamb Inn was closed on 21st February, 1859, in which year the brewery was trading as Hagger and Jope, also agents for Wilder's Burton Ales. Hagger then seems to have sold out his share. The new owners were two brothers John B.S and William S.Jope.

"Messrs Jope and Jope beg to call the attention of private families to their splendid and brilliant Christmas Ale at 1/6d and 1/8d per gallon. Orders received at the Lion Brewery." Northampton Mercury 17th December, 1859

During their short time at the Lion Brewery, the Jope Brothers carried out extensive modernisations. They converted the antiquated ill-equipped brewery into a modern steam powered concern. They developed an extensive trade at London, Towcester and Weedon and a large stores at 47 Grey Friars, Coventry. They also owned pubs in Coventry including the Unicorn from 1861.

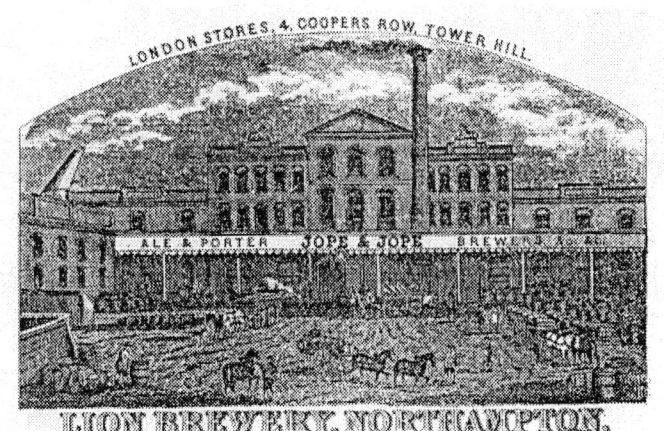

A Lion Brewery bill head from August 1865.

By 1866, the Lion Brewery had been sold to three local businessmen Thomas Coales, Phillip Allen and Henry Cooper. Their business had grown up out of a beer depot set up by Cooper at Hardingstone.

HARVEST ALES
Henry Cooper, sole agent to Ind Coope and Company of the Brewery, Burton on Trent can supply Old Ales for Harvest purposes at 24/- net per barrel (36 gallons) delivered to any railway station. Hardingstone, near Northampton. Northampton Mercury 30th June, 1860

```
WILLIAM JOPE AND JOHN JOPE
        (LATE HAGGER),
   ALE AND PORTER BREWERS,
   HOP AND SPIRIT MERCHANTS,
      LION BREWERY, NORTHAMPTON,
               AND
        BISHOP STREET, COVENTRY.
```

NORTHAMPTON
(continued)

The new owners of the Lion Brewery maintained their agency with Ind Coope, whose beer they sold alongside their cheaper own brews. However, H.Cooper is listed separately as a brewer at 4 Wood Hill, but he left the partnership in 1869 and started a photographic business.

The partnership of Coales and Allen prospered and they both lived in fine country houses. Thomas Coales lived at Great Houghton Hall, whilst Phillip Allen remained in Hardingstone.

In 1877, the Bulls Head, Sheep Street was transferred from W.Warren to Coales & Allen.

When Coales died in 1880, this left the brewery solely in the hands of his partner. This was not to remain the case for long.

"Notice is hereby given that the business heretofore carried on by the late Thomas Coales and the undersigned Phillip Allen at Northampton as Common Brewers, Maltsters and Spirit Merchants under the style of Coales and Allen will be in future carried on by the said Phillip Allen and the undersigned Frank Burnett as the firm of Allen and Burnett and all accounts with the late firm may be settled with the new firm. Dated this thirteenth day of December 1880."
Northampton Mercury 25th December, 1880

The new partnership opened offices at 6 Wood Hill, buying the shop from Henry Cooper. They ran several pubs in the town, the most notable being the Lord Palmerston on the Market Square. As well as local village pubs they had several accounts in Coventry, where Phillip Allen had strong connections.

However, Allen and Burnett began to get into financial difficulties and in November 1887, they made an approach to NBC, but the terms were not acceptable to the latter. In February 1889, they entered into fresh discussions which led to their eventual take-over through a share transfer. The following statement was issued:-

"The Northampton Brewery Company have entered into negotiations with Messrs Allen and Burnett of The Lion Brewery, Northampton for the purchase of their business. A meeting of the shareholders of the company is to be held next week to consider the negotiations as far as they have been carried; and if approved, steps will at once be taken for the raising of the capital."

The take-over was finalised and was reported at the December AGM of NBC. Phillip Allen joined the NBC Board and remained a member until his death around 1910.

The Wood Hill office was sold off to a chemist, called Kinnell, in 1890. By March 1891, the Lion Brewery was only partly occupied, with a Mr John Barford leasing part of the premises. The plant and machinery, except the boiler, were put up for auction, with NBC reserving the rights to buy some and transfer it to the Phoenix. However, the maltings continued to be used for some time.

About 1894, the brewery was converted to a mill, which was almost totally destroyed by fire some two years later. After 1896 the remaining brewery building was used as a bottle store and oddly enough as an indoor cricket training net. With the outbreak of World War Two, the Lion Brewery was used as a civil defence base.

The purchase did not prove to be to NBC's advantage, since the 70-80 properties were run-down and did not bring the expected increase in trade. Unfortunately, this was also a time of general depression which did not help sales, despite a major investment in the houses by NBC. Phillip Allen suggested that they could have sold some 3 months earlier, but his partner had said no.

The NBC AGMs from 1892 to 1894 were marked by criticism of the purchase, indeed at the latter the Chairman admitted that *"As to the capital, he said it was no use hiding the fact that they did make a most unfortunate purchase when they bought the Lion Brewery"* (Hear Hear from the shareholders).

In November 1946, NBC negotiated to take-over the site of Greenough's builders merchants (112 Bridge Street), adjacent to their Phoenix Brewery. As a result the Lion site was offered to the building firm and the remains of the brewery were demolished. The stone lion was reputely moved to Moulton Park.

Ansell, James, *Bird in Hand, 4 Regent Square.*

Ansell was at the pub by at least 1864 and is listed as a brewer in 1877. By 1900, the pub was being run by J.Burt, with no reference to brewing.

NORTHAMPTON (continued)

Ashby, Edward, *Wellington Street.*

Mentioned in a newspaper article in 1838, Ashby was presumably a jobbing brewer, since he refers to brewing at Mr Clarke's house (see entry), the latter being a baker in the same street. In 1836 Ashby is shown as the occupant of a malting and house in Abington Street, the property of William Clarke.

Banks, Thomas, *Dychurch Lane Brewery.*

In 1809, James Durham of the Spread Eagle Brewery (see entry) bought an existing brewery business in Dychurch Lane. The following year he sold this *"common brew house"*, but retained the attached maltings.

"TO BE LET OR SOLD a large convenient building situated in Dychurch lane in the town of Northampton; comprising a brew house, two cellars, stabling for four horses, and a yard with a pump of good water. The premises having been used as a common brew house will be found a desirable purchase for any person wishing to engage in that business- if not disposed of before the first day of March it will be sold in auction together with the brewing utensils casks etc.. further particulars may be known by application to Mr James Durham, Mercers Row, Northampton." Notice - Northampton Mercury 10th February, 1810

The business appears to have been sold or leased to the Banks family. William Banks had been running a brew house in Cock Lane (later known as Wood Street) since at least 1796. This may have been at the site previously occupied by William Clark (1790-96). The business passed to his son Thomas Banks, who is listed as a brewer in Dychurch Lane in 1810 until 1830. It may have been bought by Nathan Mawby who is listed in Dychurch Lane in 1830 and possibly the site which became the Black Boy (see Clark entry).

Bennett, James, *The Forget Not, 52 Bath Street.*

Listed as a publican brewer in 1866. Prior to this he had been a beer retailer on Kettering Road. The pub is still trading, but is now called the Sportsman's Arms.

Billingham, William, *Meacocks Row.*

Listed only in 1818, the location later became part of Bridge Street.

Boon(e), William, *Bearward Street Brewhouse.*

William Boon(e) was a brewer here from *c*.1790 until *c*.1818. James Wilson is listed between 1818 and 1841 at Bearward Street. Prior to this, in 1781, George York was listed as brewing in the same street.

Brooker, Ernest, *Cambridge Street.*

Brookers appeared in directories as brewers, but were producers of ginger beer.

Brown, John, *Fleece Commercial Inn, 115 Bridge Street.*

In 1845 the Fleece had been owned by a Mr Manning and prior to that Richard Phipps. However, in 1855, Brown's headed paper describes the Fleece as providing Burton and Home Brewed Ales. He is listed in 1861 as brewing at the pub and he was still there in 1864. Joseph Jules Guignol was running the pub with no mention of brewing in 1874, but in 1878, it was being kept by Mr Charles Konow as a fully licensed inn, advertising *"Burton and Home Brewed Ales"*. Mr Konow was also the proprietor of the Refreshment Saloon, Cattle Market and both properties seem to have been run by Easts (see Milton Malsor) at some point.

In 1889, the pub was being kept by William Rigby with no mention of brewing. It later became a Phipps house before being closed in 1930 and demolished for road widening in 1931.

Brown may have been related to the John Brown who was a victualler at the Hatton Arms in Gretton, which is still trading. However, the latter operated on a very small scale, since an inventory of his property when he died in 1853 valued the brew house coppers at £3 and 4 small barrels at £1 10/-.

NORTHAMPTON (continued)

Brown, John, *Garibaldi, 17 Bailiff Street.*

Brown was from Rothwell and had moved to Northampton where he is shown as a beer retailer in 1849. At some point the premises became the Garibaldi, where he is listed as a brewer and grocer in 1877. He also seems to have owned the Boot & Slipper, 10 Spring Lane, in 1864. The pub was rebuilt in 1897 by his son, also called John. John Brown was still running the Garibaldi in 1900, before selling it to Dorman Pope, of which he had become the Chairman (see entry).

Bull, Fuller, *Angel Lane Brewery, Phoenix Place.*

In 1790, Laomi Howard was a brewer in Angel Lane. Six years later, Thomas Whitmy was running the business. The Whitmy family went on to become wealthy builders, and in 1842 Pickering Phipps married Mary Whitmy, whilst his cousin and partner, Richard Phipps, married Ellen Whitmy. By 1830, the Angel Lane brewery was being run by Fuller Bull, who had previously been brewing in Silver Street (1818). Bull was still here in 1841, but the following year the business was in the hands of James Bull and the address was given as Phoenix Place. James Bull soon afterwards moved from brewing into keeping a beer house.

Burgess, Joseph, *St Mary's Street.*

Burgess is listed from 1830 to 1841 but the exact location is not known.

Butcher, William, *Race Horse Inn, Kettering Road.*

The Northampton Mercury for 3rd January, 1852, gives details of the sale of effects at the Race Horse Inn included Brewing Plant, property of Mr Butcher. The pub was tenanted by a William Ward. The address is shown as 6 Abington Street in 1864, when the pub was being run by Thomas Plumb, but with no mention of brewing. William Butcher lived at 20 Abington Street.

William Butcher was the owner of the Race Horse in 1841, when he also owned the Ship, Mercer's Row (1830-1840) and the Plumber's Arms, 16 Sheep Street. In 1836, he also seems to have been at the Half Moon, previously kept by Thomas Butcher, which was owned by a Benjamin Atkins. The Race Horse is still a pub at 15 Abington Square, but has been extensively rebuilt.

Butler, George O'Connor, *Cream of the Valley, 31 Crispin Street.*

The pub was kept by a Thomas Butler in 1858, but he is only shown as a beer retailer. However, in 1877, George is listed as a brewer. The pub was bought by Phipps in 1884 for £425 and closed in 1908, when the licence was surrendered for extention of the Overstone Arms.

Butler, Robert *(1792) Fish Lane*

Butlin, Thomas, *Bearward Street then Wellington Street.*

This may be the same Thomas Butlin who had been the tenant of the Half Moon, 163 Bridge Street between 1816 and 1826. Thomas is shown as a brewer between 1830 and 1841. In 1881, a George Butlin was a brewery traveller.

Carlsberg, *140 Bridge Street.*

Initial negotiations about the land at Bridge Street had begun in 1969. The Phipps NBC breweries were closed over the period 1973-74, and their demolition left the site clear for the construction of a brand new plant aiming to tap into the growing demand for lager. The brewery was designed by the internationally renowned architect Knud Munk and Phase I was aimed at 1m barrels per annum. The Steinecker brew house was capable of producing a brew every 4 hours.

The new business (F3576) required an initial £12m investment, which was jointly financed by Watney Mann (49%) and Carlsberg of Copenhagen (51%). Carlsberg had been imported into the UK from 1868 and supplied in the area by Phipps.

The first brew was in August 1973 with bottling in October. The formal inauguration was on 10th May, 1974. Phase II from 1974-76 saw an expansion to 2m barrels and Phase III in 1977-79 saw the building of the canning line and warehouse. The brewery site covers some 20 acres and is capable of 3m hectolitres, ie about 528m pints, per annum. It is now valued at £100m.

When Grand Metropolitan, who had acquired Watney, finally withdrew from brewing, their share in this plant was sold to Tetley, who were part of Allied-Domecq. In 1997, Carlsberg AB finally took 100% ownership of Carlsberg-Tetley and have recently made further significant investments to increase the capacity of this site and secure its status as a leading UK brewery for the 21st century.

Chance, John, *The Knightley Arms, 9 Commercial Street.*

Chance is listed as a brewer in 1866 and he had been at the pub from at least 1864. Later, in 1877, Edward C.Craddock is shown as brewing at the pub, but in 1889 it was being run by Mrs Jane Craddock with no mention of brewing. The pub closed in the early 1960s.

Chapman, James *(1790-96), Woolmonger Street.*

Chapman, Thomas *(1790-92), Bridge Street.*

Clark, Thomas, *Black Boy, 55 Upper Mounts.*

In 1854, Thomas Clark is listed as a baker, butcher and beer retailer at 53 Upper Mounts and 111 Scarletwell Street. In 1845, Mr Clarke was running the Labour in Vain, Mounts, and it may be that at some point the pub changed its name, since in 1858 the location is shown as the Black Boy. Thomas is shown as a brewer there in 1877. Prior to this a William Clark was a victualler and maltster in St Giles Street (see Ashby).

"Black Boy Beerhouse and Bakery for sale..late in the occupation of Thomas Clark." Mercury 25th September, 1879

The Black Boy closed in 1917. Thomas Clark also seems to have owned the Rifle, 59 Bouverie Street, in 1864.

Clayson, James *(1790-1792), Broad Lane.*

Colledge, Robert *(1818), Horseshoe Lane.*

Cook, William, *King's Street.*

William Cook, a carrier, at some point bought the Dolphin, which had a brew house in 1802. Although he is shown occupying a bakehouse in St Giles Street, he also owned the Red Lion, Sheep Street and a malt house at Cotton End. In 1839, a W.Cook is also shown as a maltster at Wellingborough.

Craddock, George, *Admiral Nelson, 3 The Green.*

George Craddock is shown as the brewer in 1877, having been at the pub from at least 1866. However, around 1884, the pub was being kept by Mrs Craddock and brewing seems to have ceased. By 1888, it was owned by Mannings, before becoming a Phipps pub, which closed in 1953.

Crick, Alfred William (1877), *Queen's Head, 14 Gold Street.*

In 1877 as well as being listed as a brewer at the pub, Crick also owned a cooperage at 9 Woolmonger Street, which he seems to have sold in 1884 (see Irthlingborough entry). The cooperage had been owned by the family from around 1830, prior to which it had been the Swan. Crick at been at the Queen's Head from at least 1845.

NORTHAMPTON
(continued)

However, an advertisement for the cooperage in 1865 stated that it was *"Established above a century"*. Joseph Crick is mentioned as a cooper in Woolmonger Street in 1828, whilst his son Joseph junior was also a cooper in Kingswell Street. In 1850 the following coopers were listed:- Isaiah Crick at Woolmonger Street; Joseph Crick, 4 Victoria Terrace; Joseph Harrison Crick, Kingswell Street.

In 1858, Joseph Crick was running the Royal Oak, 56 Woolmonger Street, whilst William is shown at 9 Woolmonger Street. The last mention of A.W.Crick is in 1899, when he is shown as a cooper at 42 Bridge Street, and the Queen's Head was being run by a James Perrin. The Cricks may be the same family which, prior to this, was malting in Wollaston. The Queen's Head closed in 1961.

Denbigh & Co (F3579), *16 Lorne Road.*

This company is shown as brewers in 1918 and 1922, although it is most likely that they were producers of ginger beer. The premises were taken over by Cutlers, a firm in the shoe industry, during the 1920s (SP 755 612).

Dorman Pope & Co (F3578), *Abington Brewery, 334 Wellingborough Road.*

In 1899 the local building firm of Henry Martin and Company was engaged to build a new five storey brewery in Abington village (SP 771 612). The clients were the newly formed company of Dorman, Pope and Company who owned a parcel of land between Wycliffe Road and Lutterworth Road.

The firm had three main shareholders George A.Dorman, Charles James Pope and Alderman John Brown. Prior to forming this new enterprise, both Dorman and Pope had worked for Phipps.

The Dorman family was originally from Dartford in Kent. George Dorman, the grandson of Thomas Phipps, had been a brewer at Bridge Street for nineteen years, latterly as Head Brewer, and was the brother of Thomas Phipps Dorman one of the Managing Directors of Phipps. The Dormans had also been running a wine and spirit merchants in the town. Alderman Brown, born 1854, was an important local politician and the father of John Brown, a member of an architectural partnership, the designer of the brewery.

It is possible that Charles Pope may have had links with the Biggleswade malting family which traded as William Pope in 1883. He became the Head Brewer of Dorman Pope, where his scientific knowledge was well known. He was particularly well regarded for his knowledge of brewing water and its preparation. He was pleased with the purity of the water from the well at the new brewery - *"Without pure water, it is impossible that sound wholesome beer can be brewed; let the skill of the brewer be never so great."*

Dorman Pope was seriously under capitalised and when John James Martin presented bills on behalf of his father's building firm they could not meet them. Building work ceased! In 1902 the firm raised further cash by a share issue. In a compromise deal, Martins were partly paid in debenture shares. The impressive red brick brewery was finally opened for production in 1902.

An inaugural dinner was held on 23rd January, 1903, at the Duke of York. Employees of both the brewery and the builders attended the function, along with C.J.Pope and Francis Harris the joint MDs. The latter may be the same individual previously at Long Buckby (see entry). Also present were A.E.L.Foll, the manager and two brewery pupils, Herbert H.Dorr and R.O.Raven. However, Henry Martin was absent as the result of an accident. A sadder absence, was that of George Dorman who had died before the completion of the project. A briar pipe, as a memento of the founder, was presented to each of those attending the dinner.

Alderman Brown commented on their beer being served to the tables and said that although they would miss Mr Dorman, Mr Pope thoroughly understood the business and science of brewing. He pointed out that the brewery was already inadequate for the large influx of trade and they were looking to extend the premises. However, it was emphasised that they did not aim to be a large firm, but simply wanted to brew good beer and sell it. Dorman Pope's

NORTHAMPTON (continued)

Abington Park Ale was soon offered as *"an ideal dinner beverage at 1/- a gallon"*.

The untimely death of George Dorman compounded the growing problems at the brewery. He had been a senior member of the management team and his experience was sorely missed.

Following the launch of the brewery, the company opened a town centre office, with a wine and spirits shop attached at 8 The Drapery. Further outlets for their beer were sought and they set about buying any available pubs. They purchased the Garibaldi Hotel in Bailiff Street, from Councillor John Brown the Company Chairman, for £6,000 which was well over its market value. This carelessness with money was a particular failing of Charles Pope and he was criticised by the firm's auditors for his error of judgement.

At this time, the company was able to advertise *"Our Ales & Stouts have received flattering recommendations from many doctors in the district on account of their excellence and purity"* (Northampton Independent 10th November, 1906). The range was as follows: Stingo, IPA, Light Pale Ale, Abington Park Ale, Extra Stout, Light Dinner Stout and Strong Xmas Ale. Their advertising used the slogan *"Improved types of the old-fashioned home-brewed ales and stouts"*. Their beer casks were glazed inside with a patent glaze to keep the beer sweet.

Charles Pope began to borrow money from friends as the firm began to struggle. Once again Fred Kilby, the firm's auditor, cautioned Pope but again he went unheeded. To raise additional capital, most of the pubs were mortgaged to the Northampton Union Bank.

In panic, John Brown bought the Garibaldi Hotel back from the brewery but paid well under the market value. Following criticism of this profiteering Brown contended that the pub's trade had dwindled under the ownership of Dorman, Pope. His political opponents used this to pillory the ex-Mayor in both the media and at public meetings.

The brewery muddled through, often running from crisis to crisis. In 1908 two of their tied houses (The Old Bakehouse and the Horse Market Tavern) were closed down because the brewery had allowed them to deteriorate beyond the legal minimum safety standards. At other times, their continued survival was achieved at the expense of popularity. When the landlord of a second house called the Garibaldi (this one was in Wellingborough Road) was declared bankrupt, the brewery took his furniture to pay money he owed. The action angered other creditors who had expected a share of any money raised.

During 1908, Pope's careless borrowing cost him the control of the brewery. Mr C.Harris became joint Managing Director and Messrs Souter and Hooley joined the Board. At this time, the company was offering *"4 quart bottles of fine pale ale or fine mild ale in neat cases for 1/4d"*.

DORMAN, POPE and Company SPECIAL OCTOBER BREWINGS.
THESE NOTED BREWINGS ARE NOW IN FINE CONDITION AND ARE FULL OF EXCEPTIONAL FLAVOUR, HAVING DEVELOPED THE FULL AROMA OF THE NEW SEASONS HOPS; FROM 4/- FOR A 4 GALLON CASK. FINE SOUND RELIABLE BITTER ALE 1/-, 1/2d, 1/4d AND 1/6d PER GALLON. DELIGHTFUL PALE OR NUT BROWN, MILD 1/-,1/2d, 1/4d, AND 1/6d PER GALLON DELICIOUS SWEET OR DRY STOUT 1/-,1/2d, AND 1/4d PER GALLON. SPARKLING BOTTLED ALES. SPECIAL INVALID STOUT. HIGHLY RECOMMENDED BY THE MEDICAL PROFESSION. 2/6d PER DOZEN BOTTLES. 1/6d PER DOZEN HALF BOTTLES. ABINGTON PARK BREWERY and 8, THE DRAPERY, NORTHAMPTON. (NORTHAMPTON HERALD 25th November, 1910)

In 1911, beer brewed by Dorman, Pope won a diploma in the open section of the national brewers exhibition. Sales flourished and Mr W.F.Strickland, the Company Secretary, was able to publish good figures, but soon afterwards he left to become the Conservative agent for East Northamptonshire, being replaced by Mr Bernard L.Hive.

However, only two years later, the brewery was forced into liquidation by its creditors. A meeting of the shareholders was called for Monday 31st March, 1913, and Mr Fred Kilby, incorporated accountant, Drury Chambers, was appointed as the receiver.

On Wednesday 3rd September, the Abington Brewery and a handful of other properties were put up for sale by public auction. Percy Brain conducted the sale at the Grand Hotel.

"Brewery, well built, modern, eight quarter brewery: frontage of 153 foot in Wellingborough Road, 95 foot on Lutterworth Road and 72 foot on Wycliffe Road. Ample supply of excellent brewing water on the premises, and the fixed plant to be included in the purchase. The business is being carried on by the receiver, and the lot will be sold as a going concern, the purchaser having the option of taking the loose plant and rolling stock at valuation in the usual way. Possession will be given on completion on November 11th next. The average trade for the past three years has been 8,280 barrels per annum."

In view of its record, there were no bids for the brewery. The stables in Wycliffe Road fetched £500. Lot 3 was the Duke of Edinburgh in Adelaide Street which was bought by the tenant for £760. The Oak beer house in Herbert Street sold for £670. Two *"dwelling houses one with a shop attached"* sited in Hood Street and an outdoor beer house at Silverstone were withdrawn.

In mid-October 1913, Charles Pope went to court to face bankruptcy. He had total debts of £2,041, of which £1,679 were due to the insolvency of the brewery. His sole assets were a few pieces of furniture valued at £18. Pope told the bench that his plight was a direct consequence of the collapse of his business. It was pointed out to him that he failed to heed the financial advice that he had been given and that mistakes like the cut price sale of the Garibaldi were acts of folly that he had been in the position to stop.

Until a new owner was found, the brewery was run by Fred Kilby, the auditor of Dorman, Pope. On 19th December, 1913, the Northampton Herald revealed that the brewery had a new owner, *"It will be heard with considerable interest that councillor John Martin, the principle debenture holder of Messrs Dorman and Pope Ltd, has acquired the whole undertaking as from December 1st."*

The company was re-launched under a new name a week later.

"Councillor JJ Martin who has taken over Messrs Dorman, Pope and Company's brewery and rechristened it the Abington Brewery....his interest in the Abington brewery is, of course, not a new one by any means. The firm of Martin built the brewery and Councillor Martin had a good deal to do with the supervision of the erection"

The advertising for the brewery products played on the letters ABC standing for the Abington Brewery Company. The company motif was a "martin", a play on the owner's name. John James Martin was granted a brewers license at the 1914 brewster sessions. The company opened a shop and offices at 16 Bridge Street and this building still has a mosaic, bearing the company name, on the floor of the doorway.

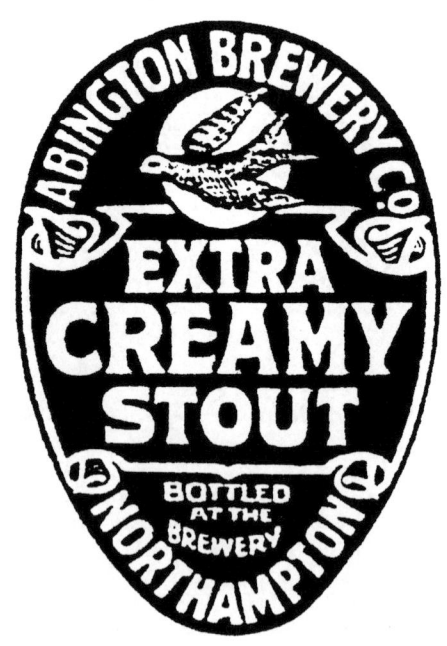

The company began to thrive and four years later J.J.Martin, who was Mayor of the town, bought Hopping Hill House a large property at Duston. In recent times this became the Hopping Hill pub.

In 1924 the brewery won a top prize in a national competition and began to advertise *"Abington Brewery Company Gold Medal Ales and Stouts"*.

Mr Martin died on 16th September, 1942, at the age of 70. He had been in poor health for several years following a fall from a horse. Ownership of the brewery passed to Lord Hesketh. Although the Heskeths were a Lancashire family, he was the major landowner in Towcester, where he had a small estate of 5 pubs, which he had leased to Phipps since 1898, but taken back in 1935:-

    Pomfret Arms, Towcester   Folly, Towcester
    Plough, Towcester   Wheatsheaf, Towcester
    Plough, Shutlanger

In February 1943, he gave Phipps notice to quit by 29th September, presumably with the intention of supplying them from the Abington Brewery.

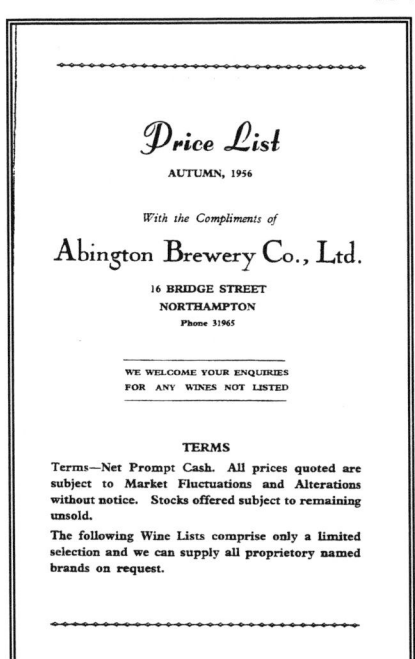

In 1946, he bought the Oak Brewery in Wisbech (F5684) but ran the two firms fairly independently. The Oak Brewery did however sell Abington bottled beers in their tied houses. The Northampton concern seems to have been looked after by a Mr Petherick.

The brewery had received investment in 1946, but much of the brewing equipment at the brewery had not been updated. Faced with a large capital investment, the company decided to cease brewing in 1958 and buy in beers from Bass Worthington. Phipps NBC retained the contract for bottling and supplying Worthington.

Upon the death of Lord Hesketh, the brewery was run by his executors, with the Chairman being his son, the Hon J.B.Fermor-Hesketh. At this time, there was an estate of 27 pubs around Wisbech and 24 hotels and pubs in the Northamptonshire and Banbury area. This included the Saracen's Head, formerly the Pomfret Arms at Towcester, mentioned in the Pickwick Papers.

In 1963 Charles Wells of Bedford made a successful bid for the company. They had long wanted to expand their operations in Northamptonshire and Abington Brewery Company's pubs offered them the foothold they sought. As a result, the Bass contract was terminated on 1st October, 1963.

The obsolete brewery was of no use to Wells and the site was sold to a property developer. The main buildings were demolished and a row of shops erected on the land. The only remaining part of the property is the brewery garage on the junction of Allen Road and Wellingborough Road, which is still a garage to this day.

Douglas, Mrs Mary Ann, *Durham Ox, 1 Augustin Street.*

The Durham Ox pub was run by a John Douglas in 1858. In 1866, a George Douglas was a beer retailer at 1 Augustin Street and Mrs Douglas was a publican brewer in 1877 at the Ox which she had run since at least 1864. The Ox later became a Phipps' pub, which was closed in 1938.

NORTHAMPTON
(continued)

Dunkley, Edward Thomas, *Wellington Arms, 19 Wellington Place.*

In 1836, property in Wellington Place was owned by a Thomas Dunkley of Crispin Street, but tenanted by John Herbert and Charles Kent. In 1858, Mary Dunkley is listed as a beer retailer at 19 Wellington Place, and in 1877 Edward Thomas Dunkley is shown as a publican brewer. He was still at the pub in 1900, but brewing had probably ceased by then. The pub was later owned by NBC, which closed it in 1937.

Durham, James and Sons, *Spread Eagle Brewery, Mercers Row.*

James Durham is in the 1781 militia listing as a victualler and on 8th November, 1783, he is shown as the owner of the Spread Eagle in Mercers Row. He brewed all the beer sold in the pub and soon afterwards began to supply neighbouring pubs as well. This expansion occurred sometime between 1790 and 1796. By the latter date, he was describing himself as a common brewer. His trade grew and by the turn of the century, he was advertising his beer in the Northampton Mercury.

1800.

> JAMES DURHAM,
> COMMON BREWER,
> MERCER'S-ROW, NORTHAMPTON,
>
> RETURNS Thanks to his Friends and the Public in general for paft Favours, and informs them he has a large Quantity of OLD and MILD ALE, and excellent PORTER, which he fells at the following Prices, viz. Old Ale 1s. 10d.—Mild Ditto 1s. 8d.—Porter 1s. 6d. per Gallon.——TABLE and SMALL BEER as low as poffible.
> NORTHAMPTON, May 24th, 1800.

IRTHLINGBOROUGH, May 8, 1800.

In 1809 Durham bought the business of a small rival brewer in Dychurch Lane (see entry). The following February he sold parts of this *"common brew house"* but kept the maltings. In 1813, he was advertising ale from his *"old established brewery"*. However, some four years later, J.C.Barrett was disputing the credibility of Mr Durham's brewery.

Durham took his sons into partnership prior to 1820. His daughter was set up in a dress shop next door to the Spread Eagle. James junior was running the business by 1830. Around this time, the Durhams also opened an inn in Abington Street.

As a result of a further takeover in 1837, Durham had a brew house in King's Street. That same year he offered for sale the Dychurch Lane maltings, describing them as *"...for many years in the occupation of Mr James Durham..."* (Northampton Mercury 21st October, 1837).

He failed to attract a buyer and had to re-advertise them the following January.

"Freehold Maltings Northampton for sale by private contract, all that old established freehold malt house with granaries over same, a drying kiln and buildings attached, centrally situated in Dychurch Lane, Northampton, and now in the occupation of Mr James Durham." (Notice - Northampton Mercury 27th January, 1838)

The last record of James Durham is in an 1841 voters list as a brewer living at Wellington Street.

Edmunds, Francis, *Horseshoe Lane.*

Listed between 1790 and 1796, Edmunds was probably a publican brewer; although the pub or inn is not known, (see entry below).

Edmunds, William, *White Horse, 64 Sheep Street.*

In 1640 when the White Horse, then shown as being in the Horsemarket, was being kept by Cicyly Hill, a malt house is mentioned. Edmunds is listed as the brewer at the pub in 1877, which he had owned since at least 1847. It was being run by M.A.Earl in 1900 with no mention of brewing. The pub closed in 1907.

NORTHAMPTON (continued)

Freeman, Richard, *The Old Bakehouse, 19 Bradshaw Street.*

This beer house, which opened in 1836, was part of a bakers and was run by Freeman *c.*1847-1874. He is listed as a brewer in 1866.

Prior to this, a Robert Freeman was an inn-keeper in 1809. In 1836, Bell-barn house and maltkiln, owned by Richard and Thomas Phipps, was occupied by Payne James Freeman, originally from Potterspury. The bakery became owned by Pickering Phipps Perry (Pickering Phipps' grandson), Duston Mills in 1860. The pub became an Abington Brewery house and closed in 1908.

Frog Island Brewery, *The Maltings, Westbridge, St James Road.*

Located in an old malt house, built 1888, and once owned by Thomas Manning & Co, this new company (F3580.5) has been in operation since September 1994. The two partners in the business are Bruce Littler and Graham Cherry. The brewery is named after the local name for the area, which used to be prone to flooding and which suffered again in Easter 1998.

The plant is self-built, using ex-Cameron cellar tanks, and capable of a 5 barrel brew. The plant also includes one fermenting vessel - FV3 - which was converted from an ex-Manns spoilt beer vessel from the local depot. At present there are two brews a week. Each brew is followed by a complete clean-down to ensure quality.

The brewery uses Maris Otter malt from Nottinghamshire and local water. The hot liquor tank (6 barrel capacity) and the grist case are filled the night before brewing and the liquor is "burtonised" using gypsum.

Over forty outlets are supplied, the brewery's main products being Best Bitter (1039°OG), Shoemaker (1044°OG) and Natterjack (1048°OG). There is also a winter brew called Croak & Stagger (1058°OG) and a range of seasonal brews. Target hops are used for bitterness and Styrian Golding for the Natterjack and Cascade for Shoemaker.

In 1997 a bottling plant, capable of 600 bottles per hour, was installed. In addition to bottle conditioned Croak, special brews with personalised labels are produced. It is intended to introduce a bottled pale ale based on the draught "Fire Belly Toad", which won a silver medal at the 1997 English Hop awards.

In January 1998, the plant was expanded to 10 barrels and re-located within the malting.

Inside the Frog Island Brewery

Photo: Authors' collection

NORTHAMPTON (continued)

Frost, Thomas, *Hare & Hounds, 48 Newland.*

A publican brewer listed in 1877 at the pub which he had taken in 1872. The address is also shown as 1 Lady's Lane. This may be the same Thomas Frost described as an *"eating house keeper"* at 61 Gold Street in 1866.

Gibson, Christopher, *Newland.*

Although listed in 1857 in the brewery section, Gibson was the agent for Salt and Company of Burton-on-Trent, though a Mrs Gibson was running the Queen's Arms, 6 Market Square. He was later shown as a commercial traveller. However, a William Gibson was a comon brewer in 1760.

Goodman, John, *Little Bell Inn, 9 Augustin Street.*

In 1854, Goodman is shown as a shopkeeper and baker in Augustin Street, when the Little Bell, at number 9, was being kept by a Pearce Cornfield. By 1861, Goodman is listed as the publican brewer, having recently taken the pub which advertises its *"Prime Home Brewed Ale"*.

However, the address of the pub also seems to have been shown as Commercial Street and in 1864 the Little Bell was in the hands of a James Gardner and there is no mention of brewing. In 1866 Goodman is still listed as a baker in Augustin Street.

Prior to this a James Goodman, Drapery, owned the Plough, Gold Street in 1827.

Harris, John, *Newland.*

John Harris is listed as a brewer in 1792. In 1831, a Thomas Harris was a victualler at the Duke of Clarence, Mercers Row, whilst Thomas junior was a maltster at Braunston. In 1861 a Thomas Harris was at the Kings Head, 15 Mayorhold and a John Harris (possibly a relative) was a maltster at Duston.

Harrison, Vincent, *25 Marefair.*

In 1866 Harrison is shown at the Saddler's Arms on Mare Fair. Although in 1877 Harrison is listed as a brewer, the beer house is not named. At some point the name seems to have changed to the Falcon Inn, later a Mannings pub.

Hobbs, William, *Bantam Cock, 1 Abington Square.*

The pub dates back to 1486, when it was owned by Gilbert Lyster, who was granted permission to brew without paying tax - a privilege usually reserved for Mayors. In 1768, it was occupied by Edward Nicholls, a victualler. In the early years of the 19th century it had been in the hands of the Perkins family, before becoming owned by James Peach around 1847 (see Peach family entry). Hobbs is listed as the brewer in 1877.

In 1883 the pub was leased by Phipps, but in 1893, Edward Major-Lucas was the landlord of the Bantam Cock (see Walker & Soames entry). The pub was for sale in 1908, but Phipps regarded the asking price of £7,000 as too dear. When NBC bought the property in 1938 its annual trade was said to be 521 barrels of Worthington. Although the pub is still trading, it now masquerades as an Irish theme pub.

Homan, T, *Green Dragon, Bearward Street.*

Homan is listed as a publican brewer in 1866, when he was keeping the Green Dragon.

Hop House Brewery (F3580.6), *Harborough Road, Kingsthorpe.*

One of the more recent addition to the Northampton brewing scene opened in November 1995 when a brew pub was located in what used to be the Cock Inn. The original coaching inn dated back to 1662, but was rebuilt in 1893.

The pub became owned by Labatt who were considering opening similar brew pub outlets in the UK. The plant came from Brewing Design Services and the ales brewed were Hopper's Original (3.6% ABV) and St David's Mercy (4.5% ABV). The latter named after the hospital located across the road.

Unfortunately, after further changes of ownership, the pub ceased to brew and reverted to its original name.

The Cock Inn housing the Hop House Brewery.

Photo: Authors' collection

Hopper, Thomas *(1792), Fish Lane.*

Horspool, Mrs Mary, *Stag's Head, 7 Abington Street.*

The Stag's Head dated back to at least 1768, when it was occupied by James Sutton, victualler. In 1805, the occupier was a Whitmill Payne, who was selling a crop of barley growing on land opposite to St Giles' church yard. In 1796, a John Sutton is listed as a brewer in Sheep Street and in 1818 at Bearward Street, but it is not known whether he was connected with the previous Sutton.

In 1830 the inn was being kept by James Castell although there is no mention of brewing.

In 1874, Mary "Auntie" Horspool took the pub where she is listed as a brewer in 1877. In 1890, when sold at public auction it was described as situated nearly opposite the Post Office, within 50 yards of the Market Square and included a brew house. Mannings bought the pub for £6,000. It closed in 1935.

Ives, Zebulon *(1792-96), Marefair.*

James, Herbert Eli, *The Hind, 2 Althorpe Street, Far Cotton.*

A publican brewer (F3580) at the Hind in 1878, but shown only as a beer retailer in 1903. In 1861, a James Eli was listed as a butcher at 132 Bridge Street and then in 1869 at Far Cotton. The address is later shown as 2 Delapre Street, when the pub was included in the 1940 Kelly's listing (see Introduction).

Jones, John, *36 Silver Street.*

John Jones is listed as a brewer at this address from c.1818 until c.1852. In 1841, William Jones is also listed, and later is shown as a *"dealer in yeast"* in 1861.

However, the 1841 Poll Book also lists William and John Jones as brewers in Bath Street, the latter shown from 1830. In addition, a Ben Jones was a brewer in Horseshoe Lane in 1818, then in 1841 at the King's Head, Mayorhold.

King, Stephen *(1818), Horseshoe Lane.*

Law, John, *Fetter Street.*

Law is only listed as a brewer in 1830, but after this he seems to have been running the Spread Eagle, 47 Hopes Place until around 1858, after which he had moved to the Blue Anchor, 3 Castle Street by 1864. The latter pub's brew house was still intact when it was an NBC property in 1887. However, Law also seems to have been running the Crispin Arms, 53 Scarletwell Street at the time.

NORTHAMPTON
(continued)

Leeson, Robert, *Fetter Lane.*

Leeson is listed at this address in 1796, then in Bridge Street from 1818 to 1841.

Linnett, William, *Little Cross Street.*

Although shown as a brewer 1830-1841, this may actually be William Linnell who was at the Ship, Mercers Row (see Butcher entry) and whose property in Little Cross Street was let to a William Warren. Linnell seems to have originally been from Fenny Stratford and at some point seems to have moved from the Ship to the Dolphin in Gold Street.

When the Dolphin and its brew house were sold in October 1802, the tenant was Thomas Linnell, although the property seems to have been owned by a Tompson, possibly Thompson (see entry). Thomas Linnell was still at the Dolphin in 1823, when he was shown as a wine and spirit merchant. In 1894, a William Linnell was listed as a brewer at Syresham.

Manning, Thomas & Co Ltd (F3581), *The Castle Brewery, 12 Black Lion Hill.*

In 1878 Thomas Manning, then aged 31, left his employment as Head Brewer with Phipps to set up in direct competition. The new firm was a partnership of Manning and Robert Blatchford Oldrey.

Manning came from a wealthy background. His father, John Manning, was a farmer at Milton and Rothersthorpe and the son of Charles Hills Watts who had married a Sarah Dunkley (see Milton Malsor). John had changed his name under the Will of John Manning esq of Harpole in 1877.

The Northampton Herald 25 July, 1863, carried an advertisement for the sale by auction of a 7 quarter malting at Moulton. This was owned by a Mr William Manning and it is possible there may have been a family connection. This strengthens the suspicion that the Mannings had earlier roots in brewing. For example an indenture of 1683 (NPL1258) not only mentions a Richard Manninge yeoman of Moulton, but a John Manninge of the City of London, a beer cooper.

The four storey Castle Brewery was completed in 1880, to designs drawn up by G.Herbert Manning, an architect from Aylesbury. It was of a traditional gravity feed design, with a capacity of 25 quarters. A stone built brewery of some character it had a floor area of 17,803 square feet. The brewery, which was opposite the station at the junction of Black Lion Hill (SP 748 603), took its name from the medieval Northampton Castle which once stood nearby. Brewing seems to have started around July 1880. The maltings stood on Elephant Lane, which ran from Green Street up to Black Lion Hill.

At the annual supper, held in February 1882, some 30 attended, suggesting the enterprise was still fairly small at this time.

THOMAS MANNING'S PRICE LIST 1884 (Robert's Directory 1884)

	per gallon	**barrel**	**kilderkin**	**firkin**
A.K (light bitter ale)	1/-	36/-	18/-	9/-
K.K (bitter ale)	1/2d	42/-	21/-	10/6d
I.P.A	1/4d	48/-	24/-	12/-
X (Mild)	10d	30/-	15/-	7/6d
XX	1/-	36/-	18/-	9/-
XXX	1/2d	42/-	21/-	10/6d
XXXX (Strong Ale)	1/6d	54/-	27/-	13/6d
Porter	1/2d	42/-	21/-	10/6d
Stout	1/4d	48/-	24/-	12/-
Double Stout	1/6d	54/-	27/-	13/6d

One of the early purchases of Manning and Oldrey was the Nag's Head on Kettering Road, which still had a brew house, from William Butcher (see entry). The partners bought the Old Millstone, with brew house at Hannington for £540 in March 1887. On the 4th December, 1888, they decided to convert their partnership into a limited company, with articles of association being issued the following February, after their financial year end. They took the positions of joint Managing Directors with an equal stipend from the company.

However, Manning appears to have been the more active member of the partnership and received £3,920 in respect of profits from their previous trading. He was also to receive £100, before payment of the stipend and had the privilege of any apprenticeship benefits.

**NORTHAMPTON
(continued)**

The capital value of Thomas Manning and Company Ltd was £100,000, which was divided into 5,000 £10 preference shares paying 6%, and an equal amount of £10 ordinary shares. The two Managing Directors each owned 2,500 preference shares and 2,497 ordinary shares. The balance of 6 shares was split equally between the families of both men.

The Castle Brewery tied estate consisted of 25 freehold pubs (14 of which were in Northampton) and 18 leasehold pubs. The Company also controlled 20 other properties (brewery, maltings in West Bridge and Elephant Lane, and ordinary houses). A wine and spirits shop was opened at 9 Abington Street. The assets were valued at £150,000. In July 1890, the business name was changed to T.Manning & Co Ltd.

In an 1895 business guide, an article on the company lists the Head Brewer as Mr C.Smith a one time pupil of Tom Manning. It goes on to describe the fermenting capacity at the Castle Brewery as follows: 6 x 40 barrels; 4 x 80 barrels; 4 x 30 barrels. The brewery at this time was powered by a 12 hp steam engine and a 4hp "Otto" gas engine.

The business became a public company in 1897, with a value of £1m. Throughout the 1890s, the company expanded its estate, for example as follows:-

1894	Admiral Nelson	Green Northampton
	Rising Sun	Broad Street
1896	Buccleugh Hotel	Kettering Road
1898	Chequers Inn	Rothersthorpe
1900	Cock	Stony Stratford

Thomas Manning acquired a very good reputation and a business rival described his as *"one of the most respected breweries in the Midlands"*. Sales continued to grow and in June 1899 the Tun Room was enlarged to increase the capacity.

The company's business was a mixture of sales through its tied pubs and off-licences, together with home trade to private individuals. To support this the brewery had several travellers covering an area within a 30 mile radius of the brewery, and the shop in Abington Street which was under the charge of Mr Freeman.

During the depression of the 1930s the Government sought to raise money by increasing the tax on beer. This threatened the continued survival of several local breweries but most notably Mannings. A spokesman for the firm was quoted in the 23rd April, 1932, edition of the Chronicle and Echo:-

"The trade outlook is far from bright and although there is no likelihood of a decrease in staff, the position is likely to become serious unless there is an improvement (in beer tax)."

That July the founder and Chairman died, aged 86. Although Major T.E.Manning took over his father's role, talks with Phipps began soon afterwards. Rumours of deals spread, but until January 1933 any mention that talks were taking place was met with official denial. Then T.E.Manning admitted to the press *"Nothing is actually fixed but negotiations are going on. It is too early to say anything definite."* Pickering Phipps was more forthcoming, *"When I was a small boy he (Thomas Manning) used to be with us and it is strange that after this interval his firm may be returning to the senior firm."*

On 25th March, 1933, the agreement was signed and the Castle Brewery became a wholly owned subsidiary of Phipps. In April a special meeting of the preference shareholders agreed to the resolution to discontinue malting and brewing and to buy from Phipps.

Phipps gained the ordinary shares through what were described as cordial negotiations, the final agreement being reached over a game of golf played by Major Manning, Mr Oldrey and Major Fraser. The purchase was covered by the issue of 60,000 Phipps' shares to the owners of Mannings, of which Hubert Cyril Oldrey, The Laws, Turvey, received 27,552 and Thomas Edgar Manning, Shrublands, Dallington, some 22,800. Manning and Oldrey also had their legal costs of up to £2,000 paid. Phipps also issued preference shares in 1939 to finance the purchase which were distributed as follows:-

Thomas Edgar Manning	7,000	Pamela Ellen Manning	3,000
Ellen Dodwell Manning	1,500	Dorothy Frances Manning	500
Lucy Eady Manning	1,500	Thomas Henry Manning	500
Richard Manning	4,000		

**NORTHAMPTON
(continued)**

It is interesting to note the appearance of Eady as a first name showing the probable family links which existed (see Little Bowden). Some of the Manning family were also living at Brewery House Old (see entry).

Major Thomas Edgar Manning became a director of Phipps, whilst the latter appointed Richard Edgar Lamb and Alfred James Fraser as directors of Mannings. A key figure would seem to be the director Edgar Claude Manning Palmer, who went on to play a major role in Phipps.

The Manning's estate consisted of 121 properties in total. Although the property was valued at some £227,000 in 1929, the Phipps' managers found the houses to be in a very poor state and the pubs were soon sporting the claret livery of Phipps. Prior to the take-over, Mannings had been averaging around 129 barrels per house compared with 146 barrels in a Phipps' house. Phipps recruited A.L.Milner from Friary, Holroyd at Guildford as their 5th brewer on £275, presumably to deal with the increased production at Bridge Street.

The Abington Street offices were closed in 1934. The fate of the old brewery was not immediately settled and production in one form or another continued until at least 1936. The final shareholders meeting was on 29th August, 1940, and the company wound up.

After that time the Castle Brewery stood empty and unused until Phipps put it up for sale on 12th February, 1947, in a public auction held at the Angel Hotel. Described as *"important freehold central site... The Castle Brewery (Disused), brewery house and two cottages"*. Local shoe makers George Webb and Company bought it for £5,000 as a storeroom for finished shoes awaiting shipment via Castle Station.

The maltings in Elephant Lane were let to the LMS railway and have now been refurbished as a bar restaurant. Those at West Bridge survived to maintain an involvement in brewing (see Frog Island).

When the town council carried out the St Peter's Way improvements in the early 1960s they demolished much of Green Street and Black Lion Hill. The Castle Brewery seems to have survived the initial onslaught, until as late as 1974, before it too disappeared under the bulldozers.

Moore, Robert *(1790), Woolmonger Street.*

Muddeman, William, *132 Bridge Street.*

Muddeman is shown as malting and brewing at Shipley Wharf Bone Mills, near to the Crown and Anchor, on South Bridge in 1864, although his home address was 30 Waterloo. He had been at this pub since at least 1845 and also ran the attached coal-yard. He also seems to have owned the Goat, 34 Gold Street, between 1854 and 1858, when the Crown and Anchor was kept by Daniel Sellers. Around this time Muddeman is also shown as a maltster in Fetter Street.

There is some confusion in that some directories also show a William Muddiman at 54 Horse Market, and it is not clear whether this is another mis-spelling or there were two individuals with very similar names. Muddiman also owned the Saracen's Head, Little Brington, in 1862 and 1877.

In 1866 Muddeman is shown only as a general merchant. He seems to have connections with John Smith Norman, who kept the Ram, Sheep Street and the latter seems to have taken over the business around 1869, when brewing seems to have ceased. In 1877, Norman is shown at the Crown & Anchor, 180 Bridge Street. The Crown & Anchor, which dated back until 1772, gave its name to the maltings of Ratliffe & Jeffrey, which were built at the rear in 1877. The pub was demolished in 1935.

Neill, George, *The Newland Brewery, 84 Newland.*

During the mid-19th century, George Neill (or Neall) was a shopkeeper at the Market Square end of Newland. His property included a brew house in which he brewed beer for sale to private customers.

An advert for *"George Neill of the Newland Brewery"* appeared in the Mercury 26th October, 1844, and is the earliest record so far uncovered. As well as brewing beer, Neill acted as an agent for several notable brewers, as shown in an another advert:-

"Bass and Company, and Allsopp and Sons, Burton and Indian Pale Ale, Campbells Edinboro' Ale, Real Devonshire Cider, Truman Hanbury and Company's Porter and Stout in casks and bottles in high perfection. G Neill, agent." Northampton. Northampton Mercury 10th May, 1845

It appears that at this time Neill also acted as an agent for the Britannia Life Assurance Company.

NORTHAMPTON (continued)

The Newland Brewery moved from the original site to new premises further up Newland on 22nd February, 1851.

"NEWLAND, NORTHAMPTON TO LET, and may be entered on Ladys Day next, all that large and spacious house and premises consisting of a large and excellent shop in front, brewery and detached offices, situated in the lower end of Newland near the Market Square, now in the occupation of George Neill."
Northampton Mercury 15th February, 1851.

Further down that same page of the paper was a second advertisement:-

"GEORGE NEILL, ALE AND PORTER MERCHANT Begs respectfully to announce his intended removal on Saturday next, the 22nd instant, to more commodious premises at the upper end of Newland, where all orders will be punctually attended to and esteemed a favour."
Northampton. 15th Feb, 1851.

> **NEWLAND BREWERY, NORTHAMPTON.**
> GEO. NEALL begs most respectfully to inform his friends and the public that he has TAKEN the PREMISES in the MARKET-SQUARE lately occupied by Mr. Pell, Solicitor, and the opposite corner to Messrs. Osborn and Stockburn, Grocers, &c.; where all orders will be received for SCOTCH, BURTON, and India PALE and Home-brewed ALES, Lane and Co.'s IRISH STOUT, and LONDON PORTER and STOUT, in Casks or Bottled. G. N. hopes this will meet the wishes of his country friends, who have complained so long of the distance.
> P.S. The BREWERY & STORES in NEWLAND as before.

George's new premises were on the very edge of town and this was to prove a disadvantage. It made him less accessible to his country customers who had a limited time in the town on market days. In August 1854, he rectified this problem by opening a shop on the Market Square. From this shop he continued to sell his own beer and a range of "national" brews.

The Market Square shop was also an "on-licensed" beer house which took the name the Britannia (linked to his agency for the Britannia). Neill also ran a second beer house across town in Green Street.

It is almost certain that Neill ceased trading in 1858. In that year the Britannia passed to the Warner family who moved there from the Tom Thumb beer house in Bridge Street. The Tom Thumb had also acted as a shop selling musical instruments and contemporary reports tell how the Britannia was decorated with musical instruments after the Warners arrived.

Ownership of the Newland Brewery passed to John Dickens Sibley, a Wellingborough grocer. Sibley was long associated with the drinks trade and owned pubs in Wellingborough and Kettering. His premises in Silver Street, Wellingborough were used as a depot for *"The Romford Brewery Company's Celebrated Ales"*.

J.D.Sibley ran the Newland Brewery until his death in December 1865. His executors took over running the company *"(for) the benefit of his widow"* until it finally ceased trading a few years later. It was purchased by William Jeffery of Bath Street, who later amalgamated it into Ratliffe & Jeffery (see entry).

Northampton Brewery Co Ltd (F3583), *Phoenix Brewery, 116 Bridge Street.*

In 1771 a Joseph Peach bought a house, called Lady Fermors, and wharf buildings in the South Quarter next to the river, from one Robert Wilkins. This property at Bridge Street was then bought in 1847, by Joseph Adnitt who also owned the neighbouring warehouses. The property and warehouses were bought by the Phillips Bros in January 1857 and converted into a brewery and maltings (SP 754 599). The maltings had originally been run by William Higgins, possibly from the Bedford brewing family, then John Gurney, before being bought by the Phillips Bros in 1863. They also bought a maltings at Weston Street from the Phipps' brewery. The site may actually date back to 1793, when Valentine Woolley in South Quarter included a brew house.

William George Phillips had embarked upon his trade in Northampton by opening a beer store on Wood Hill in November 1855. From this shop he acted as the agent of the Britannia Brewery of Stony Stratford. This may have been the brewery at the Bull Inn where a Thomas Phillips was a tenant brewer in 1859.

The Brewery, Bridge Street

THE BREWERY, BRIDGE STREET

William was the son of Edward Phillips of Coventry, who ran the Pilgrim Inn in that city, and may himself have run the pub and malt house before moving to Northampton. He lived at the Elms in Billing Road was soon joined in partnership by two of his brothers: Alfred (from Milton Malsor) and Thomas Rotherham (from Wootton, resident in Northampton since c.1841).

The Phillips dynasty had originated in Royston, where members of the family were brewing until 1949. The brothers' great uncle Joseph owned the Coventry and Stamford Brewery which traded as Joseph Phillips and Company (see entry St Martins). However, the Coventry brewery was sold in 1850, perhaps leading to the move to Northampton.

Their business letter head featured Britannia, suggesting possible links with the Stony Stratford agency. The "Steam" brewery was thought to have been started in 1856, but this would not fit with the property transfer mentioned above. The first advert in the Northampton Mercury was the following year:-

"To farmers and others Phillips Brothers are now prepared to supply parties requiring grains. Orders received at their office, Wood Hill, or at the brewery, Bridge Street.. Steam Brewery, Northampton". Northampton Mercury 18th April, 1857

Phillips Brothers brewed a clear amber beer called "stock ale" which was a vast improvement on the *"thick old fashioned beer"* brewed by rivals Phipps and Thomas Hagger. As a result it met with instant favour with the local drinkers to the detriment of the competition. The thick and turgid Northampton Milds were soon to disappear as Hagger sold up his business and Phipps frantically modernised.

Ale 10d per Gallon   X Ale 13d per Gallon
XX Ale 17d per Gallon   XXX Ale 18d per Gallon
(Northampton Mercury 23rd July, 1859)

As well as the range of full strength beers Phillips were able to offer "Table beers supplied during summer months in any quantity" and these weak beers sold for 4d and 6d a gallon.

Their first purchases in 1859 included the Gardener's Arms, Wellingborough Road and the Pedestrian Tavern. In 1860, they bought the wharf near the brewery, previously used by George Osborn and then William Higgins.

They expanded into Rugby in 1865, when they bought a stores and maltkiln in Windsor Court from John Richardson. The company was able to open a brewery at Burton on Trent (F880) in 1865 which was soon supplying the local trade with a superior brew. This move and the range of drinks mentioned above suggests that they were at the forefront of technical entrepreneurs brewing pale ales, most likely using the Union system.

PHILLIPS BROTHERS BREWERS BURTON ON TRENT AND NORTHAMPTON
Phillips Brothers India Pale Ale in 9, 18 and 36 gallon casks Phillips Brothers sound dinner ales at 10d and 1/- a gallon Delivered carriage free Phillips Bros celebrated Northampton stouts at 1/2d,1/4d, and 1/6d per gallon. (Delivered carriage free) Phillips Bros are now prepared to supply farmers and others with good sound ales at 8d and 10d per gallon. Specially brewed for haymaking and harvest purposes.

In 1868, Phillips Brothers raised additional capital by taking on a partner called Samuel Lipscomb Seckham. Although later described as a highly successful architect from Oxford who had retired at the age of 41 and who joined the firm as a *"mere matter of investment"*, his wealth arose less from being the city surveyor and architect of the corn exchange there, than from his design of "Park Town" and the related property deals, if not speculation. His initial contact with the Phillips family may have arisen from his residing at Wootton Hall, prior to moving to Lichfield, where he rented Hanch Hall before buying Beacon Place. He became a well-known personality in Staffordshire, including becoming a Deputy Lieutenant and the High Sheriff in 1891.

However, the Phillips brothers may have over-stretched themselves. In 1872, Messrs Venton, Bull and Cooper prepared a report on the Northampton Brewery and the following year the Burton Brewery was sold to Trumans.

> *"Notice is hereby given that the partnership heretofore subsisting between the undersigned William George Phillips, Thomas Phillips, Alfred Charles Phillips and Samuel Lipscomb Seckham at Burton on Trent and Northampton as brewers under the style or firm of "Phillips Brothers" was dissolved by mutual consent on and from the 30th day of September last. All debts due and demands and liabilities upon the said firm, will be received, paid and discharged by the undersigned Samuel Lipscomb Seckham, who will continue to trade at Northampton, under the style or firm of The Northampton Brewery Company (late Phillips Brothers). Dated this 30th day of December 1873."*
> Northampton Mercury 31st December, 1873

In March 1874, the brewery and property were conveyed to Samuel Seckham who was now actively running the business, with the assistance of Frank Phillips (son of Thomas Phillips). He bought much of the premises and equipment of the old company when it came up for sale in May 1874. The rest of the business seems to have been financed by Thomas Jervis. (NB in 1869, a Thomas Jarvis founded a Phoenix Brewery in Bedford). However, in October 1874, the firm lost money, when William Thomas, of the Alhambra Tavern and Music Hall in Gold Street, was made bankrupt. It is tempting to see these as being connected with the break up of Phillips Brothers' Brewery. It is around this time that it begins to use the name "Phoenix Brewery", perhaps to represent the new approach.

In 1874, Thomas Phillips moved with his wife and 10 children from Wootton Hall to Newport, Mommouth (now Gwent). There, using their share of the proceeds from the sale of the Burton Brewery, they set up the firm of Phillips and Sons Ltd. This business continued to brew at the Dock Road Brewery until 1949 when it was taken over by Simonds of Reading.

William Phillips moved to Oxford, where he bought the brewery of John Higgins, and set up W.G.Phillips and Sons at the Tower Brewery in Park End Street (F3855). It was taken over by Hall's Oxford Brewery (F3853) in 1910. Alfred Phillips moved to Caversham from where he kept in regular contact with NBC.

In 1874 Phoenix launched their *"Digestive Stout, 1/6d a gallon, brewed expressly for invalids, and highly recommended for its nourishing quality by medical authorities"*. Thus, they became one of the first local brewers to claim the healthy properties of their beer.

The brewery actively sought contracts to supply beer to the army, workhouses, schools and any other institution. They even advertised a special price list for "Public Institutes and Schools". Under such schemes the brewery expanded. In 1877 the brewery was being managed by Herbert Smedley.

In 1878 Frank Phillips also left NBC, to take control of the Coventry brewery of James Marriott and Sons which was renamed Phillips and Marriott and Company (F1217). Showing the usual brewing flair of the family, he is said to have revolutionised the brewery. The 1878 NBC Price List was:-

	Per Gallon	Per Barrel	**STOUTS**		
XX Household	1/-	36/-	SS Single Stout	1/2	42/-
AK Family Ale (Bitter)	1/-	36/-	DS Double Stout	1/4	48/-
No.2 Mild Ale	1/2	42/-	EDS Extra Stout	1/6	54/-
No.3 Mild Ale	1/4	48/-	**BITTER ALES**		
XXXX Strong	1/6	54/-	PA Family Pale Ale	1/2	42/-
NBC Imperial Stingo	2/-	72/-	IPA India Pale Ale	1/6	48/-
			EIPA East India Pale Ale	1/8d	60/-

In 1882 the maltings and warehouse at 120 Bridge Street, previously used by Phipps, were bought from John Perry. However, they were still mortgaged for £2,000 to Pickering Phipps Perry and the Keep brothers of Birmingham. The Brewers' Journal for March 1882 states that large alterations to the Phoenix brewery were to be undertaken Messrs Scamell & Colyer, brewery engineers. These included a new boiler house and entrance gate.

In 1886 sales of 52,484 barrels gave a net profit of £23,080 and it was decided to form a new incorporated company, Northampton Brewery Company (NBC) with Samuel Seckham as the Chairman and Managing Director. The business had a share capital of £150,000 made up of 7,500 7% cumulative £10 preference shares and 7,500 ordinary shares of £10. To help raise capital there was also an issue on 25th April of £150,000 of debenture shares, some £70,000 of which went to buy out Thomas Jervis.

In addition to Seckham, the initial subscribers to the business also had brewing experience as follows:-

> H.J.Gurdon-Rebow (Chairman Tamplin & Sons, Brighton and Chairman Manchester Brewery Co
> and later Director of Bohemian Breweries Prague)
> W.C.N.Chapman (Star Brewery, Canterbury)
> D.E.Cardinall (Director Manchester Brewery Co)
> H.A.Haig (Director Manchester Brewery Co)

The shares went on sale on 13th February, 1887, and were over-subscribed four times over in the first five days of trading. On 18 February the incorporation was completed. One of the early shareholders was Daniel Hipwell.

NBC was described as owning a brewery of some 28,500 sq ft, two 90 quarter maltings, 69 freehold houses and 18 leasehold. Many of the properties were in the Coventry and West Midlands area, presumably as a result of the Phillips family ownership. This also included the Molineux estate at Wolverhampton. The prospectus emphasised the capacity of 80,000 barrels and expansion potential. In terms of the share price, comparisons were made with Phipps & Co's £21 paid which were worth £41 to £42 and the City of London Brewery Co at £45 to £47. The Head Brewer was Alan Page, who carried on from the Phoenix.

The prospectus for the debenture stock showed that some of the pubs had brew houses, although it is unlikely that they produced much other than perhaps an occasional home brew:-

> Arnold Arms, Barby, Rugby   Bell, East Farndon
> Old Plough, Hartwell   Swan, Holcote
> Beer House, Little Houghton   Golden Lion, Market Street, Kettering
> Blue Anchor, Castle Street   Eastgate, Boonfield Peterborough

In the November, they were approached by Allen & Burnett, but they declined to purchase them on the terms offered. However, in December they did agree to buy the business of Mr Robert Choules of the City Hotel, Coventry for £15,000 but ran it as a separate concern until 1890. [This is presumably the business which Friedrich's Gazetteer shows as Chouler & Co (F1209)]. He became their agent in Coventry and eventually became a member of the Board. Three of the Board members were also involved with the Hull Brewery.

The first AGM was held on 16th December, 1887, at the Plough Hotel Northampton. The business reported increased trade, resulting in a Gross Profit of £49,582, enabling a final 10% dividend to the ordinary shares. The meeting was followed immediately by an EGM to rectify a problem with Mr Seckham's salary which had been set at 5% of Net Profit before debenture interest, whereas the Articles of Association had been written to say "after". The pleased shareholders not only agreed the change, but the award of £506 to cover the previous year's misunderstanding. However, there were some difficulties with financing.

> *"We have heard from Mr Burdett, Secretary of the Stock Exchange, that there is not the slightest chance of obtaining a quotation of the Northampton Brewery ordinary and preference shares or debentures until the entire amount of mortgages are absolutely paid off, and the whole of the debenture stock is absolutely free."* Messrs Panmure Gordon

In January 1888, Bassett Thorne Seckham, son of the Chairman, replaced Mr Smedley as the brewery manager on a salary of £200 per annum. He was assisted by a Mr Conner, described as a consulting brewer.

In February 1889, NBC were in negotiation to purchase a local brewery with a large tied trade, but a fresh issue of shares and debentures would be needed. The £50,000 balance of the previous authorisation of £200,000 was offered at £105 and by May, £33,195 had been raised. This was to take-over the ailing Lion Brewery. They came to a broad agreement for the take-over at the Board Meeting in August 1890, provided the shareholders consented to the issue of additional share capital. However, it took some negotiation with regard to the Nett Profit of Allen & Burnett.

"The Northampton Brewery Company have entered into negotiations with Messrs Allen and Burnett of the Lion Brewery, Northampton for the purchase of their business. A meeting of the shareholders of the company is to be held next week to consider the negotiations as far as they have been carried; and if approved, steps will be taken for the raising of capital." Northampton Herald 6th September, 1890

The shareholders' special meeting on 26th September authorised 5,000 6% Preference Shares @ £10 and 5,000 Ordinary Shares @ £10. Of which 2,290 of each were allotted to Allen & Burnett to finance the take-over. The balance went at par to existing NBC shareholders. Phillip Allen one of the partners was taken onto the Board of NBC to represent the company's interests in Coventry. For example, they looked closely at buying the Coventry business of Messrs Wilfords. Although NBC showed a Gross Profit of £63,065 for the year, they had to make a large provision for bad debts and there was £89,211 expenditure on the capital account to pay for Allen & Burnett.

In August, NBC entered into an agreement with the Committee of the Wolverhampton Wanderers Football Club for a lease to them of the Molineux Grounds, offices and dressing rooms during the football season (as fixed by the English FA) for a term of 14 years from 1 September at a rent of £50 pa. NBC also made an approach to the Manchester Brewery Co Ltd, with whom they shared directors, re supplying their Walsall houses with stout from the Walsall stores. Despite the name, this seems to be the Manchester Brewery in Derby which traded as Stretton Brothers (F1433 - see Praed entry).

In April, NBC bought out the Plough Hotel Ltd at a 50% discount since it was in a poor financial position. The property was to play an important role throughout NBC's history. At this time, the four storey brick built brewery was connected to the Grand Union Canal by a short spur which went right up to its back door. Discussions were held with Messrs Pontifex about the possible installation of refrigeration and cooling equipment for £3,500 to £4,000. They were also putting electric lighting into the brewery and properties. Alterations had also taken place at the Lion Brewery maltings.

In January 1892, it was decided to rationalise the estate by selling some of the properties. The previous year Molineux had been visited, and although it had been decided to hold on to it for the moment, NBC would consider a sale. Allen & Burnett's Thrapston stores and house were sold for £1,050, and changes to reduce costs at the Peterborough agency included the dismissal of the agent Mr Whitehead (see Helpston). However, March brought a falling-off in trade, linked to the problem of the "Long Pull" by which publicans were keeping customers through over-measure. The Board agreed to sell some of the un-licensed properties in Coventry and Northampton and it was decided to sell the Molineux Hotel and grounds. The trade depression led to the directors only taking £400 rather than the £1,400 they were due.

However, business was sufficiently profitable that employees were given an annual holiday free ticket to London for each man and wife, as well as 4/6 to spend.

The letter for that year's AGM stated that *"The Directors invite the attendance of Shareholders at the Brewery between the hours of One and Two previous to the General Meeting, to examine the working and produce"*. The examination of the latter did not reduce the criticism concerning the poor trade and, in particular, the purchase of Allen & Burnett. The following year's AGM saw the shareholders attempt to reject the Annual Report and Balance Sheet and appoint a committee of enquiry.

In 1893, Messrs Arthur Chetwynd retained a 3 year contract to supply malt on commission, but with a reduction of 4d per quarter. NBC were considering supplying themselves and there had been some controversy about the Seckham family involvement with Chetwynds. Seckham's son-in-law was Arthur Chetwynd of Longdon Hall, Staffordshire, (Viscount Chetwynd of Bearhaven).

The following year the depression seemed to have been survived with January showing an increase in sales of 379 barrels on a 3 month comparison with the previous trading year. In addition, there was a 3% decrease in costs and a fall in returned beer.

Mr Seckham's state of health led to him being relieved from active management. It was decided to bring in a brewer to assist Basset Seckham and a "Mr Tripp" from the Tadcaster Brewery Company took the job. This is presumably Howard Tripp who left Tadcaster as general manager at this time (Tadcaster p25).

NORTHAMPTON
(continued)

Trade was still difficult in 1894, consequently there was no dividend on the ordinary shares and the directors fees were held again. The Board even suggested that individual share and debenture holders should each buy a barrel of beer, carriage free, for home consumption, thus generating a trade of £2,000. Nevertheless, NBC found the £2,500 to buy 5 houses in Newport Pagnell from a Mr Pound. The AGM was again beset by shareholder criticism about the trade and the Lion Brewery properties. Messrs Cardinall and Rebow decided to retire as directors. E Bridgewater was appointed, but unfortunately, he died only two years later.

However, life was not all finance, since Mr Haig had to leave early from the directors meeting of Wednesday 27 November "*having spent yesterday in the wine and spirit department*".

In 1896 it was agreed that, on expiry of the Molineux lease, it would be sold to the occupants, financed by William Butler of the Birmingham brewery. The Hop Bitters business, stock plant and goodwill, was sold to a Mr Jones for £300. Mention is made of a fire at what had become the Lion Mills and the wharf there was for rent, suggesting that the old brewery premises were no longer occupied.

Robert Choules died in 1897 and Mr Allen "*was sent to Coventry*" to live and look after the business. Perhaps this helped reduce some of the previous criticism of the Board. At this time the total annual bill for salaries and wages was £9,023, whereas the five directors received £2,029. However, the workforce were quite happy to present Mr Seckham, JP and Dep Lieutenant of Staffordshire, with a silver bowl on his 70th birthday and the shareholders presented him with a three-quarter size portrait.

The company made a small expansion into Oxford in 1898 when they took over Daniel Halls' St Giles Brewery (F3851), with its four tied houses, for £9,000, beating Morrell's offer of £6,700. A Mr P.O.V.Hall continued as the NBC agent for Oxford, operating from the Plume of Feathers; however, he was a problem for many years. The malting contract with Chetwynds was terminated that year and NBC arranged to undertake all their own malting.

Discussions were held in 1899 with Messrs White & Co, as to whether the Lion Brewery premises were suitable for manufacturing soda water. These discussions continued into 1900, but did not progress and Major-Lucas (see entry) were considering buying the premises in the October. That year brought an arsenic scare in the Manchester area related to a Liverpool firm Bostock & Co which was supplying contaminated sugar. This caused NBC to issue a circular to customers guaranteeing their products as being "*free from any deleterious ingredients*".

Samuel Seckham died on 4th February, 1901, aged 74. His son and heir, Major Bassett Thorne Seckham DSO, who was away fighting in South Africa with the Staffordshire Regiment, was proposed as the Chairman, but he turned it down and D.J.Morgan MP was elected. After Bassett's return he became Managing Director. NBC also appointed Dr Horace J.Brown as consultant brewer and director. Dr Brown had previously been employed, since 1866, at Worthington's brewery in Burton on Trent, where he had introduced a more scientific approach to the art of brewing.

In May 1901, Molineux was sold, but the company's links with football were maintained when 2 years later they agreed a loan of £100 to Northampton Town AFC to "*encourage sport in the town*".

On the brewing side NBC were buying 500 quarters of flake maize, presumably to help head retention on the beer. Their approach to quality ingredients can be seen in that Californian malt and barley composed almost half the stock in 1902. In 1903, L.Turnell was the Head Brewer at £400 pa, Alan Page having become the General Manager and a Director. The other brewers were C.Murphy and H.L.Barnett, the latter retiring in 1906. The standard of brewing at NBC was later to lead to many pupil brewers learning their trade at the Phoenix.

In December 1904, the Milton Malsor brewers W.J.East and Company (see entry) were offered to NBC for £13,000. The final price was £10,376 including the book debts, stock, loose effects and valuation. The horses and casks etc. which were not needed were to be sold. The brewery plant was sold, the buildings put up for sale or rent and completion of the deal took place by 31st March, 1905. In the February, the Dunstable brewery had burnt down, but although NBC received an order for 69 barrels, the hoped for negotiations to supply them did not progress.

During the early years of this century the brewery, as with many others, suffered from increasing costs for raw materials and slowly declining sales all of which kept the profits at a low level. However, the share price of the company remained high. Investment in 1910 in 2 new fermenting vessels and a malt mill suggested an optimistic view of the future. They hoped to raised some finance the following year by looking to sell-off some of the unlicensed property.

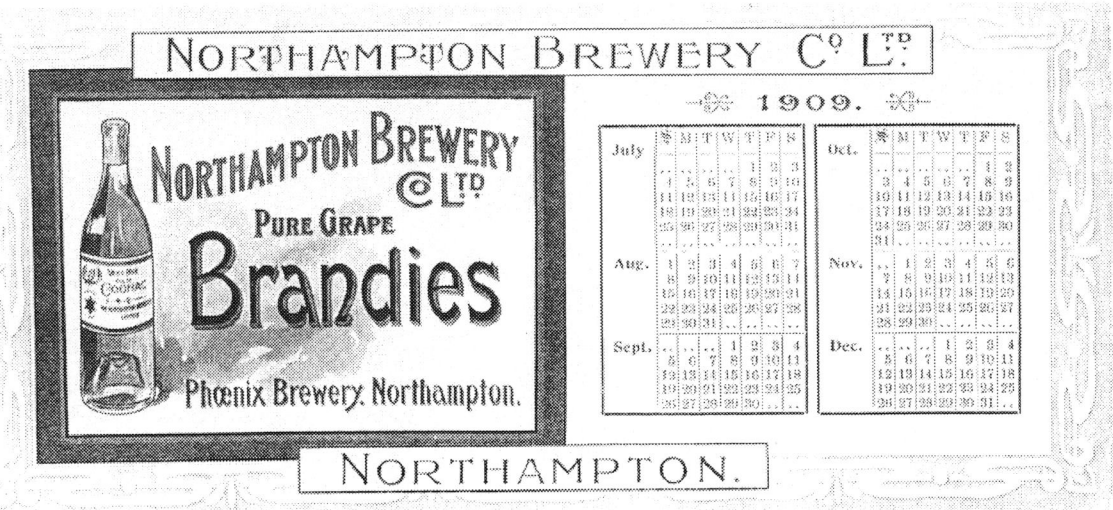

On 23rd August, 1911, the brewery workers were thanked for not becoming involved in a local strike and later that year received a special bonus. However, in April 1913 when NBC offered a 1/- rise for those on less than 26/- per week, in view of the increased cost of living, an unsigned letter said the rise was unacceptable and asked for 3/- extra. The Chairman spoke to the men and said that in the interest of the shareholders, whose dividend had already been reduced, they could not go any further. A notice was posted explaining the management view. Practically the whole of the employees, with the exception of staff and the maltsters, came out on strike. The MD "interviewed" the men at the Plough Hotel, conceded to the 3/- rise, and work was resumed. The local paper praised Colonel Seckham for his handling of the strike. The 27th Annual Report on 20th December showed profits up £3,000 to £32,753.

In 1913, to promote their beer, NBC printed and distributed a free booklet explaining the brewing processes at their brewery. The bottled beer department had a £1,500 investment to cope with expansion. In the following January the directors agreed to the novel idea of an advertising budget of £500.

The war brought the call up of many personnel, 93 from a total of 214, including two of the brewers, leaving Mr Turnell on his own. Dr Brown recommended a temporary assistant and NBC took on H.G.Heasman. For those men called up, NBC agreed to pay their wives 1/- per day, 2d per day for each child under 14, and their jobs would be kept open. However, there was some discussion as to whether this money should be for 5 or 7 days per week. The directors called up would be given leave and remuneration was to be considered, eg Colonel Seckham was initially given 6 months leave on half pay. The Board's view was that *"It was considered that it was the duty of every unmarried man, of suitable age and health, to enlist"*. In the event, 44 joined the forces out of a total staff of 145.

In July 1915, NBC made a reciprocal agreement with Bass, in which their product would be allowed in certain Northampton properties, whilst NBC Stout would be available in Bass Leicester pubs. The continuation of the war led to Colonel Seckham resigning his post as MD in April, although he remained a director. Alan T.Page and Gerald J.T.Seckham were appointed as joint MDs.

On Saturday 1st July, 1916, a major fire was spotted at 5pm when the flames burst through the brewery roof. Luckily, the brewery had a direct private wire to the fire station and the town fire brigade was promptly on the scene. In the meantime, Edward Kean, the recently appointed Company Secretary, together with the Head Brewer had braved the flames to save the company's papers. These were taken to the Plough Hotel for safe keeping. Some brewery workers were also quickly on the scene and were able to save some of the beer, which was ready for despatch on the Monday.

The work of the fire fighters was hindered by showers of red hot malt and sugar which were raining down on them. At 6pm the roof fell in! It took the firemen a further two hours to put the fire out, but by that time the top floor was completely destroyed and the third floor was extensively damaged. However, the four walls of the brewery were intact, except for a crack down the rear one.

During the night, small fires kept igniting which the firemen had to keep putting out. Their vigil carried on during Sunday morning. Although it was reported that the fire had been caused by spontaneous combustion in the malt stores, it actually seems to have broken out in the roof above No 1 hot liquor tank. The fire destroyed 2 mash tubs, grist case, cooler and malt elevator and damaged 3 coppers, underback, dissolving vessel, grist elevator and 3 hot liquor tanks. Malt to the value of £2,000 was lost in the fire and the total damage resulted in an insurance claim for £13,561. However, they also received £27,500 from the claim for profit insurance.

Messrs Bradfords (Architects) discussed proposals for restoring the brewery, Messrs Martins put in the lowest tender for rebuilding the brewery and Messrs Briggs for the plant. Temporary offices were set up in the Plough Hotel and NBC approached 12 breweries to obtain ale and stout at special discount. Eventually they made deals with Bass, Phipps, Whitbread, Dulley, Praeds and Lucas of Leamington. In addition, some brewing on commission was organised.

Unfortunately, in the October, the Ministry of Munitions refused building consent and NBC had to look at temporary repairs if they wished to resume brewing. At this time, they were receiving beer from Phipps, Lucas and Phillips and Marriot of Coventry.

The pressure of the difficulties of 1916 were perhaps too much for D.J.Morgan, the brewery chairman, who retired through ill health, to be replaced by Gerald J.T.Seckham. He died the following March, as did the hero of the fire Mr Kean. In March 1917 also NBC drew up a detailed scheme for closer working with Phipps & Co, on a commission basis of 5/- per barrel. Lucas of Leamington were also still supplying beer. It was at this time that the government introduced a restriction on output which limited NBC to 30,000 bulk barrels per 12 month period, compared with a pre-war 90,000 barrels. Nevertheless, this move may have preserved NBC through maintaining the brewing licence. In August they were looking at commencing brewing again, but it was still not possible and the agreement with Phipps had to be continued.

In January 1918, NBC were in negotiations with Phipps over a pooling scheme, but Phipps' proposed profit split of 70/30 was not acceptable. Phipps continued to brew for NBC, using NBC materials and casks on commission, but reduced to 4/- per barrel. The Board view was that: *"The idea of one beer cannot be entertained unless and until pooling of profits is arranged and acted on."*

Perhaps the negotiations presaged the problems of the later merger.

The end of the war saw the return of the men, which brought a need to recommence brewing, if only to find work for those whose jobs had been guaranteed on their enlistment. By 1919, there had been 62 applications for reinstatement of which: 38 were thought reasonable, 15 not and 9 had already returned to work. The lady clerks were given notice to quit. The men were returning to a 47 hour week with a 50/- minimum wage and 6 days paid holiday.

1924 NBC Price List	4½ gal	9 gal
XX	11/6d	23/-
PA	14/-	28/-
IPA	16/6d	33/-
DS	16/6d	33/-
XXXX	19/-	38/-
NBC	27/-	54/-
Bottled beer per dozen bottles		
	Pints ½ Pints	Nips
Pale	6/6d	4/-
IPA	5/-	
Double Stout	7/6d	5/-
Stingo	6/6d	4/6d

(Daily Chronicle 17th December, 1924)

In June the increased barrelage allowed to Phipps meant that they were unable to brew for both and NBC would have to brew a portion. In addition, Lucas could not brew for NBC because of a coal shortage. Although Phipps suggested continuing with the working agreement, NBC said no. In the meantime, the Lion Brewery which the government had tried to buy or rent the previous year had been retained because of the need to make as much malt as possible.

In 1920, NBC continued the rebuilding of their brewing equipment, for example 4 new fermenting vessels were bought in the September. Their difficulties may also have helped the decision to turn down an offer to buy Eady and Dulley in July. The Milton site was also put up for rent.

It was decided, in April 1923, to produce a 4d beer and in July Mr Turnell retired and Mr Watkins, the 2nd brewer, was appointed as the Head Brewer on a salary of £900 pa. New underbacks were installed and it was decided to advertise Stingo. NBC were also using their cash to buy back their debenture stock eg £240 on the 1887 at £87½.

In 1925, Horace Brown, the consultant brewer who had been a director for 24 years, died. July also saw the death of Colonel B.T.Seckham and his replacement by Gerald J.T.Seckham, who became the Chairman. Gerald Seckham and Alan T.Page were also the joint managers. L.C.Baillon became a director of the business. The following year, the Secretary Percy Hanafy and the Head Brewer W.J.Watkins also became directors.

NORTHAMPTON (continued)

The business was looking to expand, but Messrs Southams turned down £90,000 for their Coventry properties and NBC were also outbid for the 5 Battle houses in the September. However, the following year they were able to buy when Charringtons were selling their Birmingham houses. They were also looking to rationalise their estate by selling the remaining unlicensed properties. Plans for a new fermenting room were drawn up and this opened in August 1927.

On 16th December, 1926, NBC held an EGM which agreed that the share capital should be increased to £320,000 by the creation of 70,000 shares. This included a bonus issue of 50,000 shares from the reserves of undistributed profit and 20,000 special "Employees shares" of £1 each. However, the latter did not have a voting right nor did they entitle the holder to any future capital bonus. They could only be sold back to the brewery and not to any third party. The brewery reserved the right to refuse to buy the shares back if it suited them. Any employee shareholder who left the company had to sell his shares back *"....to the company at par (£1), or at the ruling market price of the ordinary shares, should the latter stand below par"*. Still, they did pay 2/8d free of income tax in the first year.

In February 1929, a special meeting discussed the possible take-over of Eady and Dulley of Market Harborough (F3325), with its 42 licensed properties and 10 off-licenses. This was paid for in December by an increase in the share capital to £500,000 and in the borrowing limit from £450,000 to £600,000. A further take-over was achieved in 1931, when the brewery bought the Northampton wine and spirit merchants Lankester and Wells, Mercers Row, from the executors for £18,250. In the 19th century, Lankester and Wells had been agents for the Anglo-Bavarian Brewery of Shepton Mallet, which seems to have had close connections with several members of the Northampton brewing trade. Although invited to tender for Elworthys of Kettering, their bid was too low.

In addition to transferring some brewing equipment from Eady and Dulley, NBC were also investing £244 in a centrifugal separator and £1,100 in a 400 barrel fermenting vessel. However, this was fairly small scale compared with plans drawn up in November by Messrs Bradshaws, the renowned brewery architects, as follows:-

New Copper House	£11,700	Refrigeration Room	£2,250
Coppers	£10,500	Refrigerator	£4,150
Racking Room Floor	£2,600		

The brewery also looked to bring in electrification of the malt mill, mash tun and cask hoist. Their production was around 60,000 barrels per year, including about 6,000 barrels related to the Eady & Dulley business. The average selling price in 1930 was £5 13s 5d per barrel compared with £5 14s 11d the year before, perhaps showing the economies of scale from the take-over. Gross profit from brewing had risen from £9,993 to £11,379. Mr W.J.Watkins, the Head Brewer put forward plans for new fermenting vessels costing some £6,000, but adding another 1,550 barrels capacity.

Gerald Seckham died in 1930 and Alan Page, who had retired from being the General Manager became the Chairman, with L.C.Baillon and P.F.Hanafy as the joint General Managers.

NBC continued its reputation as a good business to learn from, the pupil brewer in 1930, being a Mr Charrington! The following year, Mr Watkins, was conducting experiments with Edme, the malt extract company, he was also offered consultancy work with Duttons of Blackburn. Mr Heron was the second brewer, whilst Mr Dixon, one of the under-brewers, accepted an appointment with Holes at Newark. The Herons were a well-respected family of "scientific" brewers from Ireland, who had provided the Head Brewer at Holes amongst others.

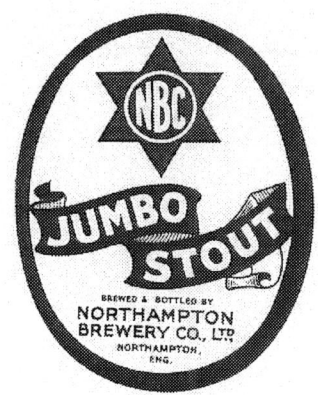 

At the start of the 1930s the company advertised their beer as being "*Good for you and for Northampton*". The emphasis on the part the brewery was playing in the local economy continued until 1937, when they still advertised that the beer was "*....brewed in Northampton by Northampton men*". The following year the approach had moved away from the general recession towards the qualities of the product. Stingo, for example was advertised as a "*drink for sportsmen*". The overall fight against the depression was linked to the Brewers Society National Action Scheme which levied 3d per barrel, requiring an NBC contribution of £800.

The NBC profit figures for the period were:-

30 Sep	1928	£59,097	1929	£60,962	1930	£65,530
	1931	£55,536	1932	£39,643		

The drop in profits was "*largely due to the additional tax on beer imposed in September 1931, which tax has now been taken off*". However, in June 1933, the financial position was healthy enough for a debenture stock issue of 100,000 5% stock at £103 per nominal £100. This was against some 41, mainly Eady & Dulley, properties valued at £81,000.

The company owned a total of 415 freehold properties of which 161 were fully licensed premises, 46 were beer houses and 64 were off-licensed premises. In addition, NBC leased 10 fully licensed premises and 4 beer houses. The overall value of the business was £993,500, of which £684,954 was the freehold and leasehold property. The debenture issue was used to reduce bank lending, discharge mortgages on the freehold property and to further develop the business.

In 1932 NBC had formed a £100 company called the Home Butler Limited, with the aim of developing the retail family trade. The intention was to build on the trade of the recent take-overs. The draught trade was mainly within a 60-70 mile radius of brewery. In 1935 the AGM was proudly told that NBC owned 54 vehicles which, despite covering 389,000 miles, had resulted in accident and damage claims of only £12 11s. They had previously turned down a proposed property exchange from Ansells and later were to turn down a bid from Atkinsons for the Walsall properties. When the Lucas of Leamington houses came up for sale in June 1934, the Board's view was that they were only trading at 3 to 3½ barrels per week and fixed a maximum of £5,000 per property. The only purchase seems to have been the White Horse at Silverstone.

However, NBC also saw wider horizons, since in 1933 they were supplying bottled beer to the Egyptian Sudan and Malta. They were also letting forward contracts for the purchase of American hops from Messrs Wood, Hanbury, Rhodes & Jackson.

In 1934/35, the Board had adopted a policy of modernising the properties, with an initial building programme of £22,600, and in August gave Messrs Martin a £7,770 contract to build the Spinney Hill Hotel. In 1938 the brewery opened the White Hills, the first of several new suburban pubs they had planned. However, World War II thwarted the company's building plans, which were destined to remain on the drawing board until the mid-Fifties.

Throughout the thirties, NBC continued to provide tuition to pupil brewers, including plans to take a Monsieur Sigard of Belgium. The Head Brewer, W.J.Watkins, was even undertaking consultancy work with Amalgamated Brewers in Stockholm. NBC also continued to invest in the brewery, for example, the 1937/38 building programme of £18,000 included new fermenting vessels and improvements to the cooling and air-conditioning. However, in April 1939, Mr Watkins reporting on Messrs Bradfords said "that the principal of this firm of architects who prepared plans of the Brewery alterations was certified as mentally unstable". The Board instructed Mr Watkins to inform the firm's successors that "we have our own staff of architects and that we shall not make use of their services in future".

ALES and STOUT				
OF HIGHEST QUALITY Brewed and Bottled by the NORTHAMPTON BREWERY Co., Ltd.				
IN CASK				
				4½ Gall.
MILD ALES—X	...	...	...	9/6
XX	...	...	...	11/6
XXX	...	...	...	14/-
XXXX	...	...	...	18/9
BITTER ALES—L.A.	...	...	...	11/6
P.A.	...	...	...	14/-
I.P.A.	...	...	...	15/9
STOUT—S.S.	...	...	...	14/-
D.S.	...	...	...	15/9
OLD ALE—Stingo	...	...	...	27/-

IN BOTTLE			
		Per Dozen	
	Pts.	½ Pts.	Nips.
PALE ALE	5/-	3/-	—
MILD ALE	5/-	3/-	—
STAR ALE	6/-	3/9	—
BROWN ALE	6/-	3/9	—
INDIA PALE ALE	8/-	4/6	—
JUMBO STOUT	6/6	4/-	—
STINGO	—	6/6	4/6
BASS & Co. PALE ALE	—	4/6	—
WORTHINGTON	—	4/6	—
GUINNESS STOUT	8/6	4/6	3/2
BARCLAY'S LIGHT LAGER	—	6/6	—
JACOBS' PILSNER LAGER	—	6/6	—

CYDER				
			Dozen	
	Quarts	Pts.	½ Pts.	Nips.
Whiteway's	10/-	7/-	4/-	3/3
Bulmer's	10/6	7/-	4/6	3/6
Gaymer's	10/6	7/-	4/6	3/6
In 6 gallon casks, 2/5 per gallon.				

A Northampton Brewery Company price list dating from 1937 which was used extensively in their Lankester and Wells off-license chain
Authors' collection

In 1940, the air raids on Coventry brought extensive damage to the properties there. Some 30 staff and 41 weekly paid employees had joined the Forces out of a total of 246 men. The Home Butler subsidiary was wound up in 1941. Despite previous complaints about the impact on trade, eg the AGM of 1941 talked of extreme difficulty from government control and shortage of supplies, the number of servicemen in the area provided an impetus. February 1942 saw Mr Watkins carrying out consultancy work at the malt extract plant of Messrs Weetabix in Burton Latimer.

The support for the war effort perhaps was wearing thin by July 1944, when the Board expressed their disappointment at the continued and widespread theft of beer, malt and sugar. They pointed out the generous beer allowance of 16/6 per week, but instructed that, in future, it was not to be taken off the premises. Furthermore, if the thefts continued they would consider ending it completely. Nevertheless, NBC did follow the Brewers Society recommendation that 5% of output should be diverted to troops serving overseas. In addition to the 602 barrels for themselves, they arranged to bottle 20 barrels per week for Hopcraft and Norris of Brackley (see entry) and 15 for Smiths of Oundle (see entry).

The end of the war brought the opportunity to re-invest in the brewery, initially some £6,500 in plant, including a 300 barrel hot liquor tank and 6 new fermenting vessels.

NBC continued to provide an excellent training ground, pupil brewers in 1945 being the son of Mr Saxby at Morlands and Arthur G.W.Brown of New Zealand Breweries. The following year one pupil was Mr Lees-Jones son of a director of J.W.Lees.

Courtesy CAMRA fund-raising

In 1947, NBC, like many other brewers, were looking at the growth of mineral waters and considering manufacturing for themselves. The initial step was to arrange a supply from Messrs Lants. In 1948, the general manager reported that foreign beers, in the form of lagers, were being imported, but NBC resolved not to purchase them.

In November 1948, there was a fire in the next door tannery occupied by Messrs Collingridge which caused some damage to the annex to the main fermenting room. This at last gave NBC the chance to buy-out their somewhat annoying neighbour. Many years previously, Collingridge had tried to rent the old East's brewery site at Milton Malsor. Having been turned down, they promptly set up next door to the Phoenix, despite NBC's objections to the likely impact of the smell.

Robert Heron had become the Head Brewer, but in 1949 he was tempted to leave to join his brother in a partnership; however, this fell through and he remained with NBC. In addition, Noel William Miller from Charringtons joined as the second brewer, whilst C.Robinson from Duttons joined as working brewer.

Another pupil brewer was Monsieur Pierre Duquesnoy of Brasserie L'Union in Jumet. These links with Belgium also led to consideration of the possibility of exporting Stingo to there. The output that year was 89,452 barrels, with an average of 1,720 barrels per week. At £850 per barrel this valued the licensed property at £1,462,000, which led to an increase of £590,743 in the books.

However, there were continuing problems with the water supply in the town. The same water diviner who had previously found the brewery's present well suggested that there was water 275 feet below the rear of the Wharfinger's Arms in Weston Street. They decided that it was worth investing £2,500 to bore a new well. The post-war upturn showed in an output of 127,685 barrels which led to a bonus for the workforce. It also gave the Board sufficient confidence to invest £34,593 in brewery reconstruction, especially the boiler house and chimney.

In 1949, the census return for weekly paid employees showed the following:-

Brewery	84	Maltings/Cooper/Transport	78

The previous property revaluation allowed an EGM on 17th April, 1950 to double the capital value to £1m by the issue of new shares. That year saw the final demise of the Eady and Dulley business at Market Harborough, when it was brought under the banner of Lankester & Wells. In September, NBC narrowly missed buying 8 properties in Coventry which Southams sold to Mann, Crossman & Paulin the day before they were due to be auctioned. That month also brought major changes of the top management, when L.C.Baillon began to discuss his retirement. W.J.Watkins became the MD and Production Manager, with H.A.Jones as the Secretary and General Manager.

Further £50,000 investment at the brewery was mainly on a new copper house and coppers. In 1951 £21,500 was spent, including a malt mill, bottle washer and filler. The under-brewers were Gordon Douglas Dobie and Alan Ernest English on a salaries of £350 each. The Annual Report noted the marked swing from draught to bottled beer.

In 1952, NBC were in the take-over market, their target this time was Phillips' St Martin's Brewery at Stamford (F4751 see entry). The purchase was financed by selling government stock. Ironically this company had been founded by Joseph Phillips, the uncle of the Phillips Brothers who had started the company out of which NBC had grown.

The company began to alter their beer range when in 1954 they launched a new draught dark mild, but it was poorly received. The company also began to back-filter some of their draught beers to combat the problems some landlords had in keeping a good pint. This was linked to the process of pouring "slops" back into the barrel, so any filtering must have been an improvement. They gained some publicity from supplying 100 cartons of cans of Stingo to the troops in Korea.

The year saw the completion of the major rebuild of the brewery. Mr Heron's son became a pupil at the brewery and Ian Gilchrist, a former pupil and owner of Hook Norton, recommended Mr Dutton Forshaw of the Burtonwood business. However, the latter was said to have given up brewing as a career later that year.

The Phoenix Brewery in 1969

Photo: Geoffrey Starmer collection

NORTHAMPTON (continued)

During 1954 and 1955 the brewery opened five new pubs as part of the suburban pub plan which had been stopped by the war. These were the Boothville (now known as the Lumbertub), the Clicker, the Sunnyside, the Westone and the Red Earl (now called the Dallington Brook). They were closing and selling uneconomic houses, eg. the Three Horse Shoes, East Farndon.

In 1955, through the Northants Brewers Association, NBC and Phipps were in a confidential agreement about the price of bottled beer and the following year there was a similar arrangement about draught beer.

The year 1956 saw the centenary celebrations of the brewery, (but see above). However, times were changing, not the least being the growth of bottled beers, especially national ones. Ind Coope came with an offer of Double Diamond in NBC pubs, in exchange for access to their own properties eg XXX Mild in the Rugby and Market Harborough areas. There were also negotiations with East Anglian brewers, such as Mowbrays, with regard to closing uneconomic houses.

In October, the NBC Board was faced with the prospect of investing £200,000 in a new bottling department. They also had a growing revenue reserve and balance sheet valuations which were higher than the market price. Furthermore, the preference shares carried voting rights which would make it possible to achieve control at lower cost. Perhaps not surprisingly, discussions with Phipps were begun.

As well as the general situation for brewers, the Suez crisis and problems with fuel shortages, Messrs Mann Crossman & Paulin were making approaches to sell their bottled beers in exchange for wines and spirits. Talks with Phipps continued into January 1957, one sticking point being that NBC did not wish to become a subsidiary company, rather they suggested a holding company for the two concerns. There was a worry that publication of the terms of the offer might lead to a bid for Phipps because the relative share prices would be reversed after the take-over and *"Phipps' shareholders would therefore, at that moment, be a body of disappointed people....ripe to an offer"*. Barings Brothers were to arrange "market support" (shades of Guinness in later years) for Phipps.

The Northampton Brewery Company Ltd.

ALL COMMUNICATIONS TO BE ADDRESSED TO "THE SECRETARY"
TELEPHONE No. 796
TELEGRAPHIC ADDRESS
BARLEYCORN, NORTHAMPTON

LCB/JMB

Northampton

1st March, 1957.

Dear Sirs,

In April the Phipps' proposals were approved and EGMs the following month saw acceptance, although not without some disagreement (see Phipps). L.C.Baillon, 58 years service, 37 as a director would take a non-executive appointment. From Phipps, E.C.M.Palmer and D.J.A.Jones would become directors of NBC. However, the final transfer of assets took until April 1959, when other interests were beginning to stir. The estate at the time included the following properties in Northamptonshire which still had brew houses standing:-

Corby, Off-license
Little Houghton, Off-license
Syresham, King's Head
Duston, Melbourne Arms
Potterspury, Reindeer

The brewery site eventually disappeared under the new Carlsberg plant.

Osborn, Francis, *The Peacock, 28 Market Hill.*

This pub dated back to 1456. In 1666, when tenanted by Margaret Billing, the Peacock was sold by Elizabeth Collis to Tom Phillipps of Rutland for £520. In 1793, Francis Osborn is described as an inn holder in Cotton End. In 1798, he was the Mayor of Northampton and owner of the Peacock when he entered into an advertising battle with John Wilson (see entry).

Osborn's daughter Sarah became Pickering Phipps' second wife. Osborn retired to a house over the South Bridge which later became the site of Thomas Hagger's brewery (see Allen & Burnett).

In 1826, his son George formed a partnership with Henry Lenton Stockburn, a coal merchant and maltster. The latter's family was from Kettering, where they had kept the White Hart (later the Royal) and also provided mortgages for other publicans, including the Battle brewers. Stockburn, who was the mayor in 1829, had inherited property which later became the Draper's Arms, 29 Drapery. In 1849, the partnership was between Stockburn and Thomas

Osborn and they were operating as hop factors. Henry's nephew married an Eliza Osborn Smith, whilst his niece married a William Linnell (see entry).

The Peacock continued to be owned by the Osborn family in the early part of the 19th century. In 1836, the pub was owned by William Payne of Oxford, with Edward Castell as the tenant. It is thought to have brewed until 1857 and the following year was being kept by Samuel Perkins. It was bought by Mannings in 1896 and was a Phipps' house when closed in 1956. The site is now a shopping centre.

In 1898, Osborn & Co owned Franklin's pleasure gardens.

Osborn, Peregrin Crosby, *South Quarter (Bridge Street)*

Osborn is listed as a brewer between 1818 and 1830. He may have been the son of the Peregrine Osborn who is in the 1781 militia list as a whitesmith in Gold Street.

Page, William B, *Bull's Head, 33 Sheep Street.*

In 1877 Page is shown as brewing at the Bull's Head; however, the following year the pub was a Coales & Allen house and later an NBC house which closed in 1917. Before this, Page seems to have been at the Plumber's Arms in 1864 (see Butcher entry).

Parker, John Samuel, *Horse & Groom, 29 Cow Lane (later known as Swan Street).*

In 1877, Parker advertised the Horse and Groom in Swan Street which was "*Noted for its Home Brewed Ales and Phipps' Celebrated Stout*". He had been at the pub from at least 1864. However, in 1888 the pub was being kept by a Mrs A.Parker and there is no mention of brewing. It later became a Phipps' house, which was closed around 1958, and was later demolished. It was included in the 1940 Kelly's listing (see Introduction).

Peach Family, *Marefair/Mayorhold*

The Peach family were important woolstaplers and maltsters in Northampton, as well as the owners of several inns. The latter they presumably supplied with malt for brewing on site by the victualler eg Thomas Ringrose a distiller/brewer in 1732. Similarly, in 1764, one of the Peach properties on the Drapery was tenanted by John Roe, a victualler. Thomas Peach's Will of 1760 left the Three Potts, Bridge Street, to his second son Thomas P.Peach. His eldest son William received the maltings in Mare Fare and the following inns:-

    Woolpack, Bridge Street (bought from the Sargeant family 1724)
    Ram Hotel, Sheep Street
    Cross Keys, Sheep Street

In 1813 a Thomas Peach is shown owning the inns and also property on Market Hill. There is a William Peach listed in 1818 as a brewer in Mayorhold. In addition, a Thomas Peach was at the Hind Inn Wellingborough in 1765, and the inn's brew house is mentioned in 1814. Around 1776 the Peach family sold property in the West End, Wellingborough, to W.Wilson (see Wellingborough entry). It is not known whether the family were related to the Peachs who had major maltings at Burton on Trent and Newark. However, a daughter did marry into the Manning family (see entry), and a Joseph Peach and family lived at the site of what became NBC (see entry).

NORTHAMPTON (continued)

Phipps (Northampton and Towcester) Breweries Ltd (F3584), *122 Bridge Street, Northampton (SP 754 598)*

WHARF, BREWHOUSE, Etc, NORTHAMPTON. TO LET. J C Barratt respectfully informs his friends and the public that in consequence of Messrs Willson, Hanson and Fascutt declining the further wish of establishing a public ale and porter brewery in Northampton, as intended and agreed, on the premises of J C Barratt in Bridge Street adjoining the River Nene or Nen and communicating with the Grand Junction Canal, JC Barratt finds his present business, independent of the above mentioned brewery falling on his hands, more than he can manage with pleasure to himself and family, is determined on declining some part of his concerns, he therefore wishes to inform the public, that he intends letting his present business at Northampton, with the addition of a large commodious house fit for the reception of a family of the first respectability...together with a new and complete dwelling house and offices in the occupation of Mr C Duke, his bookkeeper, divided from the above only by a gateway or entrance to the said wharf and premises. The outer offices consist of a newly erected and very complete brewery, cellars, storerooms etc; large maltings and malt chambers, extensive warehouses capable of containing several thousand quarters of grain, a stable etc.... The advantage for establishing a brewery viz convenience of land and water carriage, one of the best barley markets, coals cheap, no brewery in the place, a large and populous town and neighbourhood and within a short distance two sets of Barracks and deposits for Government stores... for further particulars to J C Barratt, Woodford Lodge near Thrapston... The brew house is provided with a plant calculated to be complete as any house now in use, the copper set and finished by the first workmen, and the remainder of the utensils ready for fixing up and may be taken at valuation. (Notice - Northampton Mercury 18th January, 1817)

When in 1817, a purpose built brewery became available in Northampton, Pickering Phipps, who had been brewing at a small brewery in Towcester (see entry) leased it from John Charles Barratt. However, the family may have had some earlier connections with brewing in Northampton. Their involvement with the Wagon & Horses (see entry) has been mentioned and Pickering's brother Edward may have been brewing in Northampton from around 1801.

On March 25th 1817, Pickering moved to Northampton, where he prospered enough to bring three of his sons into the business. Edward, Richard and Thomas eventually became partners in their father's brewery, whilst James, the eldest son, remained farming in Towcester until his death in 1831. Pickering also moved his desperately ill father into a house near the brewery. The other son, John Phipps, founded a drapers business.

In July 1818 Pickering's first wife Ann died at the age of 50, she had borne him five sons and three daughters. The following January, Pickering's father, James, died in Northampton at the brewery house.

On 18th November, 1819, Pickering married Sarah, daughter of Alderman Francis Osborn who formerly kept the Peacock (see entry). There were no children from this second marriage.

Pickering became involved in local politics as an Alderman and was elected Mayor in 1821. He remained involved in the town council until his death. In 1824, Pigot's Directory lists Phipps, Pickering & Son brewers and maltster, South Quarter.

On 14th March, 1827, Edward and Elizabeth Phipps had a son whom they named Pickering in honour of his grandfather. Richard Phipps christened his heir Richard junior, whilst Thomas, or Tom as he was known, had a daughter called Charlotte, following his marriage in 1832 to Mary Ann Newby.

Pigot's Directory for 1830 lists Phipps, Pickering & Richard as brewers in Bridge Street. They were also operating as maltsters and coal and salt merchants from the premises. They also owned the Fleece on Bridge Street, which was tenanted by William Odams.

Alderman Phipps, the brewery's founder, died on Monday 17th May, 1830, at the age of 58. Upon his death the brewery passed to Richard and Thomas, Edward having died the previous year. The 1831 Directory lists Richard Phipps as a brewer. Richard and Thomas also operated a malting at Bell barn.

Edward's widow, Elizabeth, remarried but their son Pickering Phipps grew up a rowdy and ill-disciplined youth. He was expelled from Mr Emery's Academy for Young Gentlemen for fighting. In desperation his uncle secured him an apprenticeship with Mr Franklin a draper with a shop on the Market Square. He surprised his family by becoming a model worker.

In 1840, the business was trading as Richard & Thomas Phipps, Bridge Street, but Richard Phipps died soon afterwards, leaving Tom Phipps in sole charge of the family brewery. In 1843 Thomas brought in Pickering junior, aged 16, to assist him with the brewery. Richard junior was brought into the business at a later date.

In 1850, Pickering, at the age of 23, married Mary Whitmy the daughter of a wealthy Northampton builder. They moved into the Brewery House where they lived for ten years prior to moving to the newly built Collingtree Grange in 1860. Richard junior married Mary's cousin Ellen on 29th March, 1860.

Tom Phipps' daughter Charlotte later married Mark Dorman, the owner of a stationers' business in the Drapery, and a leading local Tory councillor. This brought about the later involvement of this name in the concern, since their son was Thomas Phipps Dorman.

The Phipps family had been involved with Tory politics since the time of the brewery founder. It is reported that the vats at the Bridge Street Brewery were all named after leading contemporary Conservative MPs. Pickering himself became a local councillor and was made Mayor of Northampton in 1860, and laid the stone for the Guildhall extension. A story is told that he offered the council a loan to build the new hall if he could use the cellars as a beer store. His offer was swiftly rejected, despite his being the Mayor. His nomination as a JP was turned down on the grounds that he was a brewer! His son and heir also called Pickering was born on 28th July, 1861.

Following the death of Tom Phipps on June 21st 1858, the brewery began to trade as "Pickering and Richard Phipps and Co, 160 Bridge Street and Towcester". The renewed interest in Towcester was followed by the take-over of the brewery of Job Goodman Sheppard.

"NORTHAMPTON and TOWCESTER BREWERIES MESSRS P and R PHIPPS HAVING PURCHASED THE BREWERY AT TOWCESTER BEG RESPECTFULLY TO INFORM THEIR NUMEROUS FRIENDS, AND THE PUBLIC GENERALLY, THAT THEY ARE IN THE POSITION TO SUPPLY FINE ALES, STOUT, PORTER, MALT, HOPS, WINE, SPIRITS, CORDIALS, Etc. OF THE SAME QUALITY AS THOSE WHICH HAVE SECURED THEM SUCH DISTINGUISHED PATRONAGE IN THEIR BUSINESS CARRIED ON AT NORTHAMPTON. ORDERS RECEIVED BY POST OR OTHERWISE, EITHER AT NORTHAMPTON OR TOWCESTER BREWERY WILL RECEIVE IMMEDIATE AND CAREFUL ATTENTION. N.b. ALL GOODS DELIVERED FREE OF CHARGE." (Northampton Mercury March 1860)

Written accounts state that the brews produced by the Phipps' breweries were thick turgid dark beers of quite outstanding strength. When nearby rivals Phillips Brothers opened a modern Steam Brewery and began to brew a clear amber ale it had a marked effect on Phipps' sales.

Somewhat concerned, the cousins approached the London firm of Davison and Scamell, brewers engineers and architects, and asked them to design a modern brewery for them. Robert Davison submitted plans for Phipps' New Brewery in August 1864. It was an impressive five storey brewery powered by a twin cylinder steam engine (which was still operating at the end of World War II) and which used the Burton Union fermenting system. The brewery, built by Dunkleys of Northampton at a cost of £22,000, was fully operational by 1868.

In October 1865, Pickering paid £2,150 for 43 Abington Street, the property of the late Thomas Howes. Although this included a brew house, there is no indication that it had been a commercial operation. By this time, Pickering Phipps was one of the most influential men in the area. He had a second term as Mayor in 1866. Richard Phipps is often lost in the shadow of his illustrious cousin, but he too was a man of character. He was the chief of the town's volunteer fire brigade, in which he took an active role.

Between 1872 and 1877, large fermenting rooms and cellars were added to the New Brewery to increase the capacity to 600 barrels per day. This involved the demolition of certain properties in Bridge Street owned by the brewery. Included in these was an old pub called the Magpie, which dated back to at least 1763.

A new plant was also opened at Towcester in 1874. The new brewery was on the East side of the High Street and employed 70 men to produce 150 barrels of beer per day. However, these changes were obviously not appreciated by everyone, since in 1878 the Phipps' Head Brewer, Thomas Manning, left to form his own business (see entry).

In 1874 the local Tory party presented Pickering Phipps with a petition of 1,050 signatures to ask him to stand for Parliament. He won the election and became the town's first Tory MP for forty years. At the 1880 election he lost his seat to Charles Bradlaugh, arguably the most famous politician to represent the town. He therefore fought the by-election for Northamptonshire South in 1881 and held it until 1885. Pickering was also a member of the Country Brewers Society.

**NORTHAMPTON
(continued)**

In 1876 the brewery opened baths, next door to the Malt Shovel. They used the waste hot water from the brewery. Initially they were planned for the use of the brewery workers, but were later given to the town.

"Notice is hereby given that the partnership heretofore subsisting between us, the undersigned Pickering Phipps and Richard Phipps trading at Northampton and Towcester....under the name and firm of Pickering and Richard Phipps, was this day dissolved by mutual consent. And the said business will be carried on in the future by the said Pickering Phipps and Thomas Phipps Dorman, under the firm of P. Phipps and Company....dated this first day of October 1880". Northampton Mercury 1st October, 1880.

In 1880 Richard Phipps junior decided to retire aged just 43. His share in the business was bought out for £160,000 (including his part ownership of the Peacock at Welford). The new partner was his nephew Thomas Phipps Dorman, the grandson of Tom Phipps, who became the owner of a ¼ share in the business. Richard then bought a large house near Bromyard which he and his wife ran as a boys' home for Barnardos.

The change in partnership led to the business moving towards registration as a limited company in 1880, incorporation being completed in 1881. This showed a listed capital value of £500,000, under the Chairmanship of Pickering Phipps. His sons-in-law, William Henry Lamb and John James Walker were directors, with Board meetings being held at Collingtree Grange. G.R.Hornby was the Company Secretary.

The initial share issue was 13,016 ordinary shares with a nominal value of £25. Interest in these shares was considerable and they realised £286,296 as follows:-

3,240	fully paid	£81,000
9,776	£21 part-paid	£205,296

This was against assets with a total value of £380,495 of which the plant was in the books at £41,881. At that time there 165 men employed at Northampton and 36 at Towcester. They were operating some 7 maltings as follows:-

Bedford, Mr Rudyard	Pitsford, let to Youil Bros	Royston
Towcester	Thorpe Road	Woburn
Weston Street No 7		

However, in November 1881, the Brewers' Journal carried a note that Mr Black had relinquished his appointment as Head Brewer at Phipps to resume his practice as a consulting brewer at 18 Albion Place. In 1882, new offices were opened at 8 Gold Street. These were designed by S.J.Newman, a notable architect, in a decorative style popular at the time.

In July 1884, indentures were made out for George Albert Dorman and Richard Percy Phipps (Pickering's nephew), whilst Charles James Pope was an underbrewer.

In 1885, Phipps invested £196 in a new mash tun from Messrs Rice & Co of London. This may be a branch of the Northampton firm which was owned by the Phipps family. However, despite this investment, Mr Wileman the brewer left. In May, additional duty on beer of 1/- per barrel led to gravities being reduced to the following:-

No 10	36°	No 9	27.5°	No 8	25°	No 6	20°
☐☐☐	24°	☐☐	22°	☐	19.5°		
No 4	17°	ESP	27°	SP	24°	XX	21°

In 1886 Pickering Phipps III replaced his brother-in-law, J.J.Walker, as a director. The following year, the Authorised Share Capital was raised to £500,000 of 20,000 @ £25 and £200,000 debenture stock. In October 1890 James Langton of Reigate became a director, the Board noting his experience of the brewery trade. His address is shown as 52 Broad Street, with connections with the Holts Brewery.

Throughout the early 1890s, the family continued to buy shares. Richard Percy Phipps, brewer of Towcester, bought 15 in December 1887. Edward Phipps, Pickering's brother, Brewers Manager of Towcester, bought 5 in 1887, 3 in 1890 and 20 in 1892. Thomas Phipps brewer of 169 Bridge Street bought some 30 shares over the period, whilst Pickering Phipps, The Lowndes, Blisworth, bought some 23. The Dormans and the Popes were also buying small numbers of shares. Interestingly, R.S.Boddington of Manchester was also buying small numbers of shares. The Hipwell family (see below) were also shareholders.

Pickering Phipps' health had been seriously damaged by long nights spent at the House of Commons. By 1889 his constitution was so poor that his doctors would not even allow him out of the house. So the business was run by Tom Phipps, the Head Brewer and director, and Thomas Phipps Dorman as joint Vice Chairmen.

Pickering Phipps (1827-90) Grandson of the founder

Pickering Phipps died *"in the presence of a large number of relatives and friends"* on Friday 14th September, 1890, at his home in Collingtree. He had done much for the people of Northampton, but also accumulated a fortune of half a million pounds. His generosity to the church, in particular, is well recorded. Similarly, the family's involvement in the village, much of which they owned, was well-marked, for example in founding the school and providing the Reading Room. The Collingtree property was sold in 1913.

The Phipps family erected several memorials to the late brewer. The most well known being St Matthew's Church on land he had once owned and which is still called Phippsville. The parish church at Collingtree contains an ornate window and an organ dedicated to his memory.

Pickering Phipps III of Rushton Hall, Kettering, succeeded his father as Chairman of the Board. Thomas Phipps Dorman continued as Vice Chairman and Dr William Henry Lamb, who had spent several years tending the health of Pickering Phipps (his father in law), was also re-elected as a director.

Life at the brewery continued, with an order in March for Messrs Pontifex & Wood to supply a 15 ton ice-making machine for £2,000. By 1892 the Bridge Street Brewery had the largest tied estate of any Midlands brewery and the ninth largest in Britain. In 1894, they also leased the county cricket ground.

In October, perhaps indicating some different styles of management, one of the agents, Mr E Maddocks, was accused of financial impropriety, he wrote to ask for clemency. He stated that he had previously mentioned his family difficulties and that he had been forced to use his expenses as an advance of salary. He wrote later about being ordered off the premises, without a moments warning, after 33 years service and suggested that this would never have happened under the late Pickering Phipps.

In 1896, the company bought the wine and spirits business of Portals, Gold Street. This old established firm was housed in premises next to the Queen's Head Inn, which was on the corner of College Street.

In February 1897, Phipps bought the Silk Mills at Ditchingham in Norfolk and converted them to maltings at a cost of £2,800. In September the Royston maltings were sold.

In November 1898, there was a final call of £1 on the 9,776 part-paid ordinary shares. This helped the December discussions about alterations to both Northampton & Towcester (£3,641), including a new tun room at Northampton for £6,824. Towcester had previously received a new copper, hop, back and mash tun. They also bought the Shipley Wharf on Bridge Street for £2,750.

In 1899 Edward Phipps retired and there were further financial changes with the authorised capital increased to £1m. In November, it was decided that Thomas Phipps, Pickering's nephew and Richard Percy's brother, was to relinquish the post of Head Brewer as from 1st January, 1900, but retain the position of advising brewer, with a salary of £500 pa, and a seat on the Board. It seems that Thomas ran one brewery, whilst his brother Richard Percy ran the other at Towcester. If so, Thomas was only 38 at the time, and it was suggested that his poor eyesight had led to his retirement. Mr W.F.Tipler was to be the general manager. However, the changes in personnel and the financial alterations were more likely part of the impact of a major amalgamation.

"IMPORTANT BREWERY AMALGAMATION IN NORTHAMPTON

The amalgamation of the two important brewery companies of P Phipps & Co Ltd and Ratliffe & Jeffrey Ltd, Albion Brewery, which has been talked about for some time, has now been accomplished, the final arrangements having been completed this week." Northampton Mercury 23rd June, 1899

The official closure of the Albion Brewery was completed on 2nd December, 1899, and Thomas Ratliffe and his son Richard joined the Board of Phipps. The take-over involved 8,900 ordinary shares to Thomas Ratliffe, who was appointed MD, and 7,500 £10 Preference shares to the family owners. The deal brought an increase of 242 houses to the estate. Its organisation probably was the reason that Phipps turned down an offer to buy Eady & Dulley (see Little Bowden).

The Chairman's speech in December 1899 addressed the shareholder worries about capital, especially the increase through splitting would dilute their dividend. He pointed out that they had received a 20% dividend for last 3 years, and that the extra preference shares had been needed for the take-over of Ratliffe & Jeffrey.

NORTHAMPTON
(continued)

Phipps, Gold Street offices, Northampton

Photo: Authors' collection

However, the amalgamation created some internal difficulties with the departure of two executive members of the company to help start up Dorman, Pope and Company. George Dorman was not only the Head Brewer, he was also the brother of one of the Managing Directors. The relationship between T.P.Dorman and Pickering Phipps was already strained, even prior to a chain of serious problems which was to rock the company.

In April 1900, Pickering Phipps offered to resign, but the Board persuaded him to stay; nevertheless T.P.Dorman took the chair for some meetings. Unfortunately, there was also a general depression which affected all breweries.

This crisis came at a time of public concern following deaths in Manchester due to *"contaminated beer"*. The cause was traced to glucose supplements which were contaminated with arsenic. Locally, the question was raised about what was being put into the beer. Tom Phipps had argued that beer could be made out of any grain, as it all turned to sugar in the mash.

In June Pickering Phipps exchanged a £50,000 mortgage for 5,000 £10 preference non-voting shares, which he then transferred to Thomas Ratliffe. The company also loaned Pickering some £30,000. However, there was some £45,300 from the liquidation of Ratliffe & Jeffrey, which together with £100,000 debenture stock, allowed their property to be conveyed to Phipps. In July, Mr Tipler was appointed as general manager. On November 27th, Thomas Phipps retired from the Board.

In 1901 it was decided to lease maltings at Midland Road, Peterborough, and to build new brewery premises at Northampton. There was some estate rationalisation at this time with the sale of some Birmingham properties, including the stables there, and the Coventry stores were also sold. This had obviously been helped by the purchase of a 3 ton Aveling steam engine for £707.

Further problems surfaced when Bass served notice on several breweries in an attempt to protect their patented trade mark of a triangle. Phipps and Davenports both employed diamonds in their advertising and this was considered too close to the Bass design to be acceptable. Phipps contended that they had used the design for their diamond ales for *"forty years or so"* and supported Davenports with their legal costs. Talks were held with Mr A.J.Clay of Bass, and also Ind Coope who had similar concerns.

When Davenports won their court battle there was a sigh of relief at the Bridge Street Brewery. Hence, in 1906 Phipps & Co *"Celebrated Diamond Ale"* was still being advertised at 1/- a gallon in cask. However, the label design had to be changed, with Bass paying £100 for the cost of unused labels.

To stem the company's problems Pickering Phipps brought in a manager, whom he "head hunted" from the Aylesbury Brewery Company. The new man was Captain Louis Edward Walker, who on 1st July was appointed as the assistant MD in charge of the brewery on a salary of £500, which was paid for from Pickering Phipps' salary of £2,000.

The decision to rebuild Northampton was clearly forward looking, since the Towcester brewery was destroyed by a fire on December 8th 1901. Initial estimates put the damage at £18,000, but the Phipps AGM heard that this figure was alarmist and that the true figure was nearer £12,000. They were further assured that insurance covered all but a few thousand pounds, the actual cost turned out to be £10,593.

However, like their neighbours NBC, Phipps had continuing water problems. The solution which they adopted was to build a main from the old Albion Brewery to Bridge Street.

The relationship between Pickering Phipps and Thomas Phipps Dorman, joint MDs, had now deteriorated to the general detriment of the company. Pickering again offered to resign as Chairman, but the Board once more voted in his favour. Mr Thomas Ratliffe was to be allowed to attend directors meetings at his discretion, and to retain his salary.

In May 1902, further brewery alterations, according to the plans of Messrs William Bradford were discussed. This included Messrs Ramsden & Son's tender for new coppers etc, H.Martin's tender of £2,480 for a new copper house, and new hopbacks. There were also £575 of renovations to the mashing machinery by Adlams of Bristol.

Following the departure of George Dorman, the previous Head Brewer, the company had serious problems with the quality of the beer being brewed. A consulting brewer Mr Lawrence Bryant, was called in. After going thoroughly into the matter with Mr Walker, Mr Bryant said, *"Well Mr Walker, I'm sorry to say it but you haven't a barrel of beer in your cellars fit to send out"*. Mr Bryant presented a report to the directors which, together with one from Mr Walker, caused the directors to decide that there must be a change in the brewing staff.

Richard Percy Phipps, who had moved from the Towcester brewery, was forced to resign. In October 1902, Frederick Bennet Brown was brought in as the 2nd brewer to replace him. Confidence in the firm slumped and the share price fell. Rumours circulated that Pickering Phipps had personally lost a fortune.

It seems that Mr Dorman objected to the "new methods" being employed by Phipps, especially the way old trading agreements were being severed. The brewery had reduced its purchases of barley grown locally and this had caused bad feelings amongst the farming community. The Crown and Anchor maltings were being used as a store, instead there was the lease on Peterborough and the Ditchingham maltings were to receive a £12,000 extension. The latter were still operated by Messrs Rutter & Co, with whom individual brewers had previously had some disagreement.

The Board were prepared to continue with the agreed plan and pressure was brought to bear on Dorman in an attempt to get him to resign. He retaliated, just prior to the 1902 AGM, by circulating the following letter to the shareholders:-

NORTHAMPTON (continued)

"Dear Sir,

You will notice that neither the balance sheet or report is signed by Mr Thomas Ratliffe or myself. Mr Phipps wishes us both to retire from the Managing Directorship in favour of Mr Walker. We doubt the wisdom of this course. Kindly attend the above meeting and if the matter is brought forward, give us the benefit of your advice and vote.

Yours faithfully

TP Dorman. 10 December 1902"

Coming on top of the rumours, this caused a great deal of disquiet. However, the Board were in agreement about the impropriety of Mr Dorman's action in associating Mr Ratliffe with him, without the latter's consent or knowledge. In addition, it had been agreed that following the transfer of 3,600 shares to Thomas Ratliffe, the balance from 12,000 on take-over, that if his son resigned to allow Captain Walker to take a place on the Board, the family interest should continue to be represented by Thomas or a nominee.

The shareholders meeting on 10th December at the Plough Hotel had an unusually large attendance *"owing to the prospect of lively proceedings"*. Several questions were put regarding the absence of Mr Dorman's signature. Mr Dorman explained that he had been unavoidably absent from the Board meeting which discussed the Report, but he agreed his support and it was passed by the meeting. Mr Dorman had actually been on holiday on the south coast.

Pickering Phipps explained Mr Ratliffe's signature was partly an oversight and partly that it would look odd if only one signed. He assured the meeting that the Report had the unanimous support of all directors.

The agenda for the meeting included the proposed retirement of Captain Richard Ratliffe and Captain LE Walker proposed in his place, and it was decided to deal with this separately from the report. Mr Harvey and other shareholders asked about Captain Walker's qualifications, for all they had heard about him was that he was given *"great power"* at the brewery and had been *"turning things upside down"* in re-organising the concern.

Pickering Phipps replied that it was not necessary for him to say what Captain Walker's qualification were (*"Oh, oh"* from the audience). He would not have been recommended unless he was properly qualified. He emphasised that he and Captain Walker stood together.

When asked about Captain Walker, Mr Dorman expressed his opinion *"that he believed Mr Walker had been working his hardest to bring the company up. That he and the directorate had not been successful was their fault"* Mr Langton *"We have succeeded"*. Mr Dorman accepted this as far as the balance sheet, but not regarding the trade, but declined to comment further about the latter.

Several questions were raised about Captain Walker's absence from the meeting, but he was duly elected to the Board. However, there were 13 votes against him. Mr T.Montgomery then raised the issue of loss of local trade and suggested that it would help retention if the business relied more on local farmers for their malt. There was no reply from the Board, but clearly the move to increased reliance on Norfolk had not been accepted by everyone.

The matter was not at an end, firstly Mr W.F.Tipler resigned on 31st December and was given 3 months pay in lieu of notice. Then, on 14th January, 1903, T.P.Dorman was formally asked to retire from the business, and the following week was sent a letter from the solicitors. He was now isolated and seemingly at odds with the rest of the Board. They had tried to oust him privately, but when he would not go, the only solution was to call an EGM for February 1903. The resolution - that Thomas Phipps Dorman be removed from the directorate - was signed by all of the other Board members.

In a letter dated 9th February, Mr Dorman expressed his belief that the removal of himself and Mr Ratliffe as MDs would be without remuneration. He also mentioned the need to preserve the *"local and traditional element"* versus *"new imported influences"*. The letter went on to mention that the volume of trade had fallen off and the goodwill of the business had been affected.

At the EGM, Pickering Phipps set the scene *"....not without good reason Mr Dorman was duly informed that he had forfeited the confidence of his colleagues....(and had) been formally asked to resign his position, but he has declined to do so, and they (his fellow directors) being unanimously of the opinion that having regard to his continual disloyalty....(could no longer) admit him to their counsels, and have to ask that he be removed (from the board)"*.

Phipps mentioned in passing Dorman's *"unwarranted circulars"* and called his attacks of Captain Walker *"beyond contempt"*. He reiterated that the only reason Walker had been called in was to take on some of the workload that the existing joint Managing Directors were not dealing with.

Mr J.H.Jepson asked whether the matter before the shareholders was not really of more importance than the removal of Mr Dorman. Mr Dorman had referred in his circular to matters of great importance touching the welfare of the brewery. Mr Jepson then proposed that a committee of inquiry be appointed to investigate the affairs of the company and report back. Mr Dorman agreed to abide by the report from the proposed committee. Further discussion referred to Mr Dorman's circulars and in particular his use of Mr Ratliffe's name without the latter's authority and who was entirely against him (Mr Dorman: *"No he was not"*).

Captain Walker was then allowed to speak; although, some present questioned whether this was appropriate. He drew the attention of the shareholders to the fact that Mr T.Phipps Dorman was present when Mr Walker was appointed assistant MD. In terms of the brewery problems he pointed out the depression was affecting all breweries. Another reason for the decrease was that for some considerable time the beers which the brewery turned out were not fit to drink (applause). That was the state of things when he came upon the scene in July 1901.

When he came to Northamptonshire there was the bad state of things as regarding the beer to deal with and he realised directly that the only thing to do was to brew good beer. In the presence of Mr Edward Phipps he felt rather diffident in discussing one case and unless he was forced he did not think it was necessary to discuss the resignation of his son as a brewer. There was then some discussion regarding Richard Phipps and his responsibility for the state of the beer.

Pickering Phipps then explained how Mr Dorman had been disloyal in changing his mind about Captain Walker's appointment and informing Mr Tipler. He suggested that this had led to the trouble. Mr Dorman disagreed with the statement and Pickering Phipps made reference to the circulars.

Mr Dorman *"My circular was not issued until I had to do something on the defensive. I was asked with Mr Ratliffe to resign. It had never been put to him or the shareholders what benefit it would be to the company if Mr Ratliffe and himself did resign quietly, as Mr Phipps wished them to"*. He told the meeting that the only thing that he could remember was a huge scheme for rebuilding and refurbishing at the brewery and he was slightly opposed to that. Referring to Mr Phipps' wife being ill and their proposed long holiday, he suggested that *"...while he was away, Mr Walker was to have the management of the whole business, and carry out the suggestions and alterations"*. Pickering voiced his disagreement of this version of events.

Dorman told the meeting that he had always done his best for the company but in the past few years he had been taking things a bit easier, as had Mr Phipps. Then when, through bad water etc., the beer had gone wrong and everything else seemed to be going astray they had had to call in a manager. Mr Walker was brought in to help the brewers, but had drifted into general management.

A vote on the amendment was then taken with 38 votes for and 26 against. Pickering Phipps called a poll with the result that 13,380 shares were for and 65,874 against. The Board had used proxy votes to stop the amendment, which some members were not too happy with. The vote to remove Thomas Dorman, went 28 for and 20 against. However, according to the Articles the vote needed to be 3:1. Pickering asked for another poll, but taking account of the previous poll, Mr Dorman resigned.

On 11th March, 1903, Captain Walker was confirmed as the joint MD in place of T.P.Dorman. At the time, Robert Stanhope Dorman was an under-brewer, but, perhaps because of the family difficulties, he does not seem to have stayed long with the business. Mr John Trimmer was brought in from Mackesons of Hythe in Kent to run the wine & spirit department, which had previously been looked after by the Dormans.

The water problems were partly resolved by the decision to dig a new well at the Foundry Street stables for £1,500. Further rationalisation of the estate took place, with the decision to dispose of the Banbury houses. The large rebuilding plans continued in 1903. The Northampton site was enlarged and in June alterations were planned as follows:- North side - £14,580; washing shed, coopers - £5,600; roofing - £2,454.

Learning lessons from the Towcester fire, the Northampton Brewery was made "flameproof". The old wooden floors were replaced, where possible, with concrete ones and all wooden staircases were replaced with iron ones. Several new buildings were added to the site to increase the brewing capacity to include that which was once housed at Towcester. The bottling stores were also re-arranged and enlarged. The Towcester agency was to move to Wolverton, with Cosgrove being retained for stores. A sign of the times was the purchase of a Fiat motor car for the estate department for £630.

Further investment included 2 hot liquor tanks for £330 from Ramsdens. They also bought a cask washing tank for £315. Thus, a total of £47,100 had been spent on the brewery. Despite, or because of the rebuilding, in October Mr Dawkins, the Head Brewer, resigned. The minutes mention continuing problems with brewing staff. Indeed, Mr Frederick Bennet Brown on trial as head brewer, was warned not to have "differences" with Mr W.G.Rutter the master maltster. Mr Seward was given a rise of £50.

Given the problems, it is perhaps not surprising that Phipps declined Easts, of Milton Malsor, at £13,362 and the Cannon Brewery of Newport Pagnell at £7,000. They also declined the Walker and Soames houses and again in 1905, when as well, the Rutland Brewery and its 18 houses was *"not considered worth entertaining"*. At the time, bank loans had risen to £130,000 and Thomas Ratliffe and Mr Webb together loaned £20,000. These offers to buy other concerns confirm that Phipps were not the only business undergoing difficulties and indeed were well thought of by the potential vendors. For example, Salt & Co of Burton on Trent were in arrears on their account with Phipps, and by 1906 they were in receivership.

In April 1905, the Board decided to close Towcester at the earliest possible instant. On the production side, F.B.Brown was confirmed as Head Brewer with a salary of £500, whilst Gerald Seward was the 2nd brewer at £250, and A.N.Trimmer 3rd Brewer at £100. An order was placed with Messrs Garton Hill & Co for 200 tons of brewing sugar at 12/6 per ton. There were close links with the Garton family who were debenture holders in Phipps, and who were also key players in the development of Watneys.

Nevertheless, doubts about the draught beers persisted, even six years after the water and other problems. The sale of bottled beer increased, even though a gallon of draught Celebrated Diamond Ale cost 1/- whilst a similar amount of bottled cost 2/6d.

In addition, internal strife was to occur once more. In July, after Pickering Phipps had described his visit to the Pulham and Ditchingham maltings, the Minutes note:-

"During discussion, Captain Walker was remonstrated with for insolent behaviour towards the Chairman, including an accusation of ungentlemanly conduct, which the Chairman intimated he should not allow to pass, but would take notice of at the proper time."

At the next Board meeting, perhaps not surprisingly, Captain Walker objected to the minutes and was promptly dismissed as MD. In the September the Board received a writ from his solicitors for wrongful dismissal. The writ carried through into the next year, when Captain Walker was given leave to postpone notice until December 31st. Captain Walker having gone to Australia, the writ lapsed and the action was dismissed with costs for Phipps. Perhaps he had not proved to be the best choice after all. Later correspondence was to relate to bad malt and the cost of the re-building.

On a lighter note, Pickering Phipps, as President of Northampton Town Football Club, agreed to extend their loan for £600.

Unfortunately, further problems arose when the Head Brewer, Mr Brown was taken ill and died on March 15th. A.G.Seward took over, on a salary of £400, with William Leslie Lynn as 2nd brewer on £200 pa, Mr Trimmer remained as 3rd brewer but with an increase to £125 pa. Phipps were offered the Thorpe End Brewery Melton Mowbray (F3361), but declined. This concern was owned by Langton & Sons suggesting a link with the director James Langton. They did buy the small business of Hanson & Son for £2,500.

In 1907 Marston, Thompson & Evershed closed their account for stout. Perhaps not surprisingly, Mr Trimmer having been turned down for the post of 2nd brewer, resigned for a post at the Cheltenham Original Brewery, and Lesley Phipps Dorman was appointed in his place. The final transfer of brewing vessels from the gutted Towcester brewery to Northampton was completed in the September.

The firm introduced a new financial system in 1908 following the discovery that one of their agents had been defrauding them for years. Noting a simple *"clerical error"* in the books of their Daventry agent, they sent a manager from Northampton to check it out. It was only when the agent, Mr Lucas, committed suicide that they discovered how much he had stolen from them. Unfortunately, they had similar problems at the Brewery, where Mr Kilburn was taken into custody over errors in the Home Ledger. He pleaded guilty and was sentenced to six months.

The new accounts systems allowed them to cut their bad debts from £38,500 to £27,000. Mortgages too were reduced, from £162,000 to just £12,500. They were even able to introduce a Christmas bonus scheme for the workforce by 1913. Competition was still creating problems with the "long pull" in Leicester area, resulting in an agreement by the Leicestershire & Rutland Brewers Assoc to end it.

In 1908, some 19 men were still at the Albion brewery, with one in each department suggesting only a skeleton staff. We tend to assume that the paternalism of the brewing industry meant long careers, but the growth of Phipps meant that 125 of the 300 had been taken on since 1900 (presumably mainly ex Ratliffe & Jeffrey), with another 100 dating from the 1890s. Mr Dickens taken on September 1903 and Mr Joyce 1906 were discharged in 1908 *"to make room for Albion men"*. However, there were 3 workers who had been there since the 1860s. One can understand the previous managerial problems.

The view taken of the workforce was perhaps somewhat harsh by modern standards, for one individual to be unfit for work on account of ill health, meant 1 weeks notice. Similarly, in September 1907, George Barnes working in the cellars was called up to help in the bottled beer department - the record states boldly *"bottle burst lost one eye"*.

In 1910, it was decided to build new offices at Bridge Street for a cost of £3,000. There seem to have been delays with the new well, that at the Albion was back in use after renovation work. The closure of the Thrapston agency shows the change in distribution, eg. that year they bought a Swift motor car for £250 and 2 Thorneycroft Steam Engines were sold and 2 petrol wagons bought. The next year a further 5 ton petrol wagon was delivered, followed shortly by two 3 ton commercial wagons.

In 1911 a bottled beer plant installation was on a fortnight's trial. Obviously the trial was successful, since in March they placed an order for a second plant from Messrs Seton & Co. A third plant was ordered later in year at a cost of £1,857. The next year saw £7,000 invested in chilling and maturing vessels and a gas-collecting plant for the bottled beer department. Further equipment for pasteurisation of stout and more gas collecting plant was bought in 1913. The investment in bottling started to pay-off when they made an arrangement to supply bottled beer to Elworthy's houses.

Although there had been a pay rise in March 1913, there was an attempted strike in the November, after notice had been given to J.A.Fitchett and T.E.Carter. There were meetings, with Colonel Seckham and T.E.Manning, to discuss a joint approach in response to a letter from the secretary of the Birmingham district of National Union of Gasworkers and General Labourers, about conditions and hours. However, there would be no further agreements with NBC and Mannings on discounts, in future, each would *"do as they liked"*.

The transport changes meant that in 1914, they had built petrol storage tanks of 2,000 and 3,000 gallons. The increase in the delivery range thus causing the Foleshill depot to close that year, and the Bedford one in 1915. However, transporting over longer distance may have been linked to the increase in beer returns at the time. Phipps also rented Dulley's old offices at 38 Market Street, Wellingborough.

The outbreak of war led immediately to 3 staff and 14 men being called up. In 1916 a further 37 men were awaiting call-up. The fire at NBC in July and the resulting arrangement to brew for them meant that Phipps would be operating fully and would be hard pressed to lose more workers.

The view of Pickering Phipps on the arrangement with NBC was quite clear:-

"I do not propose that we should attempt a final amalgamation until after the war but that we should work up towards it by extension of the present working arrangement..... which can, and probably would, be continued permanently in any event." 14/9/1917

However, there were problems with the proposed 30:70 profit split. At the time Phipps brewed for themselves around 90,000 barrels and 30,000 for NBC. They anticipated that combination could reduce costs from around 6/- per barrel at Phipps and 7/- at NBC, to around 5/- per barrel. The shape of things to come!

NORTHAMPTON (continued)

The Government proposed concentration of brewing in 1918, led to talks with Hipwells about an NBC style arrangement, which came into force in the October. Mannings also considered such an arrangement, but did not follow up the initial approach.

Major Richard Ratliffe returned from the war to become a director once more, and manager of the Estate Department on £500 pa. The post-war confidence in 1919 led to discussions about the possibility of running railway sidings into the brewery and also buying new trade. One of these included that of Mr & Mrs Strong of Coventry, who had bought a small brewery with two pubs and wanted to know if Phipps were interested in supplying them. This concern, shown in Friedrich's Gazetteer as Elijah Strong (F1229 at Woolston, Coventry), actually seems to have been that bought from the executors of John Cave at Wolston (F5702 see also History of Brewing in Warwicks p36). However, Mr Strong was not particularly successful, since in 1923 he owed Phipps some £384.

The war had also brought a price agreement with NBC and Mannings:-

Beer	Barrel	Beer	Barrel
5d	90/-	7d	120/-
6d	108/-	8d	142/-

The complete take-over of Hipwells (F3821) was discussed, and Melville Hipwell was taken on as a pupil brewer. However, Phipps decided not to purchase Day & Sons of St Neots, with 61 licensed houses. The take-over of Hipwells in 1920 brought another two dozen tied houses and links with a key brewing family. The 1920 AGM was told:-

"During the year the company has absorbed the business of Messrs Hipwell and Company of Olney on terms which we agreed were mutually advantageous and I'm sure that neither of us will regret it."

The take-over cost some £115,000 in cash and shares, with John Charles Hipwell, receiving 7,500 share and a seat on the Phipps' Board. A further 7,500 shares each went to family members: Arthur William Hipwell, Henry George Hipwell and Samuel Edgar Hipwell. The brewery plant was valued at £23,560. Mr Burt, a director of Bass, wrote hoping that they could continue with their trade in the Hipwell properties.

NBC were still having problems and their Board wrote in the July to say they were looking for 400 barrels if necessary. In addition, Mr Langmore of the All Saints Brewery, Leicester, had inquired about the Phipps' charges for brewing for hire, but nothing had come of the approach. Captain Edmunds of the Banbury brewery, Hunt, Edmunds, also had meetings to look at the possibility of Phipps undertaking contract brewing for them. Despite what modern consumers might think, "badge brewing" has a fairly lengthy history.

In 1921 Phipps were in a healthy position with £65,805 at the bank and investment in Victory and War Bonds of £102,734. They had also been able to spend £25,463 on the new brewery.

There were still problems with the long pull. They were also forced to allow their tenants to sell Guinness stout after it was already being sold in pubs in the Kettering area. This may also have influenced the investment of £3,134 in a roasting plant at the Weston Street maltings.

The Crown and Anchor maltings had a worn gas engine and electric power was to be installed, suggesting it was being used. The Lords maltings at Olney was sold to Morgan & Eady in March 1921, and the Old Crown Maltings, Olney, in 1923. The Hipwell purchase which was completed in the October 1921 led to some estate rationalisation, with the Huntingdonshire properties being sold to Marshall Bros for £4,750.

Phipps and Ratliffe were joint MDs in 1922, but their respective salaries reflect responsibilities: £3,950 for the first compared to £375 for Mr Ratliffe. The new well, which had cost £1,663, had begun to solve the water problems.

The trade depression led to enquiries for a 4d beer to match that being sold by the Huntingdon brewers. Phipps decided to cut the price of the 5d at Kimbolton.

Impressed with what they had seen on a visit to Watney's Stag Brewery, the directors invested £5,650 in a Scott's yeast pressing system. They also purchased a new Bottling plant from Messrs Montague Sharp & Co for £3,800. However, in 1925 they were still having problems with poor malt. Luckily, when the suppliers, Messrs A.A.Clarke of Olney, went to court, the case went in favour of Phipps.

In 1926 Phipps looked at Charrington's Coventry properties, which were on the market, but like NBC they seem to have been unimpressed. They also considered Hunts of Stamford (see entry), but decided the price was so high that it was useless to attempt further negotiation. Mr Ratliffe retired as MD, sadly he died the following February.

The decision to use motor transport only, meant the retirement in 1927 of 6 draymen and stablemen. Further investment included a Goliath cask washing machine for £1,980 from Hopkins and Son, Clerkenwell, London.

Phipps were still choosy about growth and in 1928 they turned down Lucas of Leamington and the Johnson & Mason properties in Coventry, although they did buy the Bell, Bell Green, Foleshill, for £10,000. The following year they declined to buy Hopcraft & Norris (see entry).

Technical progress continued, as Messrs Ramsden & Co lined the pine fermenters with copper at a cost of £1,198 in 1929 and experimental pasteurisation in the bottling plant. The following January Messrs Pontifex installed a plant for £1,335. There was further investment that year of £7,914 in a cold store for hop, sugar and malt. A major sale of de-licensed property helped recoup some of the cost.

In 1931 Phipps decided to close their offices in Gold Street. Mr Lamb and Major Fraser were assistant MDs on salaries of £250 each. There were still problems with competition and the Guinness price had to be reduced to 5/- per dozen in the off-licences. The increase in beer tax in 1932 affected the profitability of all four major breweries in the town, but only Mannings Castle Brewery was pushed to the very edge. Concerned about the effects of *"this confounded beer duty"*, Pickering Phipps suggested that a tax on tea would be a better option.

> *"....surely it is time our blue ribbon friends (temperance groups) were allowed to make some contribution to the expenses of this country...."*.

Several local publicans had been put out of business by temperance crusaders and Phipps had personally pledged himself to fight for any licensee who he felt was being persecuted. The increased beer tax finally forced Mannings to merge with Phipps.

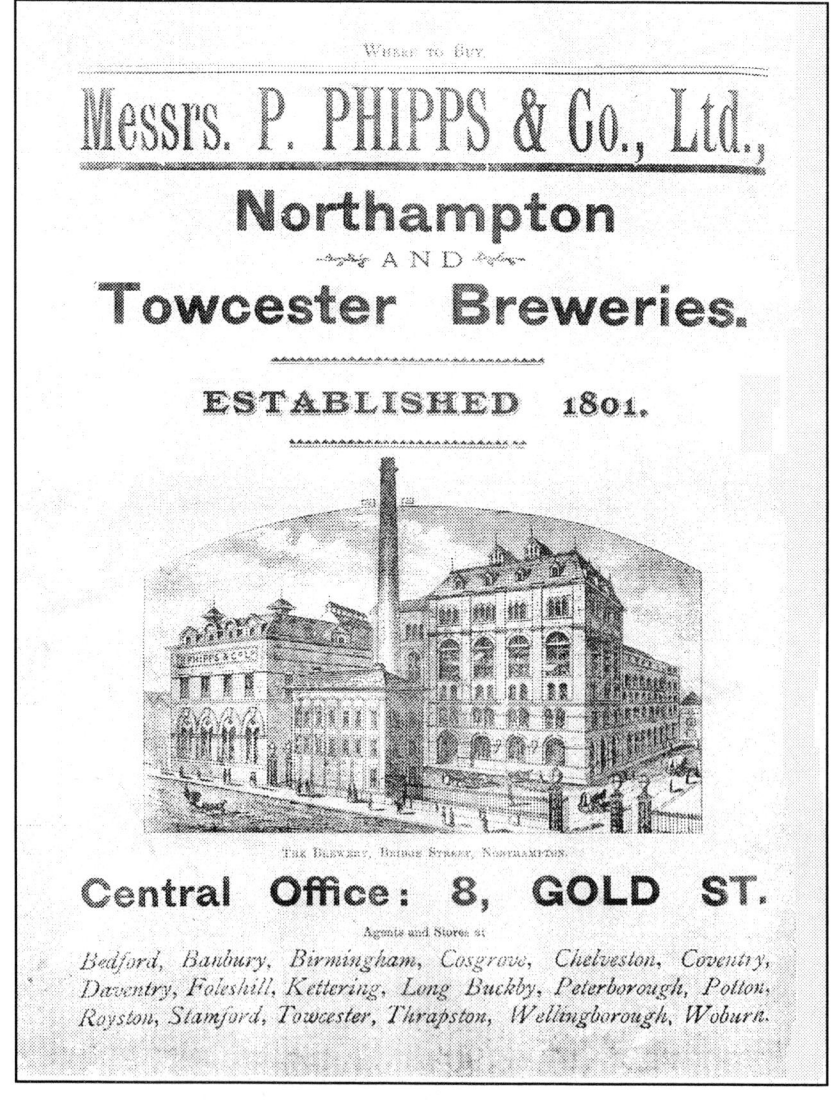

NORTHAMPTON
(continued)

In January there were meetings with Mr Manning and the take-over was agreed on 24th March and made public the next day. The Manning's estate brought a further 120 pubs under Phipps' control. It was to be financed with 60,000 unissued shares.

In addition to the extra properties, in 1935 the Board agreed the rebuilding and alterations at several properties and two new hotels, the Broadmead Hotel, Broadmead Avenue and at Hallwood Road Kettering. At the same time, 5 houses in Towcester went to Lord Hesketh (see Dorman Pope). In April 1936, Phipps were in negotiation to sell the Stag's Head and offices at 9 Abington Street.

In the September, Pickering Phipps took a reduction in salary to £1,500 and that of the assistant MDs was raised to £1,000 each, representing changed responsibilities. On Friday 8th October, 1937, Pickering Phipps died at the age of 76. He left a widow, but no heir to take over his position at the brewery. He had never been a particularly popular man, but his ruthless approach had always benefited the brewery. The finances were even healthier, with £203,514 at the bank.

Initially, Richard Edgar Lamb chaired meetings, with Major Richard Ratliffe as his deputy. However, Lamb died the next year and Major Ratliffe was appointed Chairman, as well as MD, at £2,800 pa. Arthur Gerald Seward became a director, and other appointments to the Board were Reginald P.Lamb and James Hubert Phipps Walker. In addition, Alfred James Fraser and Edgar Claude Manning Phipps were appointed to the Mannings Board.

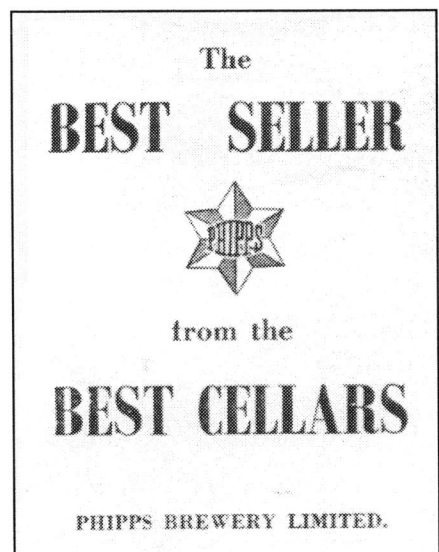

At an EGM in July 1939, the business name was changed to P.Phipps & Co Ltd, perhaps the crucial point being the removal of reference to Towcester. The meeting also agreed 5,000 2nd preference shares of £10 each to finance the Mannings purchase. However, the month also saw the purchase of 5 reinforced concrete air raid shelters for £150 each.

With the outbreak of World War II, the brewery experienced severe supply problems. They won a contract to supply the army and so could not meet the local demand. Consequently pubs in the town regularly ran dry. Maize and malt extract were used as a substitutes, as well as a whole range of other types of starch such as potatoes. The 1938 gravities of Phipps' beers had been higher than average (IPA 1048°OG, PA 1042°OG, AK 1030°OG and BS 1031°OG), but these were reduced during the war. For example, the Brewers Society, acting on behalf of the government, had agreed a 10% reduction in February 1941 and a further 5% the following February.

Nevertheless, as with NBC, the influx of servicemen proved quite beneficial to the cash flow. In June 1941, as well as bank balances of £231,829, Phipps had some £122,539 in Government War loans. However, one problem was that the Ditchingham maltings were requisitioned.

In April 1943, John Charles Hipwell resigned because of ill-health and was replaced by Frank Cecil Hipwell from Steward & Patteson. An agreement with NBC increased the basic minimum wage from 56/- to 62/- plus the war bonus. The Budget saw increases in prices:- 24/- per barrel; 1/- per dozen pint bottles; 6d per dozen half pints.

This did not appear to create too many problems, since bank balances rose to £334,879. However, the war did bring other problems, with an RAF bomber crashing on the Chandos Arms at Winslow causing its total loss, however there was compensation of £803. J.C.Hipwell died in the December.

Water supply continued to be a problem; however, Phipps were able to take the surplus from NBC's new well. Technology made further inroads, with the purchase at £2,175 from Messrs Pontifex, of a new pasteuriser for the bottled beer department. As well as draught beer Phipps had a full range of bottled brews which were easily distinguished by the colour of their crown caps. A yellow cap crowned IPA, whilst PA had a green one. The celebrated Ratliffe Stout had a red cap, No.10 a blue one and, hardly surprisingly, brown ale had a brown topper.

The Ditchingham maltings were de-requisitioned in December 1944. Although this had created problems for malt supply, this had been off-set slightly by compensation of nearly £5,000.

As well as the brewery and maltings at Northampton and Ditchingham, the business had a tied estate of some 651 licensed premises. Like NBC, they were being influenced by the growth of bottled beer, leading to the construction of a new bottling department at a cost of £30,000 on the building and £34,000 on equipment. However, a major change in the brewery was the retirement of A.G.Seward in September 1954, although he was retained as a technical adviser. He had been with Phipps for 54 years, 47 as the Head Brewer. His replacement was A.J.M.Hipwell. The

following month, the Elephant Lane maltings in Green Street were sold for £7,000 to Messrs Stimson Bros.

In 1953, Phipps also began to look at their close rivals, the Wellingborough firm of Campbell Praed (see entry for details on the background story and the initial approach from Praeds). To finance this they transferred the credit balances on their current and deposit accounts, £534,000, into a special account. They also arranged their overdraft facility to rise to £400,000 to cover trading. Their intent to brew at Wellingborough only for a very short period and then scrap the plant, was clearly influenced by the tax position.

The Praed's site at Wellingborough was sold to cover the cost of transferring the R.C.Allen soft drinks production to Northampton. They also bought Coombs Table Waters of Louisa Road for £10,000.

The take-over created some problems, not least being the prosecution of a Northampton stockbroking firm. For Phipps, it may have been one deal too far. They could raise £700,000 from liquid resources through selling government securities to the value of £280,000 to add to the cash in their accounts. However, this left £100,000, which they hoped to cover by a loan from Lloyds Bank, to be repaid by higher profits over the next 2 years. Unfortunately their application to the Capital Issues Committee for the loan was turned down. The view within the company was that the Treasury "*did not wish the amount of the purchase price to be in the hands of the general public for possible speculative purposes*" - some things do not change!

To counteract the growing sales of national bottled beers, they allowed Bass and Worthington to be sold through their houses and looked at the possibilities of Ind Coope's Double Diamond. They also added to the established bottled range a beer they called Velvet Stout which was advertised extensively as a sportsman's drink.

"Everywhere for immediate energy Phipps' Velvet Stout is being asked for. Strong....and very smooth at 1/4d a bottle. Brewed with Glucose".

This was presumably to replace the Redwell Stout which they had acquired with the take-over of Praeds.

In June 1955, Phipps decided to build new offices at the brewery. They were influenced by the fact that 8 Gold Street and the block in which it stood, including the Queen's Head, occupied a position whose value was far in excess to that of its current use. They hoped to sell the site for £200,000, with Boots the possible buyer.

On the soft drinks side, R.C.Allen was losing money, partly because of the delays with establishing the plant. It was felt that to rectify this, tenants would have to be tied for purchases.

With the sale of 8 Gold Street to Boots for £95,000, the company lost their main town centre wine and spirits shop, so they decided to close the Vine Inn in Abington Street. They had acquired the pub, with Praeds, on a lease until 2747(!), and re-opened it as a licensed shop. Like their rivals NBC, they gained publicity from supplying the troops overseas, with 120 dozen half-pints of No 10 being sent to the 1st Battalion of the Northamptonshire Regiment in Hong Kong.

There were problems with both the gross profit and trade in general, which led to a 1° reduction in the gravity of the draught and bottled IPA and PA. Problems with transport costs led to yet a further reduction of 1° on the IPA and 2° on the PA, the latter having 1° put back through extra priming. However, a 1d price increase in February 1957 led to 1° being put back on the PA.

The Board discussions in December 1956, about the need to have new contracts of service for the directors, were perhaps a good indicator that things were about to happen.

"The Boards of P.Phipps and Company and Northampton Brewery Company Ltd announce that they have for sometime been giving consideration to the future of their respective companies having in mind the close proximity of their two breweries and the fact that they both operate to a large extent in the same area they feel satisfied that there could be considerable economies in operation with resulting benefits to stockholders and improvement in the service which they could render to their respective customers if there were a closer association between the two companies. They have accordingly asked Baring Brothers and Company Ltd in consultation with their respective auditors and legal advisors to examine the position and put forward proposals." (Chronicle and Echo 7th January, 1957)

NORTHAMPTON
(continued)

The Copper House - Phipps South Brewery in 1967

Photo: Geoffrey Starmer collection

The Refrigeration Plant - Phipps South Brewery in 1967

Photo: Geoffrey Starmer collection

This announcement was met with mixed feelings. Phipps' shareholders were upset and asked about the benefits that they would see. They had heard all about such economies prior to the Praed's take-over. Instead the profits had fallen from £212,189 in 1955 to £197,887 in 1956. In contrast NBC's profits over the same period had risen £6,000.

On May 1st the merger plans were circulated. The document listed the main principles of the agreement to be:-

1. It is a merger of two companies. The take-over of NBC by Phipps is a purely technical operation.
2. The beers of each concern will continue to be available to the public generally. Both brews will be sold in suitable public houses.

The directors of Phipps called an EGM at the Angel Hotel on May 24th to vote on the proposal. In the fortnight leading up to the meeting a large group of one hundred and twenty shareholders led by Mr F.Phillips publicly voiced grave misgivings about the merger. They felt that NBC shareholders were getting a very good deal at their expense. Their anger was fuelled by rumours that a leak of information regarding the deal had been responsible for the strong rise in NBC share prices during the previous few weeks.

On the day before the EGM, a meeting was arranged between Mr Phillips and the Board. Mr Phillips emerged from this meeting and was able to tell his supporters that *"(following) full and frank discussions I now have great happiness in supporting the merger"*.

By 25th May, Phipps had received valid acceptances representing 88% of NBC's shares. At this point the "take-over" was complete. It brought the 711 Phipps' houses and the 420 NBC houses together into one of the larger tied estates in the country.

The new company was known as Phipps Northampton Brewery Company, but on advertising material it was always shown as Phipps NBC. The logo that the company adopted was the old NBC six point star, but with the addition of the Phipps' name.

It was agreed that the Board would consist of 10 members. Phipps gave a £1,500 golden handshake to Mr F.C.Hipwell whose family had been represented on the Phipps' Board since the take-over of their Olney brewery, 40 years earlier. At NBC, the Chairman L.C.Baillon was given a non-executive post after 37 years as a director of the brewery. Major Lionel Seckham, the grandson of the founder, along with Mr W.J.Watkins and Mr H.Jones received golden handshakes of the same size as Mr Hipwell's.

The policy was to gain security from outside interests by increasing efficiency and profits, whilst retaining goodwill through individual trading names and products. This would be backed by an estate programme based on *"fewer and better"* houses.

However, there would be a common in-house production of malt, despite the compulsory purchase of the Weston Street malting for road widening, and an interchange of brewing and bottling. Transport would be integrated and a tie for R.C.Allen soft drinks introduced. The NBC wine and spirit store in College Street was sold.

The first step toward integration was a hatchway through to the NBC bottled beer store for the transfer of mineral waters. However, the process was speeded up in 1958, when the Customs & Excise raised questions about the use of two brewing licenses for the one business. This led to discussion about not only combining paperwork, but also the physical integration of the two breweries. This became known as Scheme B, with phase 1 costing £22,000 taking 2 years and phase 2, a further 2 years and £76,000.

March 1958 saw the launch of Gold Star as a brand name, with the possibility of Staybright for the keg, both names alluding to the agreed logo. However, *"in view of the anticipated small sales of keg beer, consideration is being given to purchases from Watney Combe and Reid"*. A demonstration in June was followed by the necessary equipment and an initial supply the next month.

Financially, the merger was starting to pay-off, with £200,000 from the sale of properties. There was also a capitalisation of reserves which allowed the authorised capital to be increased to £2.9m through the creation of 759,000 £1 shares. This allowed £1,195,263 to be issued on a 1 for 1 basis. There was also an issue of £938,705 new debenture stock to substitute for the existing mixture. These were set against the following assets:- Freehold & Leasehold £5,058,970; Plant & Machinery etc. £510,472.

The brewing process was being looked at more closely from the point of view of the accountant rather than the brewer. To improve the keeping quality and palate of the PA it was decided to add 2 pints of priming to each barrel, together with phylax solution. On 78,000 barrels pa this would cost £20,000 which would be recouped by a reduction in gravity of 1° to 1031°, which the priming would restore to 1032°. The SPA was also reduced 1° to 1032° saving £5,000. These changes were not well received in the pubs and clubs.

The integration continued, with the introduction of a single cold store, single racking point and single pick-up points for draught and for bottled beer. It was also agreed to group all types of bottled beer. For example, although Ratliffe and Jumbo stout were brewed separately, the finished product was almost identical, albeit the latter contained a higher percentage of waste beer. IPA, PA/Starlight and Brown were brewed in both breweries but bottled under different labels.

The first stage was for all stout to be brewed in the NBC brewery, basically the same as Jumbo with 1035.24°OG and maximum waste beer inclusion of 15%. The bottled grouping would be:-

BIPA	Phipps	1041.76° OG
BPA	Phipps Starlight new beer	1032.26° OG
BA	NBC Buffalo Brown	1034.53° OG

Phipps Brewery in 1969

Photo: Geoffrey Starmer collection

January 1959 saw a strong financial position, and it was decided to press ahead with the capital building programme and to maintain sales outlets. In order to watch profit rates it would be necessary to consider shift working and the introduction of female labour into the bottling department. In the February, the pipe-line between the breweries was working and it was agreed to invest in stainless steel tanks from Burnett & Rolfe Ltd.

The labels for the new group bottled products were also available. In addition, mineral waters were being supplied to the Abington Brewery Co and the Leicester properties of Ind Coope and Bass. To help cope with this, the new accounting machine was operating, allowing even closer working of the administrative staffs. Mr Jones, bringing his experience from the war and Praeds, was pressing the adoption of a long-term Group Plan.

In March the Board, taking note that sales of lager were 2% of beer consumption and increasing, looked at producing lager from top-fermented yeast against the gravity of key brands:-

Manchester - 1037° OG   Grahams - 1032° OG   Carlsberg - 1032° OG

The first brew of "Stein" took place in the May. This was to replace total sales of 58,800 dozen for Grahams and Carlsberg. The cost was put at 4s 4½d per dozen half pints compared with 7s 7d for Grahams and 9s 1d for Carlsberg. Advertising of £1,500 would add another 1/- per dozen. The selling prices to the trade would be 11/-. This would give a profit of 5/6 per dozen at a gravity of 1034°. However, there would be a need for investment in cooling equipment.

Innovation also included experiments with Munton & Fyson malt extract, which would give a higher gross profit. PNBC were aware of 8 other breweries which were already using the extract and another 23 who were considering its use. On the malting side, Rutter & Co were trying a new malting process for increased production. The process involved "gushing" for 40 hours and then flooring for 6 days instead of 10/11 days.

Times were difficult for the industry with national beer production down by -3.37%. However, in April 1958 beer duty was reduced by 43/7d per barrel, which allowed trade prices to be reduced by 46/8d. Unfortunately, this was expected to reduce gross profit by £39,000 unless it could be offset by an increase in sales of 4.6%. One possibility was the invitation to tender for the Watford Gap service station on the new motorway. However, drinks could only be served with meals and, at a cost of £50,000, the 50 year lease was felt to be insufficient to make a tender worthwhile.

In July, the Board were once more looking at new service agreements for the directors, a sure sign that further changes were likely. The initial drive was to preserve the independence of the business, hence, there was a need to consolidate the two breweries and use the production facilities to the full.

Simonds of Reading had made an approach to form a consortium with PNBC and three other breweries, but nothing had resulted. The Board had discussions with Wells of Bedford and Hunt Edmunds of Banbury, but both wished to retain their independence. The Board were informed, by Baring Bros, that PNBC had a degree of vulnerability and were regarded as a possible target for a bid, especially with their large cash reserves.

In order to expand the estate, PNBC were in discussion with Derek William Pritchard of Ind Coope. However, they were somewhat surprised at his suggestion that they link up with Ansells. With the hindsight of the later growth of Allied Breweries, his suggestion is perhaps more understandable.

In the event, Ind Coope offered 140 ex-Brackley houses. However, they would only add 340 composite barrels, at £1,450 per barrel, indicating an average of 2½ barrels per week for each house. The barrelage was later corrected to 360 and with the offer of another 18 houses, with a composite barrelage of 97.2, the deal began to look more acceptable. It included a 15 year agreement not to take any new national brands, to take Skol, Double Diamond and Long Life and to cease to sell Carlsberg.

The houses would be paid for by a mixture of cash and shares, the latter at the market price of 64/- and with a caveat that Ind Coope would inform the Board of any future buying and selling of shares. They eventually ended up with a holding of 54,869 shares. Although there was a loss of some 60 barrels a week supplied to Hall's houses, there were other benefits in terms of potential access to Taylor Walker properties, Ind Coope purchases of Guinness bottled at Northampton and increased sales of R.C.Allen mineral waters.

The final deal was the purchase of 151 houses, 133 ex Chesham & Brackley and 18 others. The benefit was expected to be a profit of £3 on an extra 20,320 barrels, generating £60,960 per year.

The cost of the purchase was £685,436, financed by a rights issue of 199,210 shares at 1 for 12, with a price of 56/- which raised £557,788. The holders took up 95% of the issue, 188,514, leaving only a balance of 10,696 to be sold in the market. The EGM in September increased the authorised capital to £3.3m by the creation of an extra 400,000 shares.

In terms of the product profile, Stein was exceeding the anticipated demand, resulting in the purchase of 38 hogsheads from Lacons at 157/- per barrel. The links with Lacons were based not just on a common product, PNBC were also canning for them and when A.J.M.Hipwell the Head Brewer retired in August 1959, causing promotions at Northampton, C.R.Hipwell came from Lacons to be the 3rd brewer. Stein won a silver medal at the British Bottlers Institute exhibition in the Isle of Man and was offered to Wells and Melbourns of Stamford. The increased production and sales also led to consideration of whether to start canning it. In the September, it replaced Carlsberg in the PNBC tied trade. It also became available in the 39 houses of Paines of St Neots, in exchange for an agreement to buy 20 tons of malt extract.

In the 46 weeks to 14th August, 1959, sales were up 3.99% ie some 8,850 barrels. However, only 2,120 were PNBC products, the balance being 6,730 barrels of what were termed "foreign" ie non-Northampton barrels. Given that the Brown Ale contained 21.1%, and the Stout 20.5% returned beer, compared with the brewery's own maximum limit of 15%, perhaps this was not surprising. In August, returns of Jumbo from Ansells, Offilers etc. increased due to "ropiness" and had to be destroyed at a cost of some £2,000. The Board were also considering whether to reduce the 10 draught beers to 6.

One slight problem arose with paying the dividend on 300 shares held by Isabel Mary Baillon, as a result of the share allocation. The signature on the allotment letter, it was felt, had not been written by the allottee and was declared invalid. Miss Isabel was the 2 year old daughter of L.B.Baillon!

The business was now being completely merged. There was one advertising budget of £14,000, including television for the first time, with the emphasis on Stein and Bison Brown. There would be one slogan *"Phipps IS Beer"*. The North brew house would concentrate on dark beers, whilst the South produced the IPA and PA. Bottled production was also split between the breweries. The sales of Stein were growing with contracts with Paines, Wells and Abington. Phipps were also supplying 7,000 quarters of malt to Manns, and 5,000 to Guinness, and were malting close to capacity.

However, there was a continuing adverse reaction from the clubs to PA and the Board considered the possibility of supplying SPA instead. The filter-back system was now in all the tied houses, despite some poor publicity in the Chronicle & Echo, and had helped to reduce returns. The brewers were looking at continuous mashing in the experimental plant at Guinness. This was supposed to be brewing producing 200 barrels per week which were then blended with the main brew.

PHIPPS NORTHAMPTON BREWERY COMPANY LIMITED

REGISTERED OFFICE: THE BREWERY · BRIDGE STREET · NORTHAMPTON
TELEPHONE: Nº 2943 (6 LINES)
OUR REF   796 (3 LINES)

BHS Archive
Birmingham City
Library

In January 1960, Simon Combe, the Chairman of Watney Mann met Board members to discuss how to *"obtain facilities for increased production"* through amalgamation by an exchange of shares. Watneys had negotiated an agreement with Ind Coope for marketing Skol in exchange for Red Barrel and needed to produce an extra 600 barrels per week, since their Mortlake and Whitechapel breweries were becoming strained after the closure of the Stag brewery.

The proposal was that PNBC would continue to trade, and with considerably increased production and no redundancies. The Board would continue in office with normal control except for capital expenditure and national advertising. The Chronicle and Echo of 5th March, 1960, euphemistically spoke of *"a marriage"* between the local brewery and Watney Mann.

The deal was agreed by the end of January, with various permutations of share exchange being considered. Eventually, with help from the brokers Baring Bros, it was agreed 107 Watney ordinary for 100 PNBC and 110 Watney Cumulative Preference for 100 Phipps 5½% shares.

The letter to the shareholders emphasised that there was spare capacity at Northampton and the deal would give access to Watney's properties in the area, including those of Mann, Crossman & Paulin with whom PNBC had historic links. There would also be the possibility of sales into the 3,450 licensed properties of the Watney Group. Comparison was made between the two groups:-

	Watney	**PNBC**
Profits 1957	£2,816,166	£882,921
Profits 1958	£2,581,972	£908,667
Profits 1959	£3,193,528	£944,585

Watney's assets were £22m compared with £5m for PNBC. At the time of the offer, Watney's ordinary shares stood at 88/9 whilst PNBC stood at 72/6. Perhaps not surprisingly, the Phipps' shareholders readily accepted.

The Board congratulated Mr Jones on his handling of the negotiations. Mr Pritchard added his congratulations and Mr Jones expressed his gratitude to Ind Coope for their attitude towards the trading agreements. On a broader scale, the emergence of the Big Seven nationals was just starting and there were several possible ways in which the amalgamation, particularly of what was to become Allied Breweries might have gone. (NB. Allied-Domecq currently have a 15% share in Carlsberg-Tetley.)

Following the merger, E.C.M.Palmer, Phipp's Chairman, and D.J.A.Jones the Managing Director joined the Watney Mann Board. Derek Pritchard resigned from the PNBC Board to be replaced by Simon Anthony Helyar Walker Heneage of Watney Mann. Interesting how the Walker name once more showed the links between the brewing families.

March 1960 saw the first trials of Red Barrel which were initially suffering from hazing problems. In April, 120 barrels were sent down to London for comparison. The next 240 barrels were brewed using half Watney yeast and half Phipps, the former being commented on for its marked head.

There was an initial investment of £185,000 for draught Red Barrel (DRB), with anticipated production of 100,000 barrels in 1961. However, in addition they would need new bar equipment, cylinders and CO^2 containers, some 40,000 containers and 14,200 cylinders. Initially, this was expected to cost at least £0.5m, but the bill finally came to £340,000.

In August 150 barrels per week of DRB were being tankered to London. The Group decided to use only metal casks in future and that DRB would be the only national brand in the Group. In terms of bottles, national brands would be:-

Brown	Manns & Watney	Light	Watney
Red	trial	Stout	Cream Label

Locally bottled and eventually locally brewed. Perhaps it was a good time for Mr Heron, Head Brewer North, to retire. In October, the 2 IPAs were grouped although the *"trade had not been informed"*.

Unfortunately, bottled No 10 costs were rising because of short bottling runs and its gravity might have to be reduced 1° to 1083. The ex-Chairman Mr Fraser died early in 1961. From June there would be only one stout brewed, with Velvet being stopped and Cream Label being adopted. There was no comment from the trade about the merging of Ratliffe and Jumbo. Overall sales were rising, mainly from the impact of DRB.

The old claret signboards of Phipps began to disappear as did the black facade of NBC houses. The corporate Red image of Watneys, along with DRB was the new order. Although there were still racking problems, the first brews of DRB were going through the brewery and by June the output was 1,000 barrels per week. The sales of Watney and Mann labelled products were rising, whilst sales of own brands were down.

The next stage in the product grouping was the merging of the two milds, and to produce the single 1034.5°OG brew from the North brewery PA. A strike on 3-5 October led to an increase of 5/- per new working week of 42 hours. This resolved some of the difficulties about pay within the wider group. An EGM on 17 November resolved some of the financial differences by reorganising the Watney Mann Loan Capital.

Watneys were looking to increase production towards 4,000 barrels per week and so the Bridge Street brewery was vastly extended with a brand new building on the St Peter's Way - Bridge Street junction being added in 1961. This new £1,180,000 plant was purpose built for DRB. The new building had been constructed when it was discovered that the existing site was not large enough to take the equipment that was to be installed. In October 1964, the brewery was providing DRB to its pubs and clubs.

In 1964, the Northampton brewery name was shortened to Phipps' Brewery Ltd. Yet this was only a stop gap, for in 1968 the Watney management changed it yet again, *"....having regard to the considerably enlarged trading area in which the company traded with consequent diminution of the significance of the local name"*. The new title was Watney Mann (Midlands). Almost immediately the brewery ceased to brew traditional ales with the very last batch of "real ale" produced on Monday 20th May, 1968. A keg version of Phipps' PA was produced until 1970, when it too disappeared.

BHS Archive
Birmingham City Library

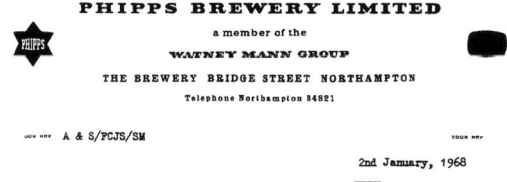

For a time Watneys were undecided on the long term future of the Northampton brewery (see Litchborough entry). Eventually the site went to Carlsberg who built their modern lager brewery on the land. Mr Guy Phipps Walker, who was related to the Phipps family, was the manager at Bridge Street at the time of the destruction of the old brewery.

NORTHAMPTON (continued)

Plackett, Richard *(1818-1830), Bridge Street.*

Ratliffe and Jeffrey Ltd. (F3585), *The Albion Steam Brewery, 16 Commercial Street.*

Thomas Ratliffe founded this brewery by 1862, but it was four years before the first reference to it being called "The Albion Steam Brewery". On 24th June, 1869, he was joined in partnership by William Jeffrey. Jeffrey (b.1832) was later to be described as one of the wealthiest men in Northampton. A quiet, unassuming man, with strong associations with Dodderidge Church, his brother-in-law was J.C.Eady of Eady & Dulley, Market Harborough (see Little Bowden entry).

The Jeffrey family owned an old established Northampton bakery/malting business at 5 Bath Street (from at least 1830), where William is shown as a maltster and hop merchant in 1862. His father was also the owner of the Forget Me Not (Sportsman's Arms) in Bath Street. William himself had bought Sibleys, a small brewery in Newland and several beer houses, which were incorporated into the firm.

Ratliffe and Jeffery's Albion Brewery - viewed from St Peter's Way

Photo: Geoffrey Starmer collection

In 1871 a local directory lists *"Thomas Ratliffe and William Jeffrey - Brewers Albion Place"*. The firm owned several properties in this street which were used as tied cottages for brewery workers. The Head Brewer, for example, lived at "The Brewery House, 4 Albion Place". At this time there was a great deal of modernisation at the brewery and old equipment, such as a Maitland's patent mashing machine, was sold off. As part of this modernisation the company new steam engines were installed.

To meet the need for additional brewing capacity a new brewery was built next to their existing one. The Brewers' Journal for September 1883 carries a description of the new building and comments on how the whole project had been undertaken within budget and timescale. The site extended from 16 to 22 Commercial Street and back to Foundry Street. Shortly afterwards they built the ornate "Crown and Anchor Maltings" on the banks of the River Nen(e). This took its name from the pub which it stood beside. Ratliffe and Jeffreys became a limited company on 23rd March, 1895. The prospectus gave the current value of the firm as £250,000. The assets included 135 tied pubs and a working farm at Duston.

The Crown and Anchor Maltings, South Bridge, Northampton, just prior to demolition

Photo: Authors' collection

NORTHAMPTON (continued)

The sad demise of William Jeffrey on the 24th June, 1895, caused disruption in the company. Alfred Page (of the Northampton Union Bank) and John Eunson (the Borough Engineer) were elected to the Board as executors of the former partner's estate. Thomas Sargent would seem to have been the brewer at this time.

It was later suggested that Thomas Ratliffe lost all motivation following the death of William Jeffrey. As a result, Phipps took over the Albion Brewery on 2nd December, 1899. Thomas Ratliffe and his son Richard were both elected onto the Board of Phipps.

Thomas Sargent, the brewer at the Albion, was informed that he would not be needed after 30th September, 1903. Together with the work at the Bridge Street brewery, this suggests that the Albion closed at this time. The Crown & Anchor maltings were used for beer storage.

At least until 1910, the title of P.Phipps & Co Ltd was followed by (with which is incorporated Ratliffe & Jeffery Limited). Physical evidence of the relationship between the two companies could be found in the black and straw-coloured mosaic signs to be found at first floor level on several of the older public houses in the Northampton area. For example, The Talbot on the north corner of the junction of Union Street and Wellington Street carried the sign *"Phipps' Noted Ales: Ratliffe's Celebrated Stout"*.

The Albion Brewery was for sale in 1919 for £8,000 and was bought by Messrs James & James. However, the sale of the whole site was only finally completed in 1929. The brewery is still standing and is used as an auction rooms (SP 753 601). The present owners proudly keep the history alive by advertising the property as *"The Old Albion Brewery"*.

The only part of the original facia remaining is the bust of Bacchus above the entrance archway. A band of carved stonework, proclaiming the building to be *"Ratliffe and Jeffreys Albion Brewery"*, had to be taken down in 1970. It had started to crumble and fall into the road below.

The Crown and Anchor maltings were taken over as a stores by Brown and Pank the wine and spirits arm of Phipps. The building was listed for its distinctive architectural style, hence surviving the demolition of the Bridge Street site, only to be gutted by fire in December 1977 and then demolished.

Roberts, Thomas Valentine, *St Giles Street.*

In 1698 Richard Benboe, a miller, paid Joseph Easton £60 for property which included a brew house in the occupation of Thomas Valentine Roberts, from at least 1690. The brew house is described as being at the lower end of St Giles Street opposite the Crown.

Robins, John, *The Sun, 2 Gas Street.*

In 1866, Robins is listed as a beer retailer in Gas Street. He is shown as a publican brewer in 1877, but by 1889 John George Robins is only shown as a beer retailer. The pub later became a Phipps property.

Roddis, John, *Old Black Lion Inn, 1 Black Lion Hill, West Bridge.*

In 1831, a George Cornfield was a maltster on Black Lion Hill, when John Roddis seems to have been at the Crispin Arms, 53 Scarletwell Street. By 1841 he also kept the Crow & Horse on Gold Street. Roddis seems to have run both pubs until at least 1858. At the time a James Roddis is listed as maltster on Horse Shoe Lane, just off Black Lion Hill. He may have been the son of James Roddis of Nether Heyford (died 1805) who was related to Robert Roddis (see entry for John Willson). If so, he was also the uncle of James Linnell (see entry).

John Roddis is listed as a brewer at the Black Lion in 1861, and the following year as malting at Weston Favell. In 1864 is also shown as running the White Lion on Kingsthorpe Road. He was still advertising his home brewed ales at the Black Lion in 1866. However, in 1874 the Black Lion was being kept by Mrs Amy Roddis, and there is no mention of brewing. The pub is still trading.

Sandes, Ben, *Mellows Row.*

Sandes is listed in 1841, but his name may actually have been Sanders and he then went on to run the Swan on Derngate.

NORTHAMPTON
(continued)

THE OLD BLACK LION INN,
WITHIN A MINUTES WALK OF THE CASTLE STATION,
WEST BRIDGE, NORTHAMPTON,
JOHN RODDIS,
PROPRIETOR.

HOME BREWED, BURTON, AND OTHER ALES.
WINES AND SPIRITS OF THE FINEST QUALITY.
Good Stabling and Lock-up Coach Houses.

Shaw, John, *Dolphin Inn, Gold Street.*

The sale details of 19th October, 1827, mention the brew house at the Dolphin and its *"pump of good water"*. Shaw was the occupant at the time, although the inn was owned by Thomas Linnell (see entry). By 1830, Shaw had moved to the Angel on Bridge Street, but is described only as an inn-keeper in the Poll Book, (see next entry).

Shaw, Thomas, *Kingswell Street.*

Thomas Shaw is listed as a brewer from around 1818 to 1830. A Mr Shaw was at the Brewer's Arms, Cow Lane in 1845. A Thomas Shaw was keeping the Angel in 1866, when his son was a coal merchant at 34a Gold Street.

Shearsby, John *(1796), Horseshoe Lane.*

Shelton, Mrs Sarah, *19 Bradshaw Street.*

Friedrich's revised Gazetteer has Sarah Shelton brewing in 1877. This may have been in connection with listings in 1877 for Thomas Shelton, a maltster on Derngate and Martin Shelton, maltster, 46 Waterloo. Thomas is shown as being a corn merchant at Oundle, where he lived.

Smart, Mrs Sarah, *Bicycle Tavern, 44 Wellingborough Road.*

Mrs Smart is shown as a publican brewer in 1877, but by 1900 the pub had changed hands and had ceased brewing. In 1858, Joseph Smart was listed as a beer retailer at 46 Wellington Street.

Sykes, Ernest William, *Britannia, 1 Victoria Street.*

Sykes' address is also shown as Lady's Lane, but he had been at the Britannia from at least 1858 and is listed as a publican brewer there in 1877. The Britannia became an NBC pub, which closed in the early 1960s.

Taylor, Thomas *(1796), St John's Lane.*

Thompson, Joseph *(1792-1796), Green (Street).*

This may be the same Joseph Thompson who occupied a brewery next to the river on Bridge Street, shortly afterwards. This was apparently owned by Alderman Brown. The brewery is described as being a 5 quarter plant and there was a newly-erected 20 quarter malting, together with granaries, a yard and coal wharf.

In 1833, Joseph Thompson senior was living in Crane Street, whilst his son Joseph junior, living at 2 Snow Hill, Birmingham, was the owner of the Red Lion, Great Creaton, tenanted by a Thomas Rollaston.

However, in 1830, the Lion & Lamb on Bridge Street was being kept by a William Thompson. This suggests that the brewery may have at one time been attached to the pub, before becoming owned by Thomas Hagger (see Allen & Burnett).

NORTHAMPTON (continued)

Thompson, Samuel, *The Pheasant, 104 Bridge Street.*

Samuel is shown as a publican brewer in 1877. Prior to this in 1858 he operated as a beer retailer at the Globe, 141 Bridge Street and the Grand Junction Wharf, Cotton End, before moving to the Pheasant by 1864. The Pheasant was kept by Edward Copson in 1892, when it was a Ratliffe & Jeffrey property, with no mention of brewing. It became a Phipps house, which closed in the early 1920s.

Threadgold, William, *32 Wellingborough Road.*

In 1869, Threadgold is listed as a beer retailer at 51 Horse Market, but from 1871 to 1876 he is shown as a publican brewer at the above address. However, in 1878 he is only shown as a beer retailer. In 1898, a William Threadgold was at the Britannia Inn, Little Brington.

Trasler, George, *College Street.*

The only entry for Trasler is in 1830, but a Thomas Trusler was at the Warwick Arms in 1851, before moving to the Swan and Helmet in Gold Street. Trasler may have been at the Boot on the corner of Bradshaw Street which seems to have been owned by the Crick family (see entry) before becoming a Phipps house. However, in 1875 NBC bought a brew house, formerly stables, on the east side of College Street from Parker Gray, wine and spirit merchants. Parker Gray continued to operate as tallow chandlers at 20 College Street until 1889. There is a possibility that the brew house may be that which was linked with the nearby Queen's Head, also owned by the Cricks.

Tresham, E and Company (F3586), *2 Tresham Street.*

Operating from 1874 to 1890, this was a wine and spirit shop which brewed its own beer and also sold hops. In the earlier period, the address is also shown as Grafton Square or Street and 1 St Andrews Terrace, the latter being the family home address.

Wagon & Horses, *34 Bridge Street.*

The original pub dated back to 1749, when it seems to have been known as the Goldsmith Inn. In 1766 James Hewitt became the victualler, but the next occupant renamed it the Blue Boar and around 1787 it became a private house. However, in 1804 it re-opened with John Bradshaw as the victualler in partnership with Joseph Chamberlain, maltster, although the old brew house had become two cottages. Interestingly, Joseph Chamberlain Eady (see Little Bowden) was called after an uncle of this name, suggesting a possible family link.

In 1822, it may have been trading as the Crispin Arms (one of two, see Roddis), when in the possession of Pickering and Edward Phipps in partnership with John Perry a local miller, and Pickering's son-in-law. The property is described as having a brew house.

The Wagon & Horses was being kept by Spencer Hoare in 1830, and in 1836 by a Seaton Lancum who owned property in Crispin Street. The brew house is mentioned again in 1884, but in 1894 it was owned by Phipps & Co and presumably supplied from the main brewery.

Walker and Soames (F3587), *Victoria Brewery, 29 Kettering Road.*

"The Victoria Brewery, whose excellent ales and stout are unsurpassed, even in this centre of the Northampton noted brews" Northampton Up to Date 1895

The original brewery on this site dated back to around 1867 when Edwin and James Youil first traded here. James lived on the premises, whilst Edwin had a home at Pitsford (see entry) where from 1884, as Messrs Youil Bros, they leased a maltings from Phipps.

"YOUIL BROTHERS and Company
Ale and Porter Brewers, Maltsters etc. Victoria Brewery, Kettering Road, Northampton
Ale supplied in 18 and 9 gallon casks at 10d, 1/- 1/1d,1/2d, 1/3d, 1/4d, 1/5d, 1/6d, 1/7d, 1/8d, 1/9d, 1/10d, 1/11d, 2/-, 2/1d, 2/2d, 2/3d, 2/4d, 2/5d, and 2/6d per gallon. These dinner and intermediate strong ales will be found of very superior quality, quite equal to that of Burton on Trent and of much greater strength. Porter, Brown Stout, Double Brown Stout, and Imperial Stout, at 1/2d, 1/4d, 1/6d and 1/8d per gallon in casks of all sizes. The trade supplied in Kilderkins of 18 gallons, barrels of 36 gallons and hogsheads of 54 gallons. The interest of the purchaser fully consulted and a liberal discount allowed. The malt being all made from the best samples of barley in the market and treated on such principles in its manufacture as to secure the greatest amount of saccharine, and consequently the largest quantity of pure and strong ales, can be most confidently recommended to all who brew their own. Youil Brothers. 1869

NORTHAMPTON
(continued)

The Victoria Brewery

Photo: Geoffrey Starmer collection

The only pub which they are known to have leased is the British Standard on Woolmonger Street, taken by NBC in 1884. The brothers ran the small brewery until 1892, when they sold it and set up as coal merchants. However, as late as 1904 they were shown as the owners of the Flying Horse at Crick. The new owner of the Victoria Brewery was Edward Major-Lucas, who traded in partnership with his brothers Joseph and John. Edward had served an apprenticeship as a brewer with Thomas Manning's Castle Brewery. He was possibly the son of Edward Munday Major Lucas, who was brewing at Rowsham near Aylesbury from around 1871 to 1876 (see Potterspury entry). Prior to this the Lucas family were maltsters at Rowsham as early as 1791.

At the 1892 Brewster Sessions, Edward Major-Lucas and James Pooley of the Victoria Brewery applied for a license to sell beer at the brewery gate. They applied to be able to sell quantities of less than 4½ gallons, but more than one gallon. The application was refused.

In 1893 the partnership between E.G.Major-Lucas and W.G.Pooler (sic) was dissolved and the company was trading as *"Major-Lucas (Victoria Brewery), Ale and Porter Brewers, Maltsters and Coal Merchants"*. That same year the company won a highly commended award at the Breweries Exhibition in London. Edward Major-Lucas was also the landlord of the Bantam Cock, Abington Square.

Around 1895, Youil's old brew house was demolished and a five storey brick built tower brewery was erected in its place. It was designed along modern principles and contained the most up to date equipment. Contemporary reports give the capacity as 8 quarters. The site also included offices, stabling, van sheds and a dwelling house.

The Major-Lucas beer range was:-

X- Mild Ale	PA - Pale Ale
XX - Mild Ale	IPA - India Pale Ale
XXX- Light Mild Ale	OK- light amber ale
XXXX- Extra Mild Ale	SA - Strong Ale
SS- Single Stout	VA- Victoria Ale
DS - Double Stout	
DS- Extra Double Stout	

The last days of the Walker and Soames Victoria Brewery in late 1989   Photo: Authors' collection

The business of the Victoria Brewery was very much aimed at the family customer.

In 1899 the Victoria Brewery was sold to Walker and Soames of Long Buckby. It is likely that brewing was then concentrated at the Northampton site, although Walker and Soames are listed as wine and spirit merchants at Long Buckby until 1906.

In October 1900 Edward Major-Lucas considered buying the Lion Brewery from NBC, but instead he used his share of the proceeds to set up The Pure Ice and Cold Storage Company, a refrigeration plant which, until the 1970s, stood next to the Bantam Cock.

Speaking at the 1909 Daventry Licensees Association Dinner, G.M.Soames denounced the changes being forced upon the industry. A report in the Northampton Herald tells how he "*condemned the proposed time limits and also Sunday closing and the suggested abolition of barmaids....*".

Walker and Soames were taken over by Hopcraft and Norris in March 1910. The squat square brick built tower brewery had its side wall painted with the legend "The American Last Works", for following its closure it was sold to a firm manufacturing cobblers lasts. The old Victoria Brewery was finally demolished in 1989 as part of the refurbishment of the bottom end of Kettering Road (SP 761 609).

West, Joseph *(1792-1818), Derngate.*

Whitney, Thomas *(1792).*

White, Eleanor Mrs, *The Flying Horse, 25 Market Square.*

The pub dated back to 1680 when kept by John Gray. It was advertising its home brewed ales in 1847 when being run by Mrs White. It later became called the Lord Palmerston around 1869, when G.Haynes was the landlord.

In 1878, it was described as a "*public house including brewhouse, 3 stables and a newly built room occasionally used as an American bowling saloon.*" At the time it was run by Mr R.Tansley.

It was bought by the Lion Brewery, before becoming an NBC house in March 1891. In 1973, it became the Lamplighter, before closing in 1980.

Wickes, William, *King's Head, 15 Mayor Hold.*

Wickes is listed in 1877, but the 1889 Stevens' Directory shows William Chaplin as a brewer at the pub (see also Jones entry). He sold the pub to Fred Dunkley in 1909. It was later a Phipps house which closed in 1971. In the 17th century, a Wickes family were inn-keepers at Welford, and their property included a brew house.

Willson, John, *South Bridge.*

A rare price war broke out in 1785. It followed the opening of a beer agency in Sheep Street by Mr Francis Osborn (see entry). For his venture to succeed Osborn tried to take trade away from the long established brewery of John Willson. One advantage that Osborn had was his ability to sell London brewed Porter. This popular beer was regarded as being far superior to Willson's home brewed Porter.

Osborn set about gaining trade from his rival by cutting his prices and offered:-

*"**Good fine ales at 11d per gallon**
FINE ALE. F Osborn respectfully informs the public that by an established connection in the brewery business he is enabled to sell exceeding fine ale at 11d per gallon at his warehouse in Sheep Street. If not approved of when tapped will be exchanged and thought no trouble."*
Northampton Mercury December, 1785

NORTHAMPTON (continued)

Willson countered this move by slashing his own prices to:-

> *"Fine ale 10d a gallon*
> *PORTER, ALE, and BEER.*
> *John Willson finds himself necessitated to inform his customers, and the general public, that he sells the above articles at the following low prices; Porter of the first quality, at 13d per gallon, with an allowance to those that sell it again; Fine Ales at 10d a gallon."* Northampton Mercury 31st December, 1785

Osborn's next move was not only to cut his prices even lower, but also set out to discredit Willson's brewing practices. He offered beer at 9½d from *"A real brewer (that is) free from those pernicious ingredients used by pretended brewers"*. In this advert he accused Willson of *"ignorance and avarice"*.

The wild claims about poisonous additives were refuted by the South Bridge brewer who offered a reward of £100 to anyone who could produce evidence to substantiate the claims. He then effectively ended the price war by selling his Porter at cost price *"To make it not worth any persons notice to employ their money in"*. He promised beer *"free of every expense. To pay only for the malt and hops at market price"*

> *"F Osborn begs leave to return thanks to the discerning public for their many favours received since commencing the ale trade and assures them that no expense (nor mean threats) prevent him from serving all those who please to honour him....Ale 11d per gallon, much superior to those sold at 15d and 16d."* Northampton Mercury 14th January, 1786

From beginning to end, the price war lasted less than a month and on 14th January, 1786, Osborn's beer was back to 11d per gallon.

Four years later John Willson died and the brewery passed to his widow. In 1790 Elizabeth Willson was advertising Porter for sale, *"....(for she) intends shortly to decline carrying on the porter business ... (but) continues to carry on the brewing and malting business in the same extensive manner her husband did...(and) has now a large stock of exceedingly fine and good ale, beer and malt which she is determined to sell on as low terms and for as little profit as possible"*. Elizabeth ran the brewery until around 1798.

However, it seems that the Wilson/Willson family may have had a wider involvement in the trade, starting with a Nathan Wilson from Cheapside in London in 1731 owning property at Bakers End/ Backers Lane. In 1739, Nathan Wilson junior sold the Wheatsheaf and White Hart in Gold Street.

In 1795, Nathan Wilson was a brewer at Cotton End, owning the Greyhound, Milton Malsor (see Easts), and in 1820 he was leasing the Three Potts. By 1824 he is described only as a merchant in Bridge Street but he is still shown as a maltster in 1830. When he died in 1831, his name is shown as Willson and his Will mentions a malting at Cotton End, the Sun in Broad Lane, the Three Crowns and granaries and warehouses, the latter being left to his brother John. However, whilst his son John received an interest in the Fountain, Silver Street, he does not seem to have followed the family business. The family also had interests in the following:-

Phoenix, Market Hill	Greyhound, Milton Malsor (see East)
Red Lion	Eagle & Child, Bridge Street

A firm called Willson, Hanson and Fascutt operated a wine and spirit merchants in the area at the start of the 19th century and was considering the purchase of J.C.Barratt's brewery (see Phipps' entry for details). In 1824, Joseph Hanson and Robert Fascutt, wine merchants, bought Robert Roddis' property on Wood Hill, described as having a brew house. However, there does not seem to be any record of them obtaining a licence to brew commercially.

In 1854, Thomas & Robert Hanson are listed as hop and wine & spirit merchants, the Angel Hotel, 23 Bridge Street, whilst John Wilson had a separate hop merchant business at 4 The Drapery.

Wilson, Joseph, *Pomfret Arms, 10 Cotton End.*

> *"Earl of Pomfret (free, public House) for sale by auction. Situated in the principal street in Cotton End.....comprising bar, tap room, 2 good parlours....cellarage for about 60 hogsheads of ale; brewhouse, granary etc.The property is situated close to the Northampton railway and possesses a frontage of about 50 feet."* Sale Notice 3rd June, 1846

NORTHAMPTON (continued)

The owner at the time of the sale was Elisabeth Norman. In 1864 Wilson was the publican and in 1877 was listed as a brewer at the Earl of Pomfret, also called Pomfret Arms. However in 1878, the pub was sold by George W. Norman to Francis Montgomery (see Long Buckby).,

Woodford, John, *154 Bridge Street.*

Although listed as a brewer in 1841, this is probably the same individual who is described as a brewer at Phillips in 1861.

Wright, Edwin, *Nag's Head, 79 Kettering Road.*

This was a beer house and shop opened in 1842, run by a Wilmer Wright. Edwin Wright is listed as the brewer in 1877. The brew house was still intact when bought by Mannings in 1881, following the death of William Butcher (see entry). The pub closed in October 1912, but the building is still standing as an off-licence and general stores.

OLD

Tomblin, Charles Stafford (F3764), *Old Brewery.*

In 1854 Joseph Tomblin was the owner of the Wold Brewery (Wold being an older name for the village) from which he traded as a brewer, maltster and wine and spirit merchant. He was originally from Wymondham, Leicestershire, but had been buying property in Old from 1845.

In December 1856 he provided a £120 mortgage for Joseph Richardson an inn-keeper of Brixworth. This was for the Horse & Hounds, tenanted by William Clark.

Joseph Tomblin's price list dating from 1855

Authors' collection

> **WOLD BREWERY. Northamptonshire.**
> **JOSEPH TOMBLIN**
> BEGS respectfully to thank his friends for the patronage he has received, and calls attention to the following LIST OF PRICES:—
>
> ALE XX .... 1s. 2d. per Gallon.
> DITTO XXX .... 1s. 4d. ,,
> DITTO XXXX .... 1s. 6d. ,,
> PORTER XX .... 1s. 2d. ,,
> DITTO XXX .... 1s. 4d. ,,
> STOUT XXXX .... 1s. 8d. ,,
>
> A good STOCK of MALT, HOPS, and SPIRITS of superior quality always on hand.
> March, 1855.

Joseph was a farmer and landowner, owning some 436 acres at the time of the 1873 census. He ran the company right up to his death in 1879, after which time Robert and Stafford Charles Tomblin ran the brewery as equal partners for the next eleven years, with Robert listed as the brewer.

> **JOSEPH TOMBLIN,**
> BREWER,
> **SPIRIT MERCHANT,**
> MALTSTER,
> HOP FACTOR, ETC.,
> WOLD,
> NORTHAMPTONSHIRE.

In 1890 Robert's son, Robert younger, received marriage settlements from both his father and uncle. His father appears to have transferred his share in the partnership valued at £1,346 14/-. However, there may have been legal problems with the transfer in that the partnership between Charles Tomblin and his nephew was formally agreed on 6th April, 1890, but it was not signed until 6th February, 1891. In the end Charles Tomblin stood surety for his partner.

The business was still trading as *"Tomblin Brothers ....brewers, maltsters and farmers"* from premises at Old and Walgrave. When audited in 1891 the business was valued at £4,280 of which Robert junior and Charles were equal partners.

In 1898 it was listed as Tomblin Bros, but in 1903 the brewery was listed in a directory as *"C.S Tomblin, Old Brewery"*, although Robert was still actively involved in the business. In 1904, Charles, perhaps taking account of his age, took out a mortgage on the property in order to provide for his wife. When the business was put up for sale in 1906 Robert was given as the sole owner. *"Five quarter brewery....having a good supply of especially suitable water....a well known and old established brewing trade has been carried out here for many years."*

However, S.C. Tomblin executed a deed of assignment for the benefit of his creditors; hence the sale of the brewery, with a final dividend of 1/- in the £1 paid in 1907.

The firm owned three tied pubs the Chequers at Old, the Fox beer house at Scaldwell and the Firtree at Spratton.

The remains of Tomblin's Brewery, now Brewery Farm

Photo: Authors' collection

Interestingly, Brewery House was occupied by Ellen Dodwell Manning (widow) and Lucy Eady Manning in 1933, when both were shareholders in Mannings of Northampton (see entry). The house, now Brewery Farm, a fine brown stone building stands between the roads to Faxton and Broughton as they meet in the village. The brick brewery buildings extend back from the house along the Faxton road and at right angles to this (SP 788 734). Contrary to some descriptions, the buildings at the rear of the White Horse are the remains of the steam-driven flour mill which the pub was originally, not the brewery.

OLD STRATFORD

Thorne, George Edward.

George Edward Thorne was a brewer and maltster here in 1854. The site of his premises is not identified, but he was living at Kingstone House at the time.

OUNDLE

Barnes, Thomas (F3844), *New Street.*

Thomas Barnes was a baker and flour dealer in 1824 and in 1830 was trading as Summers and Barnes, maltsters. He is listed as a brewer and baker in New Street off the Market Place between 1864 and 1884. He traded from a brew house, at what was once the Mermaid pub, next to the Turk's Head. Oundle School bought the property in 1884 and built School House on the site. Barnes died in 1919 aged 85.

Bullen, William.

Listed in 1831 as a brewer, he was presumably operating a small home brew pub. However, a John Bullen owned property which became part of the Oundle Union Brewery.

Clifton, John, *West Street.*

The pages of the journal of master carpenter John Clifton (Osborn & Parker) give a glimpse of life in 18th century Oundle. As well as being a builder and carpenter Clifton was a jobbing brewer. He carried out brews for several of the town's pubs using their own brew houses. The earliest brew recorded in his journal is in 1764 for Eleanor "Nelly" Chambers at the Green Man in West Street. This small pub was next door to Clifton's house. Also among his clientele was the Horseshoe, which later became the Three Tuns, and a Mr Smith from Stoke (Doyle).

Clifton also helped to build and repair at least two brew houses in Oundle. For example, in September 1771 he records working on the brew house of Mr Thomas Ellis at the Talbot - the town's most prestigious inn. In that year Clifton purchased his own brewing kettle from Nelly Ragsdell, a local ale wife. To supplement his income he hired out the kettle to his neighbours.

On 19th June, 1773, he set up his own brew house and on 9th August he records that Richard Deacon, his apprentice, had spent all day working on partitioning etc. However, Clifton wasn't always happy with his brews. A special Easter Apron Ale of 7th April, 1779, he reports as being *"..very indifferent"*. On 30th July, 1778, he describes another brew as *"fusty"*. Clifton died in 1784 at the age of 55.

McKee, Charles Frederick (F3845), *The Anchor Brewery, South Road.*

This pleasant little brewery is still standing on the corner of Mill Lane (TL 038 879). It was founded by Paul Durrans, a former bank clerk, who appears to have been residing in West Street. In 1854, Durrans is listed at Mill Lane as a brewer and maltster. The following year, his son

OUNDLE
(continued)

A recent view of McKee's Brewery

Photo: Authors' collection

Richard founded the Lascelles Hall Brewery in Yorkshire, whilst his other son, James, founded a black lead factory near Barnsley.

It was in 1866 that the brewery is first recorded as the Anchor Brewery, although it stands on the site of an older Anchor cottage. This formed part of the row of stone-built cottages, several of which still stand. The remainder were demolished to form the brewery site. The Anchor could have been demolished or it could have been the cottage which still adjoins the brewery and which, until the brewery closed, was used as the brewery offices with an entrance into the archway through which the drays left and re-entered the premises.

On 24th May, 1875, Arthur Bent Beardsley, from Torquay, bought into the business for the sum of £610 10/-. This gave him partnership rights for 7 years on the basis that he was to devote his whole time to the business. The overall capital of the business was £2,221, with the value of the stock, plant etc. at £1,221, giving an indication of its small scale. Paul Durrans was able to take out £230 per annum in lieu of rents, suggesting a non-active role. In 1876 the business was trading as Durrans & Beardsley, brewers and maltsters. In 1882, when the 7 year period was over, Beardsley took over the ownership of business but seems to have died in the mid-1880s.

Charles Frederick McKee purchased the business in 1886 and ran it and five tied beer houses in Oundle until 1906. The business also manufactured mineral waters and supplied the following pubs:-

    Anchor, St Osyths Lane
    Three Horseshoes, Benefield Road
    Red Lion, Warmington

The building was then used by a boot and shoe factor until 1940.

A recent view of the remains of McKee's Brewery - the South Road maltings in 1989

Photo: Ian P Peaty

OUNDLE
(continued)

Another view of McKee's Brewery taken in 1989 - South Road brew house and Head Brewer's house

Photo: Ian P Peaty

Oundle Union Brewery (F3845.5), *30 West Street.*

The site of this concern has long associations with malting and possibly brewing. In 1741, one Benjamin Munn was connected with a malting office there and the malting kiln and yard were in the hands of John Austin. In the period 1798 to 1809, as part of the Enclosure Acts, John Brown, Richard Nunnale, Linley Hurst and James Kirby owner of the Old Hind, previously the Unicorn Inn, next to Townley House, were involved with the property purchases. In addition to the inn and stables, there were various drying sheds and tanning pits for the leather industry.

In 1835 William Baker filled in the old tanning pits and demolished the stables and drying sheds to erect a maltings. Shortly afterwards, a brewery was built on the property of John Brown. (NRO - Zachariah Billing's statement of 1856 concerning ownership of the property).

"OUNDLE UNION BREWERY COMPANY.
Notice is hereby given to the owners or proprietors of shares in the Oundle Union Brewery Company are required to pay a call of £3 per share, on each of their respective shares in the said undertaking, to the account of the Oundle Union Brewery Company at the bank of Messrs Daniel Yorke and Company Oundle on or before the first day of February 1838. George Croxton, secretary Oundle 25th October, 1837." Northampton Mercury 4th November, 1837

The Oundle Union Brewery was brewing in West Street from 1836, the name probably originating in that given to the area under local government. The company was the brainchild of Charles and Thomas Yorke, from the local banking family. However, in addition to the bank in West Street, Jas Yorke & Son wine and spirit merchants were in West Street in 1824, followed by Charles Frederick Yorke in 1840, suggesting some family connection with the trade.

A rare example of an advertisement for the Oundle Union Brewery

Authors' collection

> **OUNDLE UNION BREWERY.**
> **W. WHITTEN**
> SINCERELY thanks his friends, for the liberal encouragement he received since his acceptance of the OUNDLE UNION BREWING COMPANY'S ALE and PORTER, and informs those who may be disposed to courage that Company, that he is enabled to sell them Ale and Porter, he warrants to be equal to any in the kingdom, on the same terms (for money) as they can be supplied at the Brewery,
> SUPERIOR BOTTLED STOUT, at *Six Shillings* per dozen

The Yorkes, together with 4 other local gentlemen, had raised some £30,000 to finance its building. In addition, there were some 13 others described as directors of the concern. However, the business had to raise a £6,000 mortgage in 1838. The 1840 AGM was attended by over 20 people, with another 4 proxy votes, suggesting that the business had indeed expanded. William Yorke chaired the meeting, but by at least 1840 the active management of the brewery was carried out by Richard Gibbon.

In 1841 it was described as a 20 quarter brewery, steam powered, fitted with every convenience by Pontifex, and capable of 300 barrels per week. Water was taken from the River Nene, filtered through gravel and then pumped by steam engine to the brewery. The site also included an 18 quarter malting. The beers were sold in Wellingborough at 6/- per dozen for the *"superior bottled stout"*.

The Oundle Union Brewery

Photo: Authors' collection

It was an ambitious, indeed perhaps over-ambitious, project which even owned three pubs in Northampton (the Three Crowns, Bridge Street; the Plumber's Arms, Sheep Street; and the Fountain, Silver Street). The difficulty in running these particular houses soon became apparent and they were sold off in 1844.

The company also owned the following:-

Chequers, Yaxley (freehold)	Milton Arms, Lutton (newly erected freehold)
King's Arms, Kettering (copyhold)	Red Lion, Oundle (leasehold - 8 years remaining)

The business had over-stretched itself and the sale of the Northampton pubs was an early indication of the troubles at the brewery. By 1847, the well respected George Gravely was the brewery manager, but even he could not stop the inevitable.

James Hutton was appointed as the official manager (receiver) on 20th January, 1850, and the business was wound up on the 16th of November. The brewery, pubs and other properties were put up for sale by auction on 31st January, 1851. The brewery did not sell, so the creditors had to keep trying to find a buyer. As late as 7th April, 1853, they were still trying to sell the brewery and maltings, although it seems the pubs, except the Chequers had been sold.

Eventually, at the auction on 9th June, Smiths purchased the company for £5,400 and closed it down. George Gravely was taken on from the failed company to act as brewery manager at the North Street brewery. In 1860, the brew house was converted into stables and leased.

The brewery offices were originally at Townley House, although this was being used as a Ladies Seminary at the time of the sale suggesting the decline in fortune which had occurred. Some buildings remain at the rear, including an old maltings now known as the Drying House. Brewery Court faces on to South Road and the old brew house tower, complete with louvres, can be seen from the street.

OUNDLE (continued)

Smith and Company Ltd (F3846), *North Street Brewery, North Street.*

The Smith family seem to have originated from Tottenham, Middlesex, since the NRO folder of their papers includes property deeds for a John Smith, the steward of this Manor in 1766. In 1774, John Smith (I), purchased the property of a Mr Coales which included a house and malting and the following Oundle pubs:-

> Three Lasts renamed the Crown
> Three Tuns later renamed Half Moon
> Red Lion bought by Oundle School in 1907 and demolished

At this time Smith was supplying malt to William Crafts of Wellingborough and in turn bought considerable quantities of beer from him. In 1775 John (I) founded the firm of Smith and Company, with the first brew on 23rd September, 1775. A contemporary report of the building of the North Street Brewery is concerned with the costs of labour and materials. Workmen, for example, earned 7/- per week and the cost of sinking a well was £6. In November 1766, John Smith (I), living at Stoke Doyle, a village about one mile south of Oundle, had a son whom he called John (II).

On 16th March, 1790, John Smith senior purchased the Woolpack Inn, Little Weldon. His address is given as Lilford Hall, but this was occupied by the Powis family, so it seems more likely that his home at Stoke Doyle was within the estate. In July 1794, John Smith (II) married Elizabeth, daughter of John Staples, Stoke Newington, whose family came from Oundle. This not only maintained the property links with Middlesex, but brought the use of Staples as family name. Around this time his father also bought property in Little Bowden, leading to the establishment there of a brewery (see entry).

In March 1797 the Oundle brewery gained a lucrative army contract to supply the prisoner of war camp at Norman's Cross situated between Oundle and Peterborough. In 1799 alone, they supplied 4,449 x 36 gallon barrels at a price of 10s 4d per barrel. Although this beer was described by a later Smith as "*not very good*" it was felt that the great expansion of the business was due to the contract. Interestingly, the troops were allowed 5 pints each per day of small beer; however, the contract allowed them to signify to the officer commanding if they wished to have 3 pints of table beer instead.

The 1799 land tax returns, in addition to the pubs listed above, mention the following:-

Common brew house and two maltings (one late Wallits)

| Maltings late Yorkes | Rose & Crown |
| Three Tuns | White Lion |

John Smith & Co are also shown having a malting office in Bridge Street Thrapston, which was being run by John's brother Richard who lived at the Inn there. Smith & Tibbits are listed there as maltsters in 1830.

On 24th August, 1805, John Smith (I) was involved in an indenture with John Hewson (a local ironmonger). When Hewson sold his property on 18-20th October, 1824, it included a small brew house and its contents, but this does not seem to have been a commercial concern.

Around 1815, John (I), moved to Bowden where his son William was running the brewery which they had established there. By 1826 the Oundle brewery was being run by John (II), and his brother Thomas. John and Thomas also ran the town's main bank having taken over the Oundle Commercial Bank in West Street and renaming it "J.and T.Smith's Bank".

The business prospered and the family became very wealthy, occupying the largest houses in the town. In 1827 John (II) purchased Oundle Rectory from the Reverend Henry Addington Simcoe, and he bought Ashton Manor in 1836.

A copy of the 1829 account books gives a flavour of the Oundle Brewery. The business was a mixture of trade and private accounts and beer was sold over a large area of north east Northamptonshire. It was selling at £1 8/- 6d for 18 gallons and grain cost 8/- for three quarters. Wages were averaging 13/9d for a five and a half day week.

In 1830 the financial arm of the business was running as "Smith and Ridsdales Bank", but this partnership was dissolved in 1831. There had also been another change of ownership at the brewery which was now called "*Smith and Tibbits - Brewers of Ale and Porter*". The new partners were John (II) and his brother-in-law, Samuel Tibbits, an attorney with offices close to the brewery.

In 1837, Samuel's son Richard Tibbits entered the partnership which traded as Smith & Tibbits, Brewers, Maltsters, Timber & Coal Merchants. John Smith (II) held two thirds and Richard Tibbits one third of the shares. In 1843, John's son - John William Smith - joined the partnership with one sixth of the total shares being provided by his father. When John (II) died the following year J.W.'s brother Herbert Staples Smith was taken into the partnership, with the three partners holding equal shares.

In 1852, J.W.Smith looked after the brewing side of the family's interests with Valentine Bliss the brewery manager, until George Gravely arrived from the Union Brewery after its take-over. However, the latter's stay could not have been that long, since William Guille is shown as the brewery manager in 1862. Richard Tibbits died in 1860 and his holding was sold to the two Smith brothers for £2,959.17s.4d. Herbert Smith died in 1865 and John William in addition to the brewery, became the owner of 13 licensed properties in Oundle and 26 in nearby villages and towns.

The family's earlier purchases of property, owning some 2,000 acres by 1841, and involvement with the local community led to John Smith being styled "lord of the manor" in Whelan's 1874 Directory. J.W.'s son John Hume Smith was born at the Rectory on 12th January, 1859, and received a public school education at Uppingham before going to Trinity College, Cambridge. In 1883, at the inaugural meeting of the Northants Brewers Association, J.W was elected Chairman of the meeting and vice-president of the association, his son was also present at the meeting.

On 30th June, 1894, Edwin Basil Ludlow (known as E.B. or Basil) joined Smiths as Head Brewer and manager. He had started his career brewing at the Swansea Old Brewery, where he was a prize winner at the National Brewers Exhibition, before moving to Showells of Stockport in 1892.

When John William Smith died in January 1897, he was the sole proprietor; hence, his son, John Hume Smith (Jack), became the owner of the brewery. Jack was active in local politics and lived at Cobthorne, Oundle. In 1899 Smiths entered into negotiations with Beans of Ketton (F2335), eventually buying the brewery. They seem to have operated from the site until around 1910, but possibly only as a depot.

"About 5 o'clock on Wednesday morning (22nd) a fire was observed at one of Smith and Co's maltings at their brewery....most of the (fire) brigade were soon present and in an hour all danger was over....damage to the extent of nearly £200 was done." (Northampton Herald 24th July, 1908)

The staff at Smiths pose for a photograph circa 1890

Photo: Andrew Cunningham collection

From the Second World War period

Jack died in February 1916. His son Lt J.H.M.Smith (Michael) had been killed in action in 1914 and it is said that Jack lost his drive after this. Ownership of the business passed to his wife Mary and daughter Marian, with E.B.Ludlow becoming a partner in the concern. E.B. was also appointed a director of Campbell Praed of Wellingborough, in place of J.H.Smith.

E.B.Ludlow passed away in November 1934, leaving £31,452, most of which went to his son Basil Guy Ludlow (Guy), who became Chairman and Managing Director of the brewery. Guy had joined the brewery after serving in the Royal Navy in World War I. His brother Rex became the Managing Director of Devenish at Weymouth in 1948. In 1986 the retiring MD of Devenish was a Mr E.W.(Bill) Ludlow who had succeeded his father.

Smith's Brewery, Oundle - the brew house is on the left hand side.

Photo: Jim Irving collection

On 23rd December, 1935, the business was incorporated as Smith and Company (Oundle) Limited. In looking at the growth of the business to some 88 pubs and 2 off-licenses, it would appear to have been organic with little take-over action, other than the Oundle Union in 1853 and the Ketton brewery around 1900. However, there had been attempts to develop at Little Bowden and Weedon (see entries).

The main area of trading in the north east of the county perhaps related to the connection with Campbell Praed and the gentlemanly approach to competition that was often prevalent in country brewing. For example, Smiths owned 7,230 shares in Praeds and the latter owned 31,000 shares in Smiths. In addition, Brigadier General H.A.Jones of Praeds was also a director of Smiths, the other directors being Guy Ludlow, E.W.Jeffreys, Major H.S.Benyon and Mrs M.G.Benyon.

OUNDLE
(continued)

The brew house - Smith's of Oundle

Photo: Jim Irving collection

Late 1950s letterhead

Courtesy: Jim Irving

The death of Guy Ludlow in August 1954 brought a large demand for death duties. In addition, the Phipps take-over of Praeds (see entry) had resulted in Phipps becoming the owner of their shares in Smiths. To buy these back would cost £4 10s per share. Hence, the following year Smith's ordinary share capital was for sale to raise the cash. The company together with the Talbot Hotel (Oundle) Company Limited, owned by the Ludlow family, was purchased by Warwicks and Richardsons of Newark in September 1955. The sale included the brewery, together with the five maltings, although malting had ceased in 1947, and 83 freehold, copyhold and leasehold licensed premises. For a time Michael Ludlow, the son of Rex managed the concern, but eventually he returned to Devenish to help run the Redruth brewery.

The new owners introduced the beer into the Yorkshire mining areas where it proved to be extremely popular. By 1962, Oundle was brewing to capacity and barely meeting the demand. At that time the brewery was brewing 5/6 times a week for its 7 x 70 barrel squares and employing some 50 staff. The products were: PA a light bitter, SM Strong Mild and XB the ordinary bitter. However, in that year the new owners were themselves taken over, somewhat ironically, by John Smiths of Tadcaster. Rather than invest in new plant, it was decided to close down and transfer brewing to Newark, with the last brew at Oundle on 11th September, 1962. The brewing plant was sold for scrap.

The property continued in use, as a depot for distribution of supplies transferred from Newark, until 1965, when demolition of the brewery and some of the adjacent building commenced.

In 1966 the site, together with those buildings still standing on it, was sold to the Welland and Nene River Authority who used the remaining buildings as stores and workshops until October 1983. It was then sold to a property development company which redeveloped the site with dwelling houses. However, the brewer's house remains standing, just before Black Pot Lane where the brewery actually stood (TL 042 883). Opposite is the No 2 maltings and the old motor transport and engineers yard.

The Three Tuns, North Street (previously the Horse Shoe a home brew pub in 1768, then later becoming the Half Moon) was reputedly the first public house to be owned by John Smith. The trade mark of Smiths consisted of three tuns and John Smith's initials. The carved stone sign which was originally located on the eastern elevation of the brewery was moved to its present position overlooking the courtyard at the rear of the Talbot hotel in 1963. In North Street itself, the door to an outbuilding at the rear of one of the houses is extensively marked from the testing of branding irons used on the beer barrels.

TELEPHONE—OUNDLE 3128 (2 lines)   ESTABLISHED 1775

SMITH & CO. (OUNDLE) LIMITED
DIRECTORS: P. R. BATTY   L. HEATON   F. R. WARWICK

THE BREWERY . OUNDLE . NR. PETERBOROUGH

**OUNDLE
(continued)**

A decorated post-war dray

Photo: Jim Irving collection

Swann, Chistopher, *Dolphin Hotel, North Street.*

In Melville's Directory of 1861, Mr Swann advertises the benefits of the hotel to include home brewed ale. He thanked the patrons who had supported his father and himself for the previously 30 years at the Swan.

```
C. SWANN,
Dolphin Family & Commercial Hotel,
OUNDLE,

Begs to return his thanks to the Nobility, Gentry, and
numerous patrons who have honoured him and his late
father with their support at the Swan Inn, for upwards of
30 years, and respectfully informs them, that to meet the
requirements of his increasing business, and to ensure the
comfort and convenience of his guests, he has REMOVED
to the

DOLPHIN HOTEL,

which has been rebuilt expressly for him regardless of
expense, and replete with every convenience for the
accommodation of those who may honour him with their
support. The Nobility, Gentry, and Commercial Gentlemen
will find every comfort and luxury provided for them,
which constant attention and experience can suggest.
    Extensive Show Rooms. Commodious and Superior
Loose Boxes. Stabling, &c. Attentive, experienced, and
careful Servants. Moderate Charges.

POSTING IN ALL ITS DEPARTMENTS.
AGENT FOR
BURTON ALES & LONDON STOUT.
HOME BREWED ALES.
BILLIARDS.
Hearse and Mourning Coach.
BATHS.
```

The Dolphin was described as having been rebuilt *"regardless of expense"* to meet the requirements of his increasing business. Now de-licensed, it is a prep school. The Swan on the corner of New Street is now used as shops.

Underwood, Richard.

One of the earliest recorded brewers in the town, Underwood's occupation is noted in the 1762 militia list.

PETERBOROUGH

Bailey, Henry, *Paul Pry, Lincoln Road, Walton.*

In 1892, Henry Bailey is described as a Vermin Destroyer, Brewer and Inn-keeper. He is listed as a brewer in Kelly's 1894 Directory, although the Peterborough directory shows him only as a vermin destroyer. There is no other mention of brewing. In 1898 a David Bailey was trading as a beer retailer on Oundle Road, Peterborough.

Baines, John, *Mason's Arms, 29 Wood Street.*

Baines is listed as the landlord and brewer here in 1884. The address is later shown as 11 Wood Street, when the pub was included in the 1940 Kelly's listing (see Introduction).

Beaver, William.

Listed in 1791 Universal British Directory as a brewer, but no location given.

Bewsher, John *(1831), Norborough.*

Buckle, Samuel, *Queen Street.*

This brewery was trading from at least 1784 when it was being run by John Cox. Along with Smith's of Oundle the business had the contract for supplying the prisoner of war camp at Norman Cross. The brewery is described as being near to a street called St John Street (which formed the southern part of what is now Queen Street) leading directly north from Cowgate. The buildings were probably ancient as they abutted on premises belonging to the Feoffees of Deacon's Charity which had been in situ for at least 80 years. Mr Cox lived in the brewery house mentioned below.

Cox traded there until his death in 1804, aged 62, when the brewery was acquired by Samuel Buckle from Cox's trustees in 1808. The first Samuel Buckle originated from Kildare, Ireland, and built up a good trade and made improvements to the premises in 1811, when the enclosure documents reveal the following tied property:-

Black Moor's Head, Ling Causeway	Blue Bell, Cowgate
Falcon, Cowgate	Fighting Cocks, Bridge Street, rebuilt 1863 as Spread Eagle.
Golden Lion, Bridge Street	King's Head, Bridge Street

There was also a maltings on Rosemary Lane/Cumbergate.

Samuel Buckle, a bachelor, died in 1813 aged 52, leaving a number of relatives with an interest in the estate which was trading as Samuel Buckle & Co. Samuel's Will had left the brewery to the trustees to run until his nephew became 21, which was in 1842.

In 1823 the business is shown as Francis Buckle & Co, brewer, near the church, and Francis is also shown as a spirit merchant. However, Pigot's Directory of 1830 shows Buckle Samuel & Co on Cumbergate as a brewers, maltsters and hop factors. Since the Red Lion was on Cumbergate, this may have been where the family lived.

In 1840, the business is listed as Samuel Buckle & Co, St John Street. The Royal Oak at Walton had been owned since 1828 by William Buckle, a brewer of Peterborough, but he seems to have died around 1845. In the 1847 directory the exors of Samuel Buckle are shown as trading from St John Street. However, in 1850 the business is shown as Samuel Buckle & Co brewers and maltsters.

In the 1851 census Samuel Buckle, aged 42 and born at Orton, is shown as a brewer, maltster and wine and spirit merchant living at 6 St John Street. Samuel Charles Watson Buckle sold much of the land and property in the late 1840s, with J.G.Atkinson buying several properties (see Cutlacks). The Ship Inn, New Road, was sold to Eyres of King's Lynn in 1848.

The brewery was put up for sale on 23rd May, 1853, at the Corn Exchange. The sale was split into separate lots:-

Lot 1	House and Garden
Lot 2	Brewery, Buildings, Pond and Garden
Lot 3	Malting
Lot 4	Store Room and Vault
Lot 5	Red Lion Inn and Malting

"The brewery is 71 feet in length, 49 feet in depth and 38 feet in height. A most extensive trade has been carried out upon the premises for a great number of years, and an excellent opportunity is offered to any persons desirous of entering into the Brewery and Wine and Spirit Business. The brewery is fitted up with apparatus and machinery entirely new within the last few years, and is capable of brewing 180 barrels per week. There is a never failing supply of excellent water."

The Buckle family also owned at least 7 pubs in the area including:-

> Packhorse, Northborough   Windmill, Orton Waterville
> Wheatsheaf, Eastfield

James Scott Bays, who had married Samuel Buckle's niece Caroline, and who was a partner in the brewery business, bought out the wine and spirit side of the firm. The business operated from 12 Queen Street and traded until being taken over by Patens in 1953. The premises were little changed from 1811 when they were thought to be have been constructed.

Lot 1 Number 10 Queen Street, the brewer's house, was occupied by Frank George Buckle who worked for the Savings Bank. In 1905 the property was bought by the coal merchants Ellis & Everard. In recent years it was used as the housing office for the City Council.

Lot 2, the brewery itself, was bought by William Proctor Stanley. Together with his partner John William Bower, he built a warehouse on the site with a general ironmongery business, and manufacture and repair of agricultural implements. Later the site became occupied by Perkins before being demolished, and is now covered by the Queensgate shopping centre.

Burkitt, Thomas, *Narrow Bridge Street.*

Listed in the 1835 Poll Book as a brewer, in May 1838, Burkitt, sold the Painters (originally the Oak Branch, Boongate) to J.G.Atkinson. He died 26th August, 1850, when his widow Rebecca is described as a liquor merchant and beer house keeper. In 1854, she was listed at the Wagon & Horses on Narrow Bridge Street.

Clarke's Brewery, *White Horse, 3 Cumbergate.*

This brewery was mentioned in a September 1858 advertisement in the Peterborough Advertiser. This was possibly the William Clarke who operated from St John's Street 1853-1866 and who is shown as running the White Horse Inn from at least 1840 to 1866. The last entry for his brewery on Cumbergate seems to be in 1876, although he was still running the pub the following year.

Cutlack & Company (F3892), *Phoenix Brewery, 32-35 Priestgate.*

In 1811, the "Inclosure" documents show Mrs Ann Smith as the owner of a brew house, now an attorney's office in the occupation of a Mr Atkinson. In 1815, John Glenton Atkinson purchased a stables and granary on Priestgate from the executors of John Johnson. However, in 1840, Pigot's Directory lists Frederick Markby as a brewer on Priestgate and he is also listed aged 35. He was bankrupt in 1843 and his property auctioned.

PETERBOROUGH
(continued)

Cutlack's Phoenix Brewery around 1900

Photo: Steve Williams collection

In 1846, Atkinson purchased from Markby, the Phoenix Brewery and the Prince Albert (previously the Chequers and prior to that the Duck's Nest). He had also bought the Blue Bell, Cowgate, from Samuel Buckle in 1844. In 1847 he is listed as a solicitor and insurance agent, and also a brewer and spirit merchant at the Phoenix Brewery.

On 17th February, 1866, Atkinson, who seems to have retired to the Parsonage at Bishops Stortford, sold the brewery and associated pubs to William and Charles Cutlack, although some property was not transferred until 1875. The Cutlacks were from a brewing family in Littleport (F2797) and it seems that William, the elder brother, remained at the brewery there.

When buying the Talbot Inn, Stilton, with attached brew house and maltings, Charles Cutlack is described as a brewer of Peterborough. He is listed in 1869 as an ale and porter brewer, spirit merchant and maltster when he also leased the Old Wind Mill and brew house at Bourne. In 1870 he was leasing the White Lion Brewery on Church Street, Priestgate from the Harrison family.

In 1871 Charles was living at 20 Priestgate with his wife and children, together with various family members and two domestic servants. At this time the brewery employed 6 men and 1

boy, with the owner's younger brother John employed as a "brewer's pupil". The company also had a maltings and brewery at Yaxley, which they seem to have bought from a Thomas Waite in 1870 (F5916).

J.G.Atkinson died 22th July, 1872, and was buried at Kensal Green; however, it was in 1874 that Cutlack paid the trustees £17,050 for the estate of the Phoenix Brewery and 14 public houses. This also included the maltings on Lincoln Road (originally Squires).

On 24th June, 1876, in addition they insured the Phoenix Brewery, an eighteen quarter malting at Boroughby and a variety of properties, at a total value of some £11,650. They had also paid £530 for the Fleece/Carpenter's Arms, with brew house, on St John's Street from William Smith a deceased publican.

Charles died in Margate at the age of 45 in 1878, leaving a widow and six children. Although John Yarrow Cutlack, one of the executors of the Will, is shown as the manager of the brewery at this time, he mainly concentrated on his business as a coal merchant. Under the terms of his Will the business was run by his executors until each child turned 21 and was offered to them in turn. However, Charles' early death created legal difficulties, in that he had been negotiating the purchase of several pubs at the time.

In 1879 they bought the King George, Boongate, for £550 from George Spriggs, who had built it in 1860 on land bought from S.C.W.Buckle. Mention is also made of a brew house on Hampden Street. Cutlacks also paid £750 for the Anchor at Farcet.

In 1883, the brewery was damaged in a gas explosion when the ground in the yard and the pavement in front were torn up after the mains had leaked into the sewer.

The eldest son, Llewellyn, took holy orders thus the business passed into the hands of Owen William, when he came of age in 1886. He presumably relied on the skills which John had acquired, with guidance from uncle William. The third brother Cecil Augustin seems to have become the brewer at the Crown Inn Whitchurch.

In 1888, the business had an agreement with Silvester Fulda a chemist of Middlesex, regarding *"a process for purifying and clarifying all kinds of ale condition within 7 days and keep for 12 months in any climate."* Cutlacks were also trying to sell their patent Eureka yeast to bakers.

William Cutlack died in January 1894 and a company was registered, on the 5th October, 1896, to acquire the business of the Exors of C.Cutlack with 23 tied houses. William Cutlack (presumably the son) being the major shareholder and Chairman and Owen Cutlack the principal. The transfer of property from the family to the Company included the Gladstone Arms, Gladstone Street for £700. This pub, built in 1855, had been bought in 1874 from a Robert Everitt, a brewer who was retiring to Beaconsfield. The incumbent tenant was William Speechley. The transfer also included the Cobden Arms, Cobden Street for £700.

The business was capitalised at £25,000 consisting of 5,000 £5 shares owned by the family. The family were living at Bridge House and at Wellington House Littleport. The Bridge House estate had been bought in 1886, when it included a 20 quarter maltings on Lincoln Road, occupied by Messrs Margetts (see Wellingborough).

Cutlack's output during the period which they brewed shows that their expansion, in terms of both number of outlets and total barrelage, matched the overall pattern of the brewery trade for this time. Thus, one sees a tripling of output between 1865 and 1885.

The site became too cramped and the company moved to Stones' brewery in Monument Street sometime around 1898 (see entry below), having sold the Phoenix Brewery on 11th August, 1897. In 1898 they were trading as Cutlack & Company Ltd. They had acquired a 25 quarter plant, large cellars and stores and the Brewery Tap fronting Monument Street. Unfortunately, hindsight shows that the good days were already over in terms of barrelage. Tied houses were auctioned in both 1905 and 1909.

They would seem to have maintained some connection with the Priestgate site until 1906, since they were still listed there; however, the site was put up for sale in August 1907. The original Phoenix brewery, which was opposite the Angel Hotel (now W.H.Smiths) stood on the site of the present Priestgate House. Cutlack & Co was registered as a private company in 1908.

PETERBOROUGH
(continued)

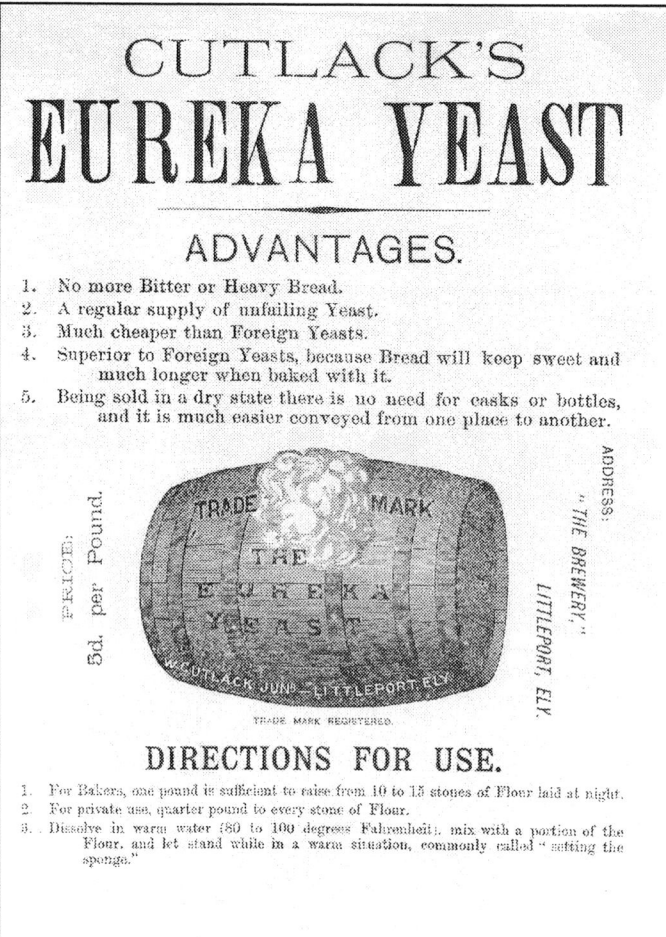

From the Authors' collection

The tower brewery, originally known as the Home Brewery (F3894), on the corner of Monument Street and Crawthorne Street had some 20 employees and produced a wide range of beers, including pale ale, mild and stout. The company took the Phoenix name with them to the new site. Of particular benefit was the spring water well at the new site. The well went down some 100 feet and the water in addition to its marvellous quality was reputed to be unaffected by anything - wet or drought, heat or cold. However, while the water was of no use for brewing it was found to be a natural soda water. The company filled 36 gallon casks which were conveyed to their mineral water factory in Chapel Street, which had been in operation since 1902.

The mineral waters were sold under the trade name "Vivaq" by Crawford & Co. This business was run by Norman Cutlack of the Parade, Margate, Kent, together with Harry Edward King of Great Tower St London. However, this side of the business did not do well and Crawford & Co were in receivership in 1912, causing financial problems for the other family operations.

Beer sales had commenced a gradual decline which lasted until 1915. Similarly, the overall number of outlets declined, partly as licensing applications became more difficult. The financial compensation schemes were designed to assist in the control of outlets: hence, the Prince Albert was compensated in 1908, the Marquis of Granby referred for compensation in 1914, Victoria compensated 1917, Huntsman de-licensed 1917 and compensated in 1923. The desire to concentrate on a few more profitable outlets is not a new idea in the brewing industry. Thus in 1915, seven pubs accounted for 50% of the brewery output, with the Cobden Arms being perhaps the jewel in the crown, with annual sales of 266 barrels.

The Peterborough company was merged with the main family concern, Cutlack & Harlock Ltd, Ely (F1639) in March 1917. On the death of Owen Cutlack in 1919 aged 53, his brother Mr Wilfred P.Cutlack took charge of the business, but brewing had ceased. The latter had written of the *"late disastrous business where so much money has been lost"* and the Peterborough end was in liquidation in 1917. Later, in 1950, a Colonel W.P.Cutlack was a joint Managing Director at East Anglian Breweries, Ely.

PETERBOROUGH
(continued)

The Home Brewery, Monmouth Street

Photo: Authors' collection

The Brewers' Journal of 15th June, 1920, carries an advertisement for the sale of surplus plant, including a fermenting vessel and 2 beer fillers at Ely. The Peterborough equipment, although mainly associated with the mineral waters, does include a 34 barrel mash tun and grist case, suggesting that brewing was being run down. Brewing at Monument Street certainly ceased in 1923. The premises were then used to manufacture aerated mineral waters, using the plant from the Chapel Street factory. When brewing ceased, some 25 to 30 men were employed, with another 10 at the mineral water factory.

In 1930 an amalgamation with Halls of Ely led to the firm becoming known as Messrs Hall, Cutlack and Harlock Ltd (F1638). Brewing was concentrated at the Fore Hill brewery which continued in operation until 1969, when it was the property of Steward & Patteson of Norwich.

Until 1932, Cutlack & Harlock Ltd were trading from Crawthorne Road with wholesale and retail spirit merchants on Long Causeway. However, in May of that year the Peterborough mineral water factory was closed and all production concentrated at Ely (Peterborough Standard 20 May, 1932 p6).

Dixon, James, *Boongate.*

Listed in the 1835 Poll Book as a brewer.

Dudley, James, *The Chequers, 22 Whalley Street.*

James Dudley is listed as brewer and beer house keeper in 1876. The beer house became the Chequers and then the Nag's Head, although Dudley seems to have moved to the Boot at Marker Deeping by 1894. In 1896, the Nags Head was being kept by William Green, but with no mention of brewing. However, it was included in the 1940 Kelly's listing (see Introduction). The pub is still called the Nag's Head and is still trading.

Elgood & Sons (F3893), *Queen Street.*

Elgoods are shown at Queen Street from 1894 to 1928, probably No 24-28. Although listed as stores in 1898, it is just possible that some brewing took place, certainly Bennett's Directory of 1901 lists them as brewers rather than as a depot. In 1884, Elgood & Harrison had been listed as brewers in Broad Bridge Street. Elgood's depot for supplies from Wisbech was at 99-101 Westgate which also handled malt for the brewery. This was presumably near to the Malt Shovel pub which they bought in 1892.

Thomas Elgood the grandfather of the current Chairman and Managing Director looked after the Peterborough end of the business (source letter from Mr N.Elgood).

English, Robert.

Listed in the 1762 militia list as a brewer.

Feast, Robert, *Eastgate House, Boonfield.*

Feast may have owned this beer house, fronting 36 Eastgate, from around 1863. When bought by NBC in 1882, the site included a freehold brewery, which Feast may have continued to operate. The Eastgate was included in the 1940 Kelly's listing (see Introduction).

PETERBOROUGH
(continued)

Fisher, George, *Stanley Arms, Brook Street.*

Fisher is listed as a brewer in 1876, when he is shown as running the Stanley Arms beer house.

Foot and Hamper, *St Leonard Street.*

This business is shown as ale and porter brewers, but was clearly a short-lived concern, since the only reference to them is in 1869. However, Edwin Foote & Co are also listed as brewers in St Leonard Street. This may possibly be the same site used by John Hilliam (see entry). The Allied Brewery History project suggests that Foot traded between 1866 and 1871, being taken over by Healy & Maddox around 1870 (see entry).

Freeman, Henry, *Three Tuns, Church Street.*

Freeman is listed as a brewer from 1851 until 1871. In 1872 the Peterborough & General Advertiser carried an advertisement for Sarah Freeman at the Three Tuns *"Home Brewed Ales, Wines and Spirits"*.

Gibson, H, *White Lion, Church Street.*

In 1864 and 1866, Gibson is listed as a brewer at the White Lion, later used by Cutlacks (see entry). In 1854, A.Harrison is shown as the licensee for the pub, which seems to have remained owned by the family.

Goodman, Feast, *Market Place.*

When Goodman's house and drapery shop were for sale in 1812, the property included a brew house. However, this may not have been used for commercial production.

Hill, James, *Broad Bridge Street.*

James Hill had a brewery on Broad Bridge Street, alongside the River Nene, and was advertising his beer in 1838. However, the Stamford Mercury of 29th May, 1840, announced a sale by auction of the brewery as a result of the bankruptcy of James and Thomas Hill. In addition to the 15 quart brewery and associated malt lofts and warehouses, the property included:-

Woolpack, Broad Bridge Street	Royal Oak, Eastfield
Star, Boonfield, owned since 1834	Chequers, Boongate
Brewer's Arms, Boongate	Elephant & Castle, Church Street
Brick Kiln Beer house	Maltings, Stanground in occupation of S Buckle

James Hill's address is given as Wisbech St Peters; however, his major claim to fame was not his brewing or other activities, but that he was the father of Octavia Hill, one of the founders of the National Trust. She was born in Wisbech in 1838 and the house is now the Octavia Hill Birthplace Museum.

Thomas Hill, who later purchased the store room and vault (Lot 4) of Buckle's brewery in 1853, also had close connections with Wisbech. He was a general merchant and operated a steam packet service between Peterborough and Wisbech, as well as maintaining an interest in the Red Lion public house (Lot 5 of Buckle's sale).

From 1864 to 1876, he is listed as a maltster at Bridge Wharf. In 1880, a C.CHill was a maltster at Peterborough. The last entry seems to be in 1901, for Thomas Hill & Son maltsters, Queen Street, established 1833.

Hilliam, John, *Brewer's Arms, 42 St Leonards Street.*

In 1874 Hilliam is shown as a brewer at the pub at the pub, having traded there since 1864 as a beer retailer. An Elizabeth Hillam also kept the Queen's Head, Broad Bridge Street in 1864. In 1866 the Hillam family are listed as beer retailers at two other locations: Robert Hillam, 18 Cowgate and Mary Hillam, St Leonards Street.

By 1891 the Brewer's Arms was owned by Charles Griffiths and no longer brewing.

Hopkins, William.

Listed in the 1791 Universal British Directory.

PETERBOROUGH (continued)

King, William, *Wellington Lane, Boongate.*

In 1866, William King is listed as a beer retailer and cowkeeper on Wellington Lane. The only entry as a brewer and beer retailer is in 1869. By 1874 the premises are shown simply as a beer house and two years later King is listed as a beer house keeper and higgler.

Kingston, Thomas.

Listed in the 1791 Universal British Directory.

Lazenby, John William, *Steam Engine, 27 Cromwell Road.*

J.W.Lazenby is listed as brewing here from 1876 when he was also running the nearby Steam Engine pub (now the Basant, 62 Cromwell Road). In 1892, Joseph Lazenby is shown as running the brewery and the pub, but the brewery seems to have closed by 1901. The brewery site is now used by several small businesses.

Malden, Aubrey, C.E. (F3896), *49 Palmerston Brewery, Palmerston Road.*

This brewery was originally used by John Weldon in 1876, the brewery having been established in 1868. He had been born in Farcet in 1817 and was the landlord of the Swiss Cottage in New Fletton in 1862. He is later shown as a brewer and grocer at No 1 Tower Street in 1871 and in 1874 as a shopkeeper in Bread Street and beer retailer in Palmerston Road.

Drawing of Weldon's dray carrying one or two gallon syphons of beer for the family trade.

Courtesy of Steve Williams.

The business traded as Weldon & Son from 1887 to 1892. By 1894 the son George Weldon is shown at 49 Palmerston Road, Woodstone, Huntingdonshire (F5778). He supplied his mild and bitter in one and two gallon syphons fitted with Barrett's patent stoppers. It seems that the beer kept well and was very popular with families.

A description of a visit to the brewery at the turn of the century comments on the novel use of high-pressure steam to clean the syphons and casks and the purpose designed brewer's dray for delivering the syphons. In the case of the latter *"For rapid delivery and saving of the ordinary attaching to more clumsy arrangements and minimising the chances of breakage, this is decidedly useful"* (Peterborough Illustrated 1892). Sound advice followed from the owner:-

"Pure malt and hops will always produce a palatable and an easily digestible beer. If nothing else were used in the manufacture very little would be heard of the evil effects of malt liquors, and doctors would more regularly recommend them, as they commonly do now in case of weak constitutions. Take a pint of good stout daily." Clearly a possible early member of CAMRA!

In 1905 Weldon is listed at Palmerston Street, but the Brewers' Journal April 1905 states that the Palmerston Brewery was for sale by private treaty, having been established in 1868. The business was described as a 6 quarter plant with machinery worked by gas power, a large covered yard etc, two good off-licences and a large jar and barrel trade.

In 1906 the site was being used by Herbert Charles Calcutt. At some point it became the property of Aubrey Malden, who was trading there in 1912.

The only other information is that, as a result of the wartime restrictions on brewing, Wells & Winch hired the brewery in 1918 and 1919 to obtain Malden's brewing certificate. This augmented production then allowed at the Biggleswade plant, gaining 512 barrels for 1918 and 2,366 in 1919 (Story of Biggleswade Brewery p27).

The property became a picture house, proprietor A.C.Malden, with the opening performance on 29th March 1920, which suggests the brewery was no longer in operation. The buildings were still standing in 1998, but the site was for sale for residential development.

PETERBOROUGH
(continued)

Malden's brewery today.

Photo: Authors' collection

Martin, Edward Victor, *143 Oundle Road.*

Martin is listed in 1925 as a brewer and beer salesman, but it is unlikely that he brewed on the premises at the time. However, the buildings, which are still standing, do appear to look as if they may have been a maltings at one time and the road opposite is called Brewster Avenue. Messrs George Martin beer agent and wholesaler operated from these premises until recently.

Mays, Thomas, *Albert Brewery, Albert Place.*

On 27th October, 1855, Thomas Mays, brewer and journeyman saddler, advertised in the Peterborough Advertiser offering *"genuine home brewed beers"*. In 1861 he is shown as a saddler and retail brewer. Mays originated from East Dereham in Norfolk. In 1867 he sold property to NBC, and in 1869 he is listed only as a beer retailer.

However, in 1876 he is shown as a brewer in Albert Place and a saddler on Cumbergate. He is also listed for 1884. His obituary makes no reference to the brewery, although it is mentioned in that of his wife in 1910.

In 1871 John Pyle was brewing in Albert Place. He was also a baker, with a shop at No 23 Albert Place. In addition, the Beehive Inn, 62 Albert Place, was included in the 1940 Kelly's listing (see Introduction).

Oakham Ales, *80 Westgate.*

In 1997 the Charter Cafe Bar bought this Rutland based brewery, planning to move it to a former unemployment office. The new site will house both the brewery and brewery tap, with an American style layout in which the brewery plant is visible through glass panels. The beers currently on offer include JHB at abv 3.8% and Bishops Farewell at abv 4.6%. A range of seasonal beers is also produced and Oakham also supplies two associated pubs and over 60 free houses.

Oakham Ales
Award Winning Beers

**Two Winning Beers at Peterborough Beer Festival
Pride of Peterborough and Champion JHB**

PETERBOROUGH (continued)

Page, Sidney John & Co (F3897), *St Leonard Street.*

In 1840 (when aged 32) and 1847 John Dauntecy Simpson was trading from the Mansion House Brewery (see Squires entry) in Westgate. Prior to this in 1830, a firm called Simpson, Mewburn and Miller. had operated as maltsters and wine and spirits merchants on Broad Bridge Street. He seems to have traded briefly in 1854 as Simpson & Collingwood, although Whincups (see Kings Cliffe) were shown at Mansion House Stores. It is interesting that an individual of a similar name is also shown at the Coach & Horses, Stamford, around this time (see entry).

In 1860, Simpson was declared bankrupt. However, in 1862 he was back in business with a new brewery, designed by Johnson of Melton Mowbray, trading as the St Leonard Street Brewery. In 1866 Simpson was again bankrupt and the property auctioned.

John Frederick Maddocks, from Chertsey in Surrey, bought the brewery in 1871 and he and Sidney Page were partners, trading in 1874, as Maddocks & Page, the Peterborough Brewery. The business then traded as J.Sidney Page & Co between 1875 and 1889. In May 1889, the brewery, plant and 5 pubs were bought by Phipps of Northampton for £7,000. This may have included the Peterborough Hotel which was located next to the brewery. In December 1891, the brewery premises were let to Samuel Boyer. In 1902 they were sold to a William Brown for £1,875.

The brewery was demolished in about 1911 to build the eastern abutments of Crescent Bridge.

Palmer, Judith, *The Crown, 749 Lincoln Road, New England.*

In 1884, Palmer is listed as a brewer at the pub which she had kept since at least 1877. William Garner was at the pub by 1892, and is listed in 1894 as a brewer, but in 1896 when still shown at the Crown, he is not listed as a brewer. The pub was rebuilt in the early 1900s.

Percival, Thomas, *Fitzwilliam Arms, Wood Street.*

Although the later version of Friedrich's Gazetteer shows Percival as brewing from 1871-76, there do not seem to be any other entries other than as a publican in 1869 (however see Spriggs entry). In 1876, a Levi Percival was running the Wheatsheaf on Midgate and in 1894 a J.T.Percival was at the White Hart, New England.

Redhead, Lucy, *Wellington Road.*

In 1892, a Lucy Redhead is shown as a publican in Wellington Street, but the only entry as a brewer for Mrs Redhead is in Kelly's 1894 Directory. Prior to this William Redhead was listed as a beer retailer at the Cherry Tree, Wellington Lane, from 1869.

Rofe, Gabriel.

Listed as a brewer in the 1791 Universal British Directory.

Rudd, William Hilliam, *Plasterer's Arms, Newtown.*

In 1866, Rudd is shown as a beer retailer on Westgate. In 1884, he is shown as the brewer and landlord at the Plasterer's Arms, the site of which is now under Queensgate bus-station and John Lewis.

Scoley, Thomas, *The Bull Hotel, Westgate.*

The first entry for Scoley as a brewer is in 1862, by 1864 he is shown as the publican and brewer at the Bull. He is still shown as a brewer in 1866, but by 1870 he is shown only as a publican. The pub is still trading.

Sewell, George, *The Windmill, Lincoln Road, Millfield.*

Listed as brewing from 1884 to 1891. Prior to this in 1877, the pub was kept by Edward Jackson. The Windmill is still trading.

Sewell, Thomas, *Wheelwright's Arms, 61 Eastfield Road.*

Thomas Sewell is first shown as a beer retailer on Eastfield Road in 1866. In 1869 Sewell is shown as a beer retailer at the pub (now The Sportsman). However, between 1884 and 1891 he is also mentioned as a brewer. In 1892, the pub's address is shown as Cemetery End and although Sewell was still running it, there is no mention of brewing. The pub was included in the 1940 Kelly's listing (see Introduction), when it was run by a George Hill.

PETERBOROUGH (continued)

Slator, Henry, *Lion Brewery, Church Street.*

Slator is shown as an ale and porter brewer in 1869, and also as a wine and spirit merchant at the White Lion. The pub brewery was leased by Charles Cutlack in 1870. The pub is still in business, but has been extensively rebuilt.

Smith, John, *Wheatsheaf, Midgate.*

In the 1791 directory, John Smith is shown as a victualler. Not long afterwards, the Peterborough inclosures refer to Messrs T and J.Smith as using a malting at Swanspool. In 1830 John Smith is shown as a brewer and maltster at Swanspool, whilst a Thomas Smith kept the Horse & Jockey on Boongate. By 1840 Swanspool had become Midgate and as well as a brewer he is the shown as the landlord of the Wheatsheaf. Smith died in February 1849 aged 69. His executors demolished some buildings, laid out Swan Place and sold building plots at auction, although some maltings remained until about 1860. Presumably at this time the Wheatsheaf passed into the hands of Cutlacks.

Smith, William, *Boongate.*

The 1847 Poll Book lists William as the occupier of a copyhold brew house and blacksmith shop. In 1876, Cutlacks bought the Fleece/Carpenter's Arms, with brew house, on St Johns Street from William Smith, a deceased publican.

Speechley, Edward, *Broad Bridge Street.*

Listed in 1850 as a brewer and the agent for Hunt & Co carriers. This is the only mention of brewing, although in 1864, a Richard Speechley was a publican at the Star on Fengate.

Spriggs, Charles, *Boonfield.*

In 1864, a Charles Spriggs is shown as a brewer at an un-named beer house which the family had run since 1840. This may have been the Fitzwilliam's Arms, Newtown which was kept by John Spriggs in 1830.

George Spriggs is shown as a brewer in Boonfield in 1869, although he seems to have become a builder and owner of pubs (see Cutlack entry). He was the licensee of the King George beer house on Hampden Road in 1870, which he owned until at least 1896. In 1877 he was also shown as a builder on Gladstone Road North. In 1883 George also owned the Beaconsfield Arms, Midland Road.

Squire, William and Co, *Broad Bridge Street.*

Wright Thomas Squire married into the Biglands family and thus inherited property which in 1778 is mentioned as having a malt kiln. In 1779, his son William is described as a merchant and common brewer. In the 1811 enclosure, he is mentioned as occupying a malting and brew house on Westgate, formerly owned by the Biglands. His property included a malt kiln and the following inns:-

Black Boy and Trumpet Long Causeway (Later Patens)	Horse & Jockey, Boongate
Rose & Crown, Broad Bridge Street	White Hart, Long Causeway

At the same time, William Thomas Squire is shown as the owner of warehouses and offices, formerly the property of Wright Thomas Squire. Pigot's 1824 listing shows William Squire & Co as brewers on Westgate. However, on 2nd June, 1826, his nephew William Walcot Squire, in addition to the Mansion House on Westgate, also inherited the malting, brewery and brewing utensils. The brewery was to be run with Christopher Jeffery (d.1842) as a partner.

The 1830 Directory lists Squire & Co as brewers and wine and spirit merchants at Broad Bridge Street and maltsters on Westgate. They were also coal merchants and iron dealers. The brewery was at the entrance to Lincoln Road and stretched back into Boroughbury past what was known as the Square Pond, so named because in 1833 it was covered with water.

In 1837 Squire went to live in Cheltenham and the brewery was sold for £8,500 to Buckles. They pulled down most of the brewery (see entry) and built North Street and sold building plots along it, although retaining the maltings on Lincoln Road. The maltings were sold in 1857 to J.G.Atkinson, (see Cutlack entry). The site was subsequently the location of the Liberal Club and Masonic Hall. The Cavell Court building now covers the area.

Stones, Thomas (F3895), *Home Brewery, 33 Monument Street.*

In 1866 John House was a confectioner on Church Street, prior to this he seems to have been a market gardener living in Kings Cliffe. By 1869 he had taken on the Vine, 9 Church Street. The pub also operated as a fruit and flower shop and John House was listed as a brewer and nurseryman in 1870 and a victualler in 1874. However, by 1877 he is shown as a confectioner, fruiterer and florist and as late as 1890 is recorded at Cowgate and Church Street.

In August 1875 a planning application was made for a brewery in Monument Street. The 1877 Directory lists George House, from Kings Cliffe, in Monument Street and also owning dining rooms at 27 Narrow Bridge Street. In 1881 he is shown as a confectioner and brewer, but the brewery employed only 2 men which suggests it was a rather small concern. Given the commonality of birthplace, name and occupation a link between George and John House seems probable!

In 1887 the property was sold to Thomas Henry Stones, who had moved here with his family from Wakefield. A new brewery, designed by Henry Milnes Townsend (the first trained architect in Peterborough), was built in 1888. This was a 12 quarter brewery which would be worked independently and in addition to the existing one. In 1891 he is shown as living in Granville House, Monument Street, together with his son Sidney who was also a brewer.

The business traded as House & Stones from 1888 to about 1894, when it is listed as Thos Stones, Home Brewery. Stones advertised his *"celebrated invalid stout"*. However, in 1888, a G.F.House was also advertising home brewed ales at the Commercial Hotel, 27 Narrow Bridge Street, which he was still running in 1896. Somewhat surprisingly the 1894 directory lists Watts & Sons as brewers at the Vine Restaurant, but this is the only mention (In 1896, a John Watts was running the Northern Dining Room on Cowgate). In 1901 when Mrs G.F.House was running the Commercial there is no mention of brewing.

In June 1897, the brewery trading as the Home Brewery, Monument Street and Crawthorne Street was for sale by auction. This was after it had been taken over by Warwicks and Richardsons, who already had a depot in Church Street. The brewery was bought by Cutlacks in 1898 (see above). The plant was described as being 25 quarters, which suggests that further building may have taken place. The sale also mentions an aerated water factory.

Stones continued to manufacture mineral waters in Towler Street, a site later used by Barber & Ross. In 1898 Stones are shown as mineral water manufacturers, spirit merchants and beer dealers, Long Causeway and Towler Street.

The buildings remain at the rear of Colourscope copy centre.

Swallow, Joshua, *Bell & Oak, Market Place.*

Swallow is listed as a publican brewer in 1864 and 1866. This was at the Bell, which he had kept from at least 1862. He was still at the pub in 1874, but there seems to be no further mention of brewing and two years later the pub was being run by John Bean Tilbury. In 1901, Timothy Rawlinson is described as the manager of the pub.

Washington, Francis.

The 1762 militia list shows Washington as a brewer.

Webb, John, *The Ostrich, 17 North Street.*

John Webb, presumably after buying one of the plots from the Buckles, traded here from 1837 to the late 1860s at what was the Ostrich brew pub. He also seems to have bought the maltings on Lincoln Road in partnership with J.G.Atkinson (see Cutlacks).

PETERBOROUGH
(continued)

In 1869 Craig Joseph Brown was at the Ostrich commercial inn, as a wine and spirit merchant. In 1874 it was being kept by George James Isley; however, two years later, Herbert Morris is shown as a brewer and running the pub. It seems to have been owned by J.Webb junior until May 1899, when it was bought by Elijah Eyres brewery of King's Lynn. The property is now the Good Beer Guide listed Bogart's Bar.

White, Catherine, *Bull & Dolphin, Bridge Street.*

In 1874 a Mrs White was offering the Bull & Dolphin for sale in consequence of the death of the owner, presumable Francis White who was at the pub in 1862. It was described as the oldest established inn in the town and having its own brewing plant. The site was described as forming an excellent location for a common brewery, being in close proximity to the River Nene and two minutes walk from the railway station. However, in 1884, a Catherine White is listed at the Bull & Dolphin, Bridge Street, suggesting that the sale and development had fallen through. The property, on what became Rivergate, was later owned by Paten & Co a firm of wholesalers and bottlers.

In 1888, the Bull & Dolphin was being kept by C.White, whilst the Bull was kept by Mrs C.White.

Whittle, James (1854), *Bridge Street (see entry on Eye).*

PITSFORD

Underwood, John, *Old Bakehouse, Main Street.*

John Underwood is listed as a baker in the village c.1849. He took up brewing soon afterwards, being shown as a brewer and baker in 1854. In 1861 he is only listed as a baker and publican, but in 1866 is shown as a brewer and baker. The old bakehouse is still standing in the village opposite the green

The Fox and Hounds which used to stand in Moulton Road also brewed from the 18th century. In 1854 it was in the hands of Jas Whitsey Benbrook who was also shown as a maltster. In addition, "Brew House Stable" in the village is so named because beer was originally brewed in the cellar.

Youil, Edwin.

Harrod's 1876 Directory lists Edwin as brewer, but this seems to have been his home address rather than a separate concern from the Victoria Brewery in Northampton which he owned with his brother (see entry under Northampton). However, Youil Bros did lease a maltings here from Phipps .

POTTERSPURY

Gurney, John, *Reindeer, Watling Street.*

In 1836, John Gurney bought the Reindeer, which he sold to NBC in 1879. The pub closed in the 1960s and is now an antiques showroom. However, the brew house and extensive maltings are still intact at the rear.

In 1830 Gurney junior is shown as a maltster in the High Street, at nearby Towcester. George Gurney was at the Talbot and Thomas Gurney was a cooper in the High Street. In 1840 George Gurney was malting in Park Street and owned and victualled at the nearby New Dolphin on Watling Street. In addition, they owned several pubs in neighbouring villages, eg. the Peacock, Long Buckby in 1874. The family later went on to run a small brewery at Rowsham near Aylesbury (F4356), which they bought from Edward Major-Lucas (see entry).

RAUNDS

Blow, William, *Golden Fleece, 4 Rotten Row.*

William Blow a publican brewer at the Golden Fleece is listed in the brewers sections of the 1861 and 1869 trade Directories. During the last decades of the 19th century the inn changed hands several times, before becoming a Praed's house. For a brief spell it was kept by John Billingham, a foreman at the local ironstone quarry, so presumably it had ceased brewing by this time. Closed in 1925 it is now a private house.

In addition, when the Robin Hood & Little John was for sale in 1859, it was described as having a brew house.

ROADE

Warwick, John.

On 4th July, 1785, John Hedges, a mason, presented a bill of £35 for building a brew house for Augustus Henry, Duke of Grafton (NRO G1007). The property being tenanted by a John Warwick.

ROTHERSTHORPE   Poplars House on the north side of North Street is a Grade II listed building (DOE listing S Northants). It is a two storey house formerly a farmhouse built around 1700 and altered in the 18th and 19th centuries. Some 15 metres to the NE of the building are what are described as outbuildings and a brew house. The latter is a low single storey 18th century building with a pantiled roof. Many farms would have brewed for their workers in the past to supplement both their wages and indeed their food. This is one of only two surviving examples in the county (see Braybrooke entry).

ROTHWELL

Cross, Joseph, *Chequers Inn, Bridge Street.*

When sold as part of the 1890 auction of Tebbutt's of Sudborough, the Chequer's Inn, in the occupation of Joseph Cross opposite the Market House, is described as having a brew house. The pub was being supplied by Mannings in 1904 and they seem to have bought the property in 1910. Now de-licensed, the pub, which dates back to around 1734, is still standing.

Gotch, T.H. & J.D., *The Rowell Brewery, High Street.*

Rowell is the old name for the town. In 1666, Jonathan Wells a carpenter built a cottage on the High Street. At some stage, and certainly by 1788, this became the Crown & Boot Inn. In 1830, William Vialls was the victualler at the inn, which on 2nd May, 1832, Mary Watson, widow, purchased for £1,075. In 1836, Thomas Watson is described as a victualler at the inn with the Gotch family, when in November a mortgage, which included assignment of the brewing vessels, secured a sum of £1,000. In 1840, Mary took out a further mortgage for £2,000.

Around this time the name of the inn seems to have been changed to the New Inn. This may have been linked to the fact that there was a separate and nearby pub called the Crown. In 1840, Thomas Watson, is described as the landlord of the New Inn, and is listed as a brewer.

The Rowell Brewery was originally a small 8 quarter plant, described as a quaint old fashioned brew house powered by a treadmill, operated by a horse, but in reality these were normally the domain of a donkey.

Thomas Watson died in March 1844 and Mary Watson, widow, decided to place the brewery up for sale.

"TO BE SOLD BY PRIVATE CONTRACT.
A capital and well established brewery with a public house....situated at Rowell....The above will be found a very desirable purchase for any person wishing to embark in the brewing business, and who can command a comparatively small capital. A considerable sum has recently been expended in rendering the establishment complete....The whole was late the property Mr Thomas Watson deceased; and the brewery and public house are now in the occupation of his widow."
(Northampton Mercury 6th April, 1844)

This is slightly contradictory, in that she had previously been the owner of the property and described as a widow, which suggests that she may have been Thomas' mother. Six months later she still had not sold the business. In desperation she advertised the New Inn on its own for sale on 19th October, 1844.

Mary died in 1845, and as a result of the earlier mortgages, the property became owned by the Gotches. The Gotches were a prominent Kettering family, with Rothwell connections in that the founder John Cooper Gotch's wife was from Rothwell. He built up a substantial business in the leather and shoe trade and ventured into banking. The family business was then organised between his two sons, such that Thomas Henry looked after the bank and John Davis the leather and shoe side.

In 1847, the brothers were running the brewery as a partnership- "T.H.and J.D.Gotch Ale and Porter Brewers". The partnership traded in Rothwell High Street. Thomas Henry Gotch is listed at Rothwell in 1850 and also as malting at Broughton. However, the Gotches were not listed in 1854, when the New Inn was kept by Richard Mason.

In 1857 the Gotch & Sons bank collapsed dragging down the whole family business. This incident, famous to students of banking, led to the passing of the Limited Liability Act of 1858, which in turn was to have an important influence on the financing of the brewing industry towards the end of the century.

"TO BE SOLD BY AUCTION,
Mr G Bates, by order of the assignees under the bankruptcy of J.D and T.H GOTCH on Friday 18th December, 1857 at the New Inn, Rowell.. The brewery consists of 8 quarter plant complete with horse power for mashing and pumping, large underground tanks with an unfailing supply of water..."

The brewery at Rothwell was estimated to be worth £3,000, which suggests that it had developed from supplying just the pub. Its details, in a letter mentioning the bankruptcy, suggest that it was a 25 barrel plant. However the business had been neglected because of the bankruptcy and a "*most unfortunate sale*" meant that the family only received £500.

Although the Gotch's brewery went out of business, George Briggs is still listed as a wholesale brewer at the New Inn in 1862. However, there is no mention of brewing in the 1874 Directory when the pub was being kept by a William Capp.

At some point the New Inn became owned by Praeds of Wellingborough who may have bought it from William Ball & Son in 1899. In a 1914 directory, the address is given as Kettering Road. Hence, when Praeds were bought in 1954, their property included both the New Inn and the Crown (see Marriot entry). There is no sign of the New Inn.

In White's 1896 Directory, Albert Pentelow is shown as operating stores for the "Garddington Brewery", this seems to be a mis-print for the Cardington Brewery (F974) in Bedfordshire. In 1898 he is shown as agent for Charles Wells who had bought the goodwill of the Cardington Brewery the previous year.

Jesson, William Ward, *The Blue Bell, Bell Lane.*

The first mention of the Blue Bell is for 1850, when it was being kept by a Samuel Shortland. A William Jesson was at the George in nearby Desborough in 1877. Jesson is listed at the Blue Bell as a publican brewer in 1892. He was still at the pub in 1898, but with no mention of brewing. The pub is said to have been converted from a police house and is still trading.

Marriott, Miss Maria, *Crown Inn, High Street.*

In 1815, an advertisement to common brewers and others mentioned the sale of the Crown Inn with brew house, now in the occupation of Mrs Ann Daulby, *"who is about to retire from business"*.

In 1850, the pub was kept by Thomas Marriott, who was also a maltster from at least 1824. In 1869, he is shown as a farmer and butcher. The brew house seems to have been retained, since Miss Marriott is shown as a publican brewer from 1895 to 1902.

The Crown sign still hangs over the rebuilt frontage of the latter, now closed, pub which stands on the High Street and some of the buildings may remain at the rear.

SLIPTON

Bland, Amos.

Amos Bland is listed as a brewer and beer retailer in 1854 and in 1862 Catherine Bland is shown as such.

ST MARTINS near STAMFORD

Aldwinckle, Bartholomew (F4743), *Exeter's Arms, 1 Water Street.*

Listed as a publican brewer in 1892, in the area of Stamford which came within the Northamptonshire boundary. He had been at the pub from at least 1877. In the 1880s, there were 15 publican brewers and 5 common brewers operating in Stamford. Bartholomew was followed by Mrs Harriett Aldwinckle in 1894. Four years later the Aldwinckle Brothers are shown as owning the Exeter's Arms, which they had owned since at least 1874. The pub was last listed as brewing in 1921, when being kept by Bartholomew William Aldwinckle.

The Exeter, which dated from 1803, closed in 1931 and the site was recently cleared for housing.

Dabbs, Arthur John.

The Brewers' Journal for February 1880 mentions Dabbs' business as being liquidated.

Hunt, George & Henry Robert (F4747), *8 Water Street.*

In 1811, a consortium of common brewers is described as acquiring premises in the town. This consisted of William Harper, William Brown Edwards (founder of the All Saints Brewery in the 1820s) and Robert Hunt. The latter went on to open a brewery on Water Street in 1814. In 1816, he bought the Rose & Crown, Wilbarston, for £180, but only four years later he sold it to Henry Chapman of Weldon.

Robert Hunt (exors of) brewers and spirit dealers Water Street are listed for 1847. In 1850 George Hunt is shown as brewer and maltster at Water Street and Broad Street. In 1854 he is also shown as dealing in spirits, but by 1869 Mrs T.Hunt is listed as the brewer. In 1874, the business was trading as Hunt & Co. However, G.Hunt were looking to be represented at the inaugural meetings of the Northants Brewers Association in 1884. In 1894, the business was trading as Hunt, George & Robert Henry.

In 1904, they supplied a small number of pubs in Northamptonshire as follows:-

Talbot, Gretton	Blue Bell, Collyweston
Plough, Nassington	Swan, Woodnewton

They also had a beer house at Warmington and another at Yarwell. In addition, the King's Head at Wadenhoe was owned the exors of George Eden Hunt.

Henry Robert Hunt died on 6th February, 1925 and left his half share of the brewery to his two brothers, Robert and Charles. However, as a result, the business together with some 70 houses, was for sale in October 1926. Frederick West Kent was the manager and Arthur Grant was the brewer. The business was bought in 1927 for £100,000 by Mowbray & Co of Grantham and brewing probably ceased around this time. The name can still be made out on a wall in Water Street.

Phillips Stamford Brewery Ltd., *Water Street.*

The first listing is for a Joseph Phillips as a brewer in 1791. In 1789, he had acquired the brewery of Thomas Trueman recorded as the first common brewer in the town in 1780 and who may have been trading as early as 1770. Joseph was from the Phillips family which had founded a brewery in Royston, Hertfordshire. Together, with his wife Judith, he is shown living in front of the brewery at 16 Water Street, where he erected Welland House in 1834.

His son, Joseph II, took over the running of the Stamford brewery and around 1825 he seems to have acquired a brewery in Coventry from David Lloyd and William P.Summerfield. He then traded in Coventry as Josh Phillips & Son (Coventry & Stamford), with the Coventry end run by Henry Phillips, his younger brother. In 1847, Joseph is shown as living at Stamford, when he owned a pub at Maxey, tenanted by Thomas Robinson.

In 1850 the Coventry brewery was sold to William Ratliffe (F1222), when Henry seems to have emigrated to New Zealand. However, in 1878 Frank Phillips left NBC (see NBC entry) to take control of the Coventry brewery of James Marriott & Sons which was renamed Phillips and Marriott and Company (F1217). On the death of William Ratliffe in 1900, his business was amalgamated with Phillips and Marriott, thus bringing it back into the family fold for a brief time until Frank Phillips death in 1901.

In 1851, the Stamford brewery and maltings was employing some 17 men. Joseph II died on 21st September, 1865 and the brewery was then run by his son, Joseph Phillips III (b.1824 Coventry) who had been practising as a solicitor in the town.

On 14 October 1868, a serious fire at the brewery destroyed the malting room and the ale stores.

Joseph III was assisted by his brother Charles until 1873, when the latter moved from Stamford. Joseph then became the sole owner, running the business through a manager. He also became an important figure in local government, including holding the offices of Under-Sheriff for Lincolnshire, Northamptonshire and Rutland.

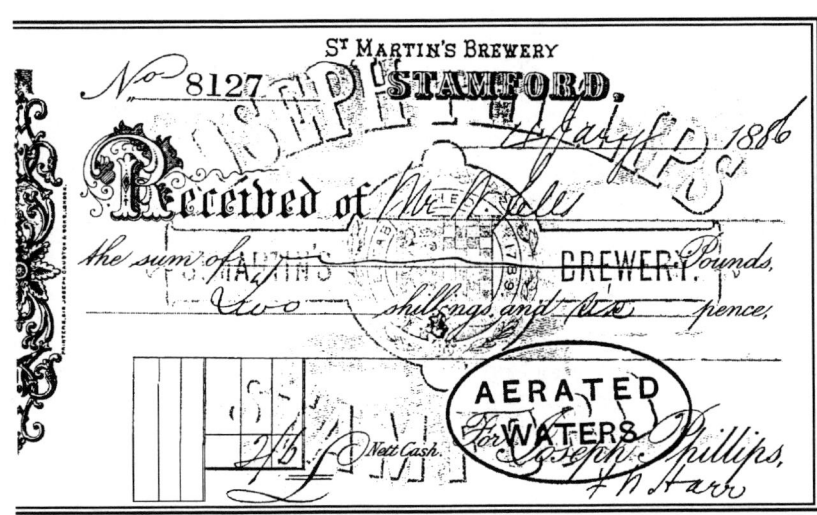

A rare example of a Joseph Phillips, St Martin's Brewery cheque used in 1886.

Authors' collection

**ST MARTINS
near STAMFORD
(continued)**

> # THE ST. MARTIN'S BREWERY, STAMFORD,
> with Commodious Residence and Pleasure Grounds,
> **THREE MALTHOUSES,**
> AND THE NUMEROUS
> PUBLIC AND BEER-HOUSES, COTTAGES AND LAND BELONGING THERETO.
>
> Particulars and Conditions of Sale
> OF THE ABOVE
> OLD ESTABLISHED & WELL-KNOWN
> ## ST. MARTIN'S BREWERY,
> COMPRISING
> A Perfectly Equipped Brew-house fitted with a 20-quarter Plant,
> **TWO MALTHOUSES**
> STEEPING TOGETHER 58 QUARTERS,
> AN ENJOYABLE RESIDENCE, LAWNS & GARDENS,
> Yards, Offices, Stabling and Stores, the whole lying compactly together and of
> **FREEHOLD TENURE,**
> ALSO
> **94 PUBLIC AND BEER-HOUSES,**
> COTTAGES AND LAND CONNECTED THEREWITH,
> SITUATE IN
> STAMFORD and the neighbouring Towns and Villages extending to OAKHAM and UPPINGHAM, BOURN, PETERBOROUGH AND WHITTLESEA,
> In the Counties of Lincoln, Rutland, Leicester, Northampton, Huntingdon & Cambridge.
> (66 of the Licensed Houses are of FREEHOLD or COPYHOLD tenure, and 28 Leasehold, Annual, or Loan Holdings.)
> The foregoing, including the GOODWILL of the several BUSINESSES in Beer, Spirits, and Aerated Waters, affording to an investor a property and trade of the best class,
>
> will be Sold by Auction,
> BY
> **Messrs. ALFRED THOMAS, PEYER & MILES**
> AT THE MART, TOKENHOUSE YARD, LONDON, E.C.,
> **On MONDAY, 24th JULY, 1893,**
> At 2 o'clock precisely, IN ONE LOT.
> By Direction of JOSEPH PHILLIPS, Esq.
>
> Particulars, with Plans, may be obtained of Messrs. PHILLIPS, EVANS & PHILLIPS, Solicitors, Stamford; and of
> Messrs. ALFRED THOMAS, PEYER & MILES,

However, the brewery, together with 66 freehold and 28 leasehold houses, was for sale by auction on 24th July, 1893. It was described as having sold 11,244 barrels of beer at a value of £25,882 in the previous year. Interest was very limited and after failing to reach its reserve price, the business was withdrawn from the sale at £60,000. The poisoning scares at the turn of the century led to an advertisement in the Stamford & Rutland Guardian which informed customers of the *"Absolute Purity of All Ales and Stout"* (4th January, 1901). The analysis had been undertaken by a Mr John Heron FIC FCS.

When he died in August 1902, Joseph's estate, presumably including the brewery and houses, was valued at £87,186. In addition to his involvement in politics, Joseph was well-read, with a wide range of interests, reflected in the extensive collection of manuscripts and books which form the nucleus of the Phillip's library in Stamford Town Hall. His son, John Henry Joseph, was the brewer, living at No 43 Water Street. The brewery tap, the Beehive, was at No 12 and the mineral water manufactory at No 7.

In 1910, the Stamford brewery was still trading as Joseph Phillips, St Martins Brewery, the business being carried on by his executors, his sons John Henry Joseph and Charles Percy (solicitor); however, the latter died in 1913. John Henry Joseph died in January 1936. Hence, when the concern became incorporated as a company on 28th September, 1937, Lionel Charles Whitehead Phillips, the majority shareholder, was described as the Governing Director. He was the son of Charles Phillips. His own son, John Savile Phillips, and Harold Alexander Jury, the brewer, were the other directors. The 1st Annual Report for the year end 30th September, 1938 showed a net profit of £4,342 giving a 12% final dividend.

The company traded reasonably, earning dividends of 10% during the war years, despite H.A.Jury being away on war service. The end of the war saw a commitment to a 3 year investment of £10,000 in a bottling plant. This began to operate in late 1948 to meet the increased sales of bottled rather than draught beer.

The Board Meeting of November 1949 records that the firm's auditors, Messrs Saffrey, had been approached by another brewery with an offer to buy Phillips for cash or shares. This could possibly have been Praeds of Wellingborough, who certainly expressed a later interest in the business. The Board rejected the proposal. However, L.C.W.Phillips died in July 1951, his place on the Board being filled by Patrick Edward Phillips of Kingsmead, Little Somerford, Chippenham. His son-in-law, Edward Randal Chadwyck-Healy (of Charringtons) also joined the Board.

The new members clearly had doubts about the future of the business when they discussed it at the January meeting in 1952. As a result, J.W.Greens of Luton were to be permitted to make an offer for the shares of the business. However, the negotiations fell through and on 29th July, 1952, a joint meeting was held with the men from NBC, the business which the Phillips family had founded.

The meeting recorded the resignations of the Phillips directors and their replacement by NBC appointees. In addition, the transfer of shares was recorded and that the registered office of the Company be changed to 116 Bridge Street, Northampton.

The Stamford business was not in a very healthy state. Of the 70 pubs, some 42 were selling less than 2 barrels of beer a week. The pubs as a block were valued at £120,000, or £168,100 individually, and the brewery and maltings £25,000. In NBC's eyes the business was worth less than these values when mortgage liabilities and loans were taken into account, although they were looking at one stage to offer £230,000.

NBC paid nearly £170,000 cash for the whole business with the transfer of mortgages and a £30,000 compensation fund. By October they began to sell off barrels and a bottle washing machine to Melbourns. In December, the Boby Mill was sold for £250 to Ridleys of Chelmsford. The meeting also recorded the purchase of all the properties of the late L.C.W.Phillips.

NBC took on J.S.Phillips as a consultant for 7 years at £1,300 pa and C.R.Jury, the assistant brewer was also given a contract, for 5 years on £800. In January 1953, it was decided to wind up the business. Hence, Phillips ceased trading on 10th February, with a surplus of £30,949. The winding up notice was in the London Gazette for 11th November, 1954, and an EGM on 9th December completed the paperwork. The liquidators sold the remaining plant and machinery to NBC for £9,382. The site itself was sold for £12,000.

Although NBC considered selling the maltings, previous investment eg £2,300 in September 1953 to increase the output from 1,100 to 2,000 quarters, meant they were worth retaining. They operated until 1966.

Phillip's Stamford Brewery in 1986 shortly before demolition.

Photo: Authors' collection

ST MARTINS near STAMFORD (continued)

Simpson, John, *Coach & Horses, 19 High Street.*

The earliest record of the pub is 1797, when George Betts was the victualler. However, in 1850, John Simpson is listed as the brewer at the pub, and a George H.Betts was a maltster in the town. In 1854, Mrs D.Simpson was running the pub, but there is no mention of brewing. The building, now delicensed is to the left of St Martin's church.

Whincup, Henry, *George Hotel, St Martin Street.*

Henry Whincup, Mayor of Stamford in 1845, is shown at the George in 1850 and was still listed as the brewer in 1874 (see also Kings Cliffe).

STOKE BRUERNE

Phipps, Samuel, *Stoke Plain.*

In 1869, the property of the late Samuel Phipps was for sale. Although this included a brew house and vessels, this seems to have been a domestic brew house with no commercial trading. Samuel does not seem to have had any direct family links with the brewers of Northampton.

Woodwards, *Boat Inn.*

The Boat Inn dates from around 1805 and reputedly brewed until about 1900 (English Country Inns p201). Stevens 1889 Directory shows William Woodward as a butcher and owner at the Boat Inn, whilst White's 1896 Directory lists Mrs Anne Woodward. However, in 1922 Mrs Woodward was described as very ill and Phipps of Northampton were looking to buy the property. Rebuilt internally in 1960, it is still owned by the Woodward family.

SUDBOROUGH

Tebbut, Frederick (F4950).

In 1812 Jonas Tebbut appears in a directory as a farmer. However, he is also described as a common brewer and seems to have taken possession of property from a Nicholas Worthington, which included a brew house and malt house. A Sanders Tebbutt, presumably his brother, is also described as a common brewer.

By 1830 Jonas was trading as "*Jonas Tebbut Ale and Porter Company*" at Sudbury (sic) and sold his beer in Thrapston through his agent Joseph Dicks - a cabinet maker and joiner.

Sanders died in 1831 and Jonas Tebbut died on 2nd February, 1836. The latter's business passed to his wife Mary and his son John Chew Tebbut. In 1840 William Brown was their agent in the High Street, Peterborough. In 1841, Tebbut's Porter and Stout were available from T.Leigh, wine and spirit vaults in the Market Place, Wellingborough.

J.C.Tebbut ran the brewery, as a sideline to farming, up until his death on 19th November, 1873. The day to day affairs of the business were then handled by the executors of the Will, who were Sanders Tebbut Lette and Francis Allen. They were charged by the estate to offer the business to Frederick Tebbut, the eldest son, at a reasonable price. If he did not wish to buy it they were told to sell it as they saw fit.

In September 1874, various parts of the farm appeared up for sale - "*38 acres of arable and pasture land near Sudborough for sale by order of the executors of the late John Chew Tebbut*".

Frederick John Tebbut took his younger brother Joseph into partnership and bought the brewery on 1st December, 1874, for £6,450. The business then traded as F.&J.Tebbutt.

Twelve years later, on 20th July, 1886, Joseph Alfred Tebbut died. His widow Mary sold out to Frederick for £336. The business was described as "*a brewery....brewing plant, dwelling house, offices, stables, coach house, large yard, the whole replete with every convenience, and in excellent repair*".

Three years later, the Sudborough Brewery was up for sale by public auction. The brewery did not sell at the October 1889 auction and was at auction again on 7th March, 1890, at the Royal Hotel, Kettering. At this time it was described as having a copper and furnace, malt mill, 5 quarter mash tun, 2 steam pumps and 4 horse-power vertical steam engine. However, it was put up for sale yet again only four months later.

"This estate calls for especial attention being situated at the entrance of Sudborough...well built of brick and slate, in excellent repair, and where a good trade has been done for many years."
(Northampton Herald 5th July, 1890)

The tied estate at the time was as follows:-

Chequers Inn, Rothwell	King's Arms, Thrapston
Lord Nelson, Stanion	Mason's Arms, Twywell
Old Friar, Twywell	Coach & Horses, Woodford

Red Lion, Aldwinckle   Castle, Aldwinckle
Round House, Sudborough and two beer houses

Mannings bought one pub, NBC bought the Red Lion and one other, Phipps bought the Chequers and John Elworthy bought four properties. However, Kelly's Directory of 1898 continues to list Frederick Tebbutt as a brewer.

Brewery Cottage, Sudborough

Photo: Authors' collection

The brewery site was purchased by Lord Barnard who already owned most of the property in the village. The buildings were converted into cottages and the old maltings were later turned into flats. Brewery Cottage is still standing on the edge of the village. It is just up from the round house, an old toll house built in 1660 on the main road. This became the "Ye Olde Round House" inn sold to Elworthys.

SYRESHAM

King's Brewery & Stores (F4998), *Royal Crown Brewery, Broad Street.*

Towards the end of the 19th century the Kirby family had a grocer's shop in Broad Street. In the 1890s this grew, and a row of cottages was knocked together to become *"the department store in the country"* selling a wide range of goods. More importantly, a brewery was built adjacent to it. Around 1900 the property was bought by Herbert King whose mother was a Kirby.

King bought a horse and van which he converted into a mobile shop. He toured the local villages selling beer, provisions and oil. Advertisements for King's ales and stouts appeared in all of the local newspapers and there were promotional gimmicks like the production of advertising jugs.

The King's delivery van

Photo: Andrew Cunningham collection

SYRESHAM (continued)

In 1903, he erected a four storey brewery which he christened the Royal Crown. This red brick brewery was extended several times during its lifetime. The company was now trading as King's Royal Crown Brewery Company.

The Royal Crown was laid out in fairly typical tower brewery design, including:-

Top Floor:	Cold liquor tanks and cooling vats
3rd Floor:	Hot liquor tanks
2nd Floor:	Mashing and fermenting room
1st Floor:	Boiler house and hops room
Ground Floor:	Offices, bottle and crate stores, bottle washing department, barrel steaming department, bottling and racking areas, boiler room, and pump room. 2 large vats

Water was at first supplied from mineral springs near to the brewery, but later a reservoir was built opposite the rectory.

By the outbreak of World War I, King's had seven horse drawn vans on the road and claimed to visit every village within twenty miles of Syresham. At the time, the brewery employed some 60 people. A number of motor cycle "outriders" toured villages almost as far afield as Oxford, Northampton and Bedford to take orders for the vans to deliver later in the week. In addition, King's took over Wood's grocery store in Brackley as a subsidiary outlet.

A fleet of customised motor vans, built by a local garage, had special roofs to accommodate beer crates and side panels designed to hold oil or paraffin. These red painted vans were a common sight on the highways and byways of South Northamptonshire.

From his first marriage, to a Jane Wilding, Herbert King had two children: the elder was Robert (Bob King) who took over the management of the shop side of the business. Herbert's second marriage was to Isabel James of Kensington, and they had a son (Edwin) Roy. Herbert King died in 1916 and his widow struggled on until the end of the war when Robert came back from France. The youngest son was still at public school but he joined the business soon afterwards; however, the business brain and the power behind the firm was Mrs King. She spent considerable money in proving her descendence from Captain Cook, but she created a sensation in the village by using the laws of an American state to marry her own stepson Robert, thus keeping the firm in the family's hands. The family had built for themselves a commodious house behind the brewery.

"The brewery stands in open country amongst ideal surrounds.... this well established business continues to grow by leaps and bounds." (Northampton Herald 3rd December, 1926)

King's Brewery

Photo: Andrew Cunningham collection

SYRESHAM
(continued)

King's Brewery

Photo: Andrew Cunningham collection

By 1924 the name had been shortened to King's Brewery. The business was the largest employer in Syresham, where all of the employees lived. It was estimated that it had 8,000 customers in an area stretching from Wendover to Coventry. Beer was only supplied to private householders and never to public houses. It was normally sold in bottles, but barrels of Golden Drop Bitter or XXX mild could be ordered. The staff were obviously keen salesmen since Isabel King's draymen were fined for hawking beer from a lorry at Banbury in 1925.

Mrs H.G.King of the Firs, Syresham, sold up the business in 1955 and the brewery was demolished for housing, after having suffered the indignity of being used as a pig farm (SP 629 416).

King's Brewery

Photo: Andrew Cunningham collection

SYRESHAM
(continued)

1927 Advertisement from the Authors' collection

> **In Lovely Country Surroundings**
>
> Drinks worth Drinking.
> Prices worth Studying.
>
> | | | |
> |---|---|---|
> | 12 Pint Cases KING'S BITTER ALE | 5s. 0d. | per Case. |
> | 4 Quart Crates KING'S GOLDEN DROP BITTER | 2s. 6d. | per Crate. |
> | 12 Pint Cases KING'S XXX MILD ALE | 5s. 0d. | per Case. |
> | 4 Quart Crates KING'S XXX MILD ALE | 2s. 6d. | per Crate. |
> | 12 Pint Cases KING'S SPECIAL INVALID STOUT | 6s. 6d. | per Case. |
> | 4 Quart Crates KING'S NOURISHING STOUT | 3s. 6d. | per Crate. |
>
> IN ADDITION TO ABOVE WELL-KNOWN BRANDS, WE ARE BREWING A MUCH STRONGER ALE KNOWN as 'SPECIAL DINNER ALE'
>
> AS WITH ALL OUR BEVERAGES, WE GUARANTEE TO USE ONLY THE VERY BEST AND PUREST MATERIALS OBTAINABLE. THIS, AND THE FACT THAT WE BREW IN THE LOVELY COUNTRY, ACCOUNTS FOR THE ENORMOUS SUCCESS OF ALL OUR VENTURES.
>
> 2-Pint Cases, KING'S "Special Dinner Ale" ... 7/- Per Case
> 4-Quart Crates, KING'S "Special Dinner Ale" ... 4/- Per Crate
>
> **At Your Service!**
> **KING'S BREWERY**
>
> Post: Syresham, Brackley.   Phone: Syresham No. 2.   Grams: King, Syresham.
>
> OUR TRAVELLERS COVER A VERY WIDE AREA AND ARE ONLY TOO PLEASED TO ACCEPT YOUR ORDERS.

King's Head, *Abbey Road.*

The NBC property insurance of the late 1950s describes the brew house at this pub as being intact, standing next to the larder. The pub, which dates back to 1630, was part of the Blencowe estate sold in 1925.

Linnell, Sarah, *Bell Lane.*

In 1847 Sarah Linnell (b.1796 Buckingham) is listed as a maltster and beer retailer at the bottom of Bell Lane. By the mid-1850s she is listed as a brewer. In 1861, her son William (b.1821) was also listed as a maltster and brewer. He traded until as late as 1898. In 1877 Sarah is shown as the maltster.

The site where the Linnell's had operated from became known as "The Maltings", but was demolished in 1924 for the construction of a property known as "The Gate House". However, despite the location, the actual Bell Inn was supplied by Stuchberry of Buckingham before being sold to Hopcrafts in 1853. In 1841, the Compasses at nearby Silverstone was owned by a victualler called William Linnell (see also Northampton) until 1869, when it was run by Richard Linnell.

THORNBY

Emerton, John (F5068).

In 1831 William Emerton is listed as a malt dealer in "Thurnby", and in 1849, Elizabeth Emerton is shown as a beer retailer and maltster. However, in 1854 she is shown as a brewer, whilst John Emerton is shown as a maltster. By 1866, the brewing business had passed to her son John who continued to brew and malt until at least 1898. In 1903 Frederick William Emerton is recorded only as a maltster in Thornby.

However, it seems that the family did not have any connection with the two main pubs of the village, the Red Lion and the George and Dragon. In 1884 John Emerton is described as a tenant of the Thornby Hall Estate in concern with property including Thornhill Close, but there is no clear indication of his own tenancy.

THRAPSTON

Allen & Burnett (F5078).

Although Friedrich's Gazetteer lists this for 1887, it seems to have been a depot, with Alexander Drage the agent. Certainly, Allen & Burnett's predecessors had an agency in the town as early as 1869. Photographs taken in 1903 of the White Hart in the High Street show an NBC stores in the next door buildings. At this date the depot was run by Fred Tarry.

TITCHMARSH **Rippin, Thomas.**

In 1862, Thomas Rippin is listed as a maltster and by 1866 had also become a baker, and in 1870 he seems to have added brewing. He is also listed four years later. In 1854 William Rippin, presumably his father, had been shown as a farmer and maltster. The 1851 census states that the village had a baker who was also a beer retailer, and a separate maltster is listed.

In 1884 Frederick Morris was a baker at the Rose & Crown (now Crown Cottage, Crown Street), but it is not known if he had taken over the earlier business. However, the Rose and Crown was included in the 1940 Kelly's listing (see Introduction).

There may be a connection with John Rippin of Geddington, who was a baker and owner of the Angel in that village from 1849 to around 1875.

TOWCESTER **May, John,** *The Crown, High Street.*

Listed as a publican brewer in the Kelly's Directory for 1877. The pub was owned by Walker and Soames in 1904.

Mayo, Mrs Harriet, *Bull's Head, Park Street.*

Listed as a publican brewer in the Kelly's Directory for 1877. George Mayo kept the pub in 1866. The pub was a Walker and Soames house in 1904.

Meads, Edward, *Plough, High Street.*

Listed as a publican brewer in the Kelly's Directory for 1877 - which he had kept from at least 1866. The pub was later a Phipps house and is still trading in the Market Square.

Phipps & Co (F5161), *High Street.*

The story begins in 1771 when James Phipps, a Bugbrooke farmer, married Elizabeth Pickering. A year later they had a son who they called Pickering (thus creating a first name that occurs several times in the family history). They remained at Bugbrooke until 1810, when they took a farm at Handley, Towcester.

In 1782, whilst still a boy of 10, Pickering was sent to work for his uncle at the White Horse Inn at Towcester. His father James married three times, so it is possible that Elizabeth had died causing Pickering to be sent to live with relatives.

There appear to have been two inns with the name of the White Horse. The 'New White Horse' was at 163/5 Watling Street. This had originally been the George built in 1708, but after a fire in 1749 it was rebuilt and renamed, and from 1796 it was occupied by the White family. The "New" closed in 1840 and seems to have become used by the Vernon family, wine and spirit merchants, before later being used as council offices. Its sale in January 1840 mentions a brew house in addition to the extensive stabling and accommodation. Interested parties should apply to William Higgins, corn merchant at Northampton or Charles Higgins at the Swan, Bedford, suggesting a link with Higgins brewery (F228) at the latter town.

In 1777, John Smith, presumably the uncle, is listed as a victualler at the Red Lion, No 138 Watling Street. Hence, when he and Pickering Phipps are shown as being at the 'Old White Horse Inn' in 1795, located opposite the Saracen's Head, one can only assume that the location of the two pubs and the reference to a maltings in an adjacent yard suggests that they were literally trading side by side. It is also possible that it was the same building which had changed names at some point.

The Saracen's Head had its own brew house in 1742, but it is not known when brewing ceased. In 1827, it was being kept by William Inns a friend of Pickering Phipps.

TOWCESTER, May 9, 1801.

P. PHIPPS, Wine and Brandy Merchant, returns his sincere Thanks to his Friends and the Public for the numerous Favours received, and begs Leave to acquaint them that he has on Sale a constant Supply of PORTER of the best Quality; and has likewise entered into the *Brewery Business*, and will be able to supply his Friends with good ALE, in any Quantity, on the most reasonable Terms.

TOWCESTER (continued)

Upon his uncle's death Pickering inherited £10 and the pub. In addition to running the inn he started a malting in the adjacent Red Lion yard. An indenture shows him buying property in Ambrose Yard near Branson's Lane and map shows that he owned half of the land that is now the recreation ground at the rear of Willis Way (Towcester p189). He also started a wine and spirit business and in May 1801 set up a small brew house (SP 693 486).

The brewery was very small and unable to cope with the increase in trade. Beer was delivered by a single horse and cart which was able to deliver as far as Northampton. In 1817 Phipps moved the centre of operations to Northampton when he leased a brewery from J.C.Barratt. (See entry under Northampton for history of the main company), although there is a suggestion that he had a brewery there from 1805/6. Pickering Phipps the first died in 1830 and was buried in Towcester church yard in a family tomb near the south door of the church.

The main concern in Northampton continued in the hands of two of his sons, Richard and Thomas, whilst the business continued trading at Towcester as brewers, wine and spirit merchants, maltsters and hop factors. William Ebenezer Vernon was the manager at the High Street premises, but it is possible that they were no longer brewing at the old site.

In 1840 and 1847 Thomas Phipps (b.1801) is shown as a maltster at the Wagon & Horses, Bugbrooke, whilst Phipps, Thomas and Richard were still listed as brewers, corn merchants in Towcester.

By 1861 the Red Lion was known as Victoria House and had become a private residence. The Victoria House Hotel now occupies the site. The adjacent site became a fishmongers and finally a car salesroom. The inn sign from the Phipps' White Horse, which is thought to have closed sometime between 1830 and 1840 was made into a table which was still owned by the Jenkinson branch of the family in the 1890s.

In 1860 Pickering Phipps, the second, and his cousin Richard were running the Northampton based concern, and purchased the Shephard's Towcester brewery, presumably to meet local demand. In 1870 John Charley Harvey is listed as a brewer in Towcester but he was probably employed at Phipps' brewery. Around this time Pickering's brother Edward was in charge of the brewery and lived in Brewery House (64 Watling Street), although W.E.Vernon was still manager. In 1874 Pickering and Richard Phipps built a new 32 quarter brewery on the Sheppard site, the original brewery presumably becoming the bottling store. They were also adding a new 40 quarter brewery to the Northampton plant.

In November 1879, they added a new 20 quarter plant to Towcester, the designs of Davison Son & Mackenzie. The new brewery employed about 70 men and could produce about 150 barrels per day. In 1885 the Brewers' Journal for June carried a list of tenders for rebuilding kilns and altering the maltings to the designs of H.Stopes & Co. By 1877, Phipps were the sole maltsters in the town from the four which had been registered in 1830.

In 1900, new boilers were installed at the brewery, the size of which can be judged from the fact that there were at least 18 fermenting vessels. Unfortunately a serious fire on 8th December, 1901, gutted the Towcester Brewery causing damage estimated at £18,000. The annual shareholders meeting was told that these figures were alarmist and that actual costs of repairing the damage were nearer £12,000 and that the insurance covered all but a couple of thousand pounds. The final cost was £10,593.

However, Phipps in 1903 began to rebuild and expand their Northampton plant and in 1905 the Brewers' Journal for April stated that the Towcester brewery had been closed. The brewing equipment from the gutted Towcester brewery was transferred to Northampton. A Mr Jepson, possibly the Phipps' shareholder who is mentioned at the infamous EGM of 1903, was looking to buy the site for £5,000, but the Board turned the offer down.

The majority of the obsolete Towcester brewery was sold off in 1919, but there were continuing problems with the mortgage on the property. Messrs Montgomery, Weston and Thomas who had bought the property went bankrupt in 1924 and the site ended up back with Phipps in 1928. They managed to remove the tenants in 1934 and the site was sold to Lord Hesketh in 1935. The brewery kept a couple of buildings to act as storerooms, but these too were sold off in 1938, when the Towcester Mill and Trading Company put in a bid for them.

The Old Brewery House, previously two thatched cottages with parts dating back to the 16th century, is still standing at 64 East Watling Street, next to Malthouse Court.

TOWCESTER (continued)

Sheppard and King, *High Street/62 Watling Street.*

In 1824 William Sheppard was a cooper in High Street, although the name Sheppard occurs in various trades in the town eg butchers and blacksmiths. In 1854 the partnership of King and Sheppard was trading as brewers of ale and porter, wine and spirit merchants, timber merchants, and coal and slate merchants. They operated from property on the east side of Towcester High Street and from a site leased at the Northampton Corn Exchange.

In 1859 the business was being run by Job Goodman Sheppard (b.1820) who, in the Northampton Herald on 9th April, thanked the public for their increased patronage since the retirement of his partner. However, in the December of that year he was made bankrupt. In 1861, Thomas King (b.1805) is recorded as living at 209a Watling Street.

Phipps bought the brewery and the site later became the location of their new brewery (SP 695 484).

Walker and Soames, *High Street/97 Watling Street.*

The business of Montgomery & Harris had been trading from 1869 as brewers at Buckby Wharf (see entry on Long Buckby). In the mid-1870s Francis Montgomery of Heathencote, a village about one mile south of Towcester, started a mineral water business on Watling Street. Kelly's Directory of 1877 lists him as a soda and mineral water manufacturer at the Watling Well/Sun pub.

In the early 1890s, Francis Montgomery was also the landlord of the Peacock Inn opposite and is listed as mineral water manufacturer, ale and stout brewer and bottler. The site had been used for malting in the 18th century, but the pub was rebuilt around 1840, when owned by John Norris.

The business was taken over by Walker and Soames in the mid-1890s. In 1896 Walker and Soames built a warehouse and bottling area next door to the Peacock Inn. The initials "W & S 1896" are clearly visible on the wall of the property (SP 694 484). It is likely that the mineral water business was taken over by C.H.Naylor who used the same trade mark and in the 1920s was owned by a Mr Jones.

The mineral water was known locally as "Spruce" and was produced between 1870 and 1920. The Watling Well is still trading and retains its wall crane and first floor door to the store room at the rear of the pub. The Peacock has recently been renamed.

WANSFORD

Eayrs, George (F5352).

Both Friedrich and "A Century of British Brewers" show George Earys as brewing in 1892. However, his name was actually spelled Eayrs (mis-spelled as Eyres in another directory of 1892), and he had previously been a cooper, before adding small scale brewing by 1877.

The Haycock, one of the county's most famous pubs, did have a brew house in the courtyard. However, it was de-licensed in 1887 and became a farm before re-opening as an inn in 1928, suggesting that this was not the site used by Eayrs, nor does his name occur in connection with the other village pubs.

However, a WE Eayrs had a general supply stores in the village between 1896 and 1901. A John Vincent Eayrs ran the Cross Keys Inn at nearby Oundle from 1853 to 1913 and in 1898 a Kingston Wells was a cooper at Eayrs Yard, Bridge Street, Peterborough.

WAPPENHAM

Howes, John.

John Howes offered for sale a *"well established bakery lately gone into brewing"* (Northampton Mercury 3rd December, 1859). He had been listed as a baker and grocer in 1854 and is shown as such in 1861, suggesting that the venture into brewing had not proved successful. However, in the following year he is listed as a beer retailer.

WEEDON

Smith & Son, *Weedon Bec & Bowden.*

Smith being a not uncommon name, it is often difficult to track down which one is which. This is exacerbated both by the connections with brewing in Weedon and the use of the first name John.

One John Smith was Steward of the Manors of Weedon Bec, Everdon and Bledlow for Eton College. He lived on Road Weedon High Street in a house which had become the Horseshoe Inn by 1775, together with owning most of the surrounding land after 1777. For at least six generations, the eldest son of the family was called John; hence, his son was also called John and when he died in 1802, his son John then aged 11, inherited ownership of the Horseshoe (later a Ratliffe and Jeffrey property). However, his mother, as the widow, had a life interest in the property, and she continued to live there as the licensee, even after she re-married and became Ann Heesom.

In 1817 this last John sold a half-acre site fronting Bridge Street at Weedon to John Humphrey who built a malt house. In 1835, John Humphrey went bankrupt and John Elliott bought his malt house; however, in 1838 he sold it for £1,300 to a William Smith, who proceeded to build a brewery at Weedon (SP 632 598), having owned the nearby Wheatsheaf since 1820. In addition, he also owned pubs in Daventry and Roade, and was supplying the canteen of the nearby garrison.

William Smith (b.1778) was the son of John Smith of Oundle (see entry) and had previously set up the Little Bowden Brewery (see entry). William installed Richard Bull (b.1805 Market Harborough, but who had lived in Burton on Trent and Birmingham) as the manager of the Weedon brewery. In May 1840, the Wheatsheaf on Weedon Turnpike was for sale, with particulars available from Messrs Smith & Son, Weedon and Bowden Breweries, Northamptonshire. At this time William Smith & Son are listed as maltsters, brewer and wine and spirit merchant Weedon Road.

However, in October of 1840 a notice from Messrs Smith & Son thanked customers for the patronage they had experienced *"since the erection of their brewery at Weedon"* and to inform friends and public that they were relinquishing the concern in favour of Mr W.M.Smith *"who having hitherto conducted the manufacturing department"* they were confident he would give satisfaction. On commencing business on his own account he mentioned his production of genuine ale and porter and stocks of superior foreign and British spirits.

William Smith, then living at Wadsley House, Ecclesfield, Yorkshire, wrote a Will in 1844, in which leaves to his wife Milicent the following:- *"Brewery in occupation of Adolphus Blumenthal; George (previously Robert Stephenson), Roade, tenant Mary Parish; Wheatsheaf, Weedon Bec, tenant Thomas Barrett; Quart Pot, Sheaf St, Daventry, tenant Thomas Brown."*

The executors of the Will were his son John and son-in-law George Wartnaby, the latter being a member of the legal family of Market Harborough. The brewery was sold for £2,100 to John Short a grazier of Weedon Bec and originally from Whitchurch, Buckinghamshire. On 1st September, 1845, Short and Richard Bull set up a partnership. The partnership deeds mention that Bull was living in the house next to the brewery and owned the stock in trade and utensils. However, in 1847 Short was then sued in Chancery for the purchase price of the brewery which should have been paid by October 1845.

The brewery was equipped with *"....a steam engine, brewing plant and dwelling house occupied by R. Bull"*.

Despite the legal proceedings, Bull and Short are still listed for 1847 and 1849, but in 1851 Bull and Short's Brewery again was up for sale, described as *"complete brewery with plant, steam engine, and every necessary apparatus for carrying out the brewing trade...."*. The brewery was described as a short distance from the LNWR station and the Grand Junction canal. The sale also included the Wheatsheaf.

In 1852 John Short was made bankrupt and the pub, maltings and brew house were put up for sale yet again in March. The executors of William Smith seem to have regained ownership of the property, which remained occupied by Richard Bull, used as a wine and spirit business.

In July 1853 there was a further resale on the order of the trustees of the late William Smith which included: *"A substantial brick built and slated brewery with an excellent malt office and drying kiln, large yard .....in the occupation of Mr R Bull."* The sale also included the George Inn at Roade and details were available from John Smith, Bowden Brewery, Market Harborough.

In August 1853 the brewery was still for sale at the premises in the occupation of Richard Bull and described as:- *"An excellent and complete Brewing Plant and Steam Engine, recently fitted up by Messrs Pontifex and Co consisting of:-*

"20 barrel copper with brass tap and furnace Wort back, liquor back, hop back with cast iron perforated bottom, underback, three fermenting squares, all of 3 inch deal bolted together. Also an eight quarter mash tun (English Oak) with an improved mashing machine and perforated cast-iron bottom and two large deal coolers with fans. The whole admirably constructed, calculated, fixed and arranged for an eight-quarter brewing plant. Also one of Messrs Pontifex & Co's improved roller malt crushers, with hoppers complete, for grinding three quarters of malt per hour. A single-throw brass barrel and valve, hot and cold liquor pump; also an excellent two horse-power steam engine, with metallic packings boiler and force pump complete, in perfect order, by which the whole of the above apparatus and machinery is worked."

At this time brewing seems to have ceased at the site; hence the sale of the plant. Although in the Stevens and White Directories from 1889 to 1896, Richard Bull's son Alfred is shown as a brewer and commission agent at Upper Weedon, he was only acting as an agent and from a different address.

The Smith's brewery was largely demolished before 1900 when the site became the White House, an imposing residence for Edmund Crosse of Crosse & Blackwell. Later used for flats, the building was eventually demolished by Rogers Engineer Ltd, who now have an agricultural machinery depot on the site.

Smith, John, *Bull, Road Weedon.*

In 1833, John Smith's (see Queen's Head entry) second son, also called John, took over the Bull and is later listed at there as a brewer and farmer. Prior to this he had been a butcher and victualler at the Plume of Feathers, Lower Weedon.

The Bull seems to have been a separate pub brew house from those of the other Smiths. However, there seems to have been a slow decline in its trade reflected in the rent which he paid to Eton College, owners of the land. Nevertheless, John Smith was an important public figure, holding a succession of offices in Weedon, indeed the Manor Court met at the Bull. The lease on the Bull expired in 1861 and John moved to Upper Weedon to farm land which had been bought by his brother George. The site of the Bull is now Manor Farm.

Smith, William, *Queen's Head, Dodford.*

John Smith, a baker in Dodford, bought 2 acres of land for £140 in 1792, and by 1795 he had built the Queen's Head on the site (SP 614 602). It is not clear when brewing commenced on the site, but when he died in 1823 a detailed inventory included a brew house and malting.

John's widow Mary took over the pub, but by 1831 their eldest son George was occupying the premises. The second son, John, went on to run the Bull at Road Weedon (see entry). However, it seems to have been this John's son, William, who remained as the brewer at the Queen's Head, since he is listed as a brewer and mineral water manufacturer in 1841.

George Smith was the tenant of the Queen's Head until his death in 1851, when his brother and executor John leased the property from the widow, Maria, with William becoming the landlord. John eventually purchased the property in 1862. William, aged 41, continued to be listed as the brewer.

An advert in 1864 for "*an active married man, used to brewery work*" puts the location as the Hilltop Brewery. William is still listed as a brewer in 1869 with his wife Elisabeth running the pub. It seems to have remained a small concern in that William only employed two staff at the time of the 1871 census.

William it seems died around 1872, since in 1873, the Dodford Brewery, as it had become known was owned by Elisabeth. It seems that William had no male heir to take-over the brewery. In 1873, William York, the brewery manager, placed an advertisement for a maltster "*who will make himself generally useful*".

In 1876 William Farmborough (F5450 - possibly Farnborough) is shown as a brewer at the Queen's Head and is also listed in Kelly as brewing in 1877.

However, by 1881 the Dodford brewery was occupied by Herbert R.McMullen from New Cross, Kent. In addition to his wife and two young children he also had a boarder, a Thomas Ansell from Middlesex who was an 18 year old apprentice brewer. Mrs Elisabeth Smith was a private resident at Bay Cottage.

The Brewers' Journal for April 1882 mentions the sale by auction on the 18th of the entire contents of the Dodford Brewery, all modern appliances of a 5 quarter plant, including a 3 hp steam engine. The location is given as being one mile from Weedon station.

Kelly's Directory of 1885 does not list any brewers in Weedon and the Queen's Head was being kept by Samuel Waters, and in 1888 the pub was owned by Mannings of Northampton.

The pub, now a private house called appropriately "The Old Queen's Head", stands on the A45 opposite the lane to Dodford village. In the mid-19th century, the other village pub in Dodford, the Swan, in the hands of a Mr Foster, was well known for its excellent home brew. This pub dated from the 16th century and straddled the brook to the NE of the church. When sold in 1877, the inventory included a 120 gallon copper with grate, 20 gallon copper, 2 deal coolers, mash tub and oak underback. However, by 1884 it had become a Phipps' house.

Watson, Joseph, *Globe Hotel.*

Joseph Watson had bought land from John Smith (III) in 1837 on which he built the Globe Hotel. In 1847 he also bought the Horseshoe from John, which stood next door, presumably to extend his property. Watson is shown as brewing there in 1849 and the 1850s. The hotel is still trading next to the main A5 crossroads.

WELDON

Chapman, Robert.

Pigot's Directory 1830 lists Robert Chapman as a maltster and it is possible that Chapman was also brewing. In 1767, he was involved with property owned by Joseph Stockburn innholder of Kettering (see also Battle entry). In 1820, a Henry Chapman of Little Weldon bought the Rose & Crown, Wilbarston from Hunts of Stamford.

Wade, Thomas, *The Weldon Brewery.*

Thomas Wade was a brewer and carpenter in 1861 to 1870 in Little Weldon. In October 1870, a notice for sale by auction on the premises, described as the Weldon Brewery, stated that he was relinquishing the brewing business. Despite the name, this seems to have been a very small concern, since Wade's account book shows him mainly involved in building work, including a new brew house at Pen Green Lodge, Corby.

However, his accounts are written in books which contain details of buying £4-500 hops in 1803-05 from Harveys in Kent. This suggests a somewhat larger business had been operating at the earlier time.

Webster, Daniel

Daniel Webster was a brewer and agent for Lord Winchilsea from 1841 to 1850. The Earl's surname was Finch-Hatton and the family estate included a brew house at which Thomas Wade later undertook some building work. However, by 1854 Webster is shown only as a farmer and grazier.

WELFORD

Peacock.

The Peacock dated back to 1736. In the early years of the 19th century, it was being kept by a James Brown, who died in 1828. His daughter Ann married a Thomas James Freeman of Husbands Bosworth, Leicestershire and ownership of the inn passed to William and Thomas Freeman.

The 1854 sale details mention a brew house, and the following year the inn, tenanted by a William Woodford, was sold to Thomas Revis of Olney, a farmer and maltster, suggesting that brewing may have still been taking place.

In June 1865, Revis sold the property for £360 to Phipps of Northampton. Although the brew house is mentioned, the purchase probably meant the end of its time as a home brew. Although now de-licensed, the building is still standing.

WELLINGBOROUGH

Cannon, Parker & Son Brewers Ltd, *The Cannon, Cannon Street.*

The Cannon Public House.

Photo: Authors' collection

The Brewery was founded in January 1993, by publicans Bernie and Andrew Parker in the old bottle store of the Cannon pub. The equipment came from Banks and Taylor. It supplies the pub and 10 free trade outlets. Brewing ceased during the summer of 1998, but with the intention of re-commencing in the autumn.

Charter, Charles (F5455), *33 Market Street.*

Charles Charter was a brewer, beer retailer and corn merchant for a period 1862-1887, although he was residing at 35 Knox Road. Harrod's Directory for 1876 lists him at No 43 Market Street, but this seems to be an error. In 1888, he was advertising special bottled stout at 3/- per dozen. The site is now occupied by shops.

Coombs, Thomas, *Chequers, 11 Cambridge Street.*

Friedrich's Gazetteer includes Coombs as a brewer in 1887. This was presumably at the Chequers, where he is shown as a victualler in 1874. The pub is now owned by Charles Wells of Bedford. A Coombs family operated a mineral water manufactory on Louisa Road until the 1950s.

Crafts, William.

In 1780, W Crafts advertised for sale a 300 gallon copper from his brew house at Wellingborough because a larger one was being fitted in its place. Bailey's Directory lists Crafts as a brewer in 1784 and he is described as such in the 1777 militia lists. The only other information available is that he was supplying John Smith of Oundle, before the latter set up his own business. However, Andrew Wilson (see below) bought the brewery of Henry Croft, possibly of the same family, and with whom John Smith had later property dealings.

Dulley, W & Sons (F5456), *Swan Brewery, 20 Sheep Street.*

In 1802, David Dulley (b.1773 Rickmansworth), officer of Excise, paid £750 to John Gibbs for the Golden Lion, tenant John Smith and 3 properties tenanted by Francis Odell, John Hopkins and William Neale, respectively. Around this time, he is thought to have built the brewery house. The Dulleys may have originated from the High Wycombe area, certainly they maintained family connections with the area. However, their property papers of 1745 for St John Street do mention a "Tobias Dally" in the Wellingborough area. David's father William died in 1811, aged 84, leaving legacies to several members of the family.

In 1811 David Dulley is recorded as a brewer in Sheep Street. He was also in business with James Whitworth, also described as a brewer, trading as Dulley and Whitworth, liquor and hop merchants. Around 1812, Dulley arranged a series of loans and it is likely that he used the family legacy money to expand the brewery and its estate. The brewery was located at the bottom of Sheep Street behind the Golden Lion Inn. The name Swan was taken from the nearby Swanspool.

In 1815, Dulley & Whitworth bought the Chequers, Grendon, tenant Thomas Chearney, for £260; however, four years later it seems to have been re-mortgaged for £280 to Robert Whitworth. They continued to trade until at least 1816, and David Dulley and James Whitworth were still involved jointly in assignment of property as late as 1835.

The statement from 1840

"STOUT" David Dulley from an 1893 drawing

David's son William (b.1797) was at the Swan Brewery c.1827. By 1830, he also acting as a wine and spirits merchant, whilst David Dulley senior is shown as operating the malting side of the business. William's brother David junior had become a chemist in Silver Street, maintaining a family connection with medicine.

In 1839 William bought his father's brewery, including the goodwill and equipment for £7,000. He also entered into an agreement to pay rent on the property, including the public houses for £360 pa payable quarterly.

A statement drawn up on 1st January 1840, valued the total property at £9,065. This included 5 pubs in Wellingborough, 7 in the surrounding villages and, perhaps somewhat surprisingly, the Lamb at Bedford. In 1847, the rent was reduced to £320 pa, but with an agreement to provide for his mother.

On 15th April, 1853, David Dulley, Rosehill Cottage, died and was buried in the little Baptist Chapel he had helped to build. His wife Mary, who died in 1855, and five of his children are interred beside him. The little chapel was replaced ten years later by a new church built, by William, on the junction of Great Park Street and Park Road.

The Dulley family built several buildings around Wellingborough, perhaps not surprising given their connection with the Wellingborough Brick & Tile Co. They can be spotted by the chequer board pattern of the two different colour bricks used. An example of a Dulley built property is the house beside the Golden Lion at No 20 Sheep Street. The bricks were brought in by barge from the Peterborough brickworks.

William Lucas of the Sun Brewery, Hitchin, recorded in his 1859 journals that he supplied malt to Dulley & Sons of Wellingborough. This seems somewhat strange given the town's strong malting industry, particularly since one firm was run by the Woolston family who were related to the Dulleys (but see later entry). However, Dulleys did have their own maltings to the right of the brewery entrance.

BREWERY, WELLINGBOROUGH.
"Notice is hereby given, that the business of a brewer and spirit merchant, heretofore carried on by William Dulley the elder, at Wellingborough in the county of Northamptonshire, under his own name solely, will on and after the first day of January 1865 be carried on and conducted by the undersigned William Dulley the elder, William Dulley the younger, and David Dulley the younger, under the name and firm of W M Dulley and Sons." Dated this 29th Day of December 1864.

In 1869, James Dulley (b.1842), 17 Sheep Street, was described as a brewer's assistant, but by 1876 he was living in Rose Cottage in front of the brewery, whilst shortly afterwards Joseph Dulley (b.1836) is shown at the brewery address. The first mentioned was William's son James Henry Dulley, brewing at Little Bowden in 1884 (see entry).

In 1891 the Sheep Street brewery was extensively modernised by Francis Dulley (possibly a relative from High Wycombe). The old brewery tuns were dismantled, polished and used as panelling in the offices, and a refrigeration plant was installed. Alongside the new brewing plant the firm also built a swimming pool at a cost of £1,530. The modernisation also led them to open a depot in Birmingham, since in 1892 they are listed at 9 Great Colemore Street (F344). They also had a depot at Nottingham and Dulley's beers were also available in Leicestershire as far north as Quorn.

WELLINGBOROUGH
(continued)

William Dulley junior died in 1873 and his father died in 1880, leaving David junior (b.1833) responsible for the brewery.

In the late 1850s, a pumping house was built next to Kilbourn's mill to pump water from the Red Well to Sheep Street. Dulleys bought the rights to the famous Redwell Spring for £2,000. In the days when Wellingborough almost became a spa town, King Charles I and Queen Henrietta had paid a visit, in 1628, to partake of the waters. Dulley's well-respected stout was named Redwell in honour of the water.

The Dulley's Swimming Pool - now the site of the new heritage centre

Photo: Authors' collection

In 1892 the Dulley Baths were opened for the use of brewery workers. The brewery itself was temperature controlled by a 15-ton Pontifex Ice Machine, with upwards of a mile of 5in cast-iron pipe filled with brine. The waste water from this machine was then used to warm the baths (Wellingborough Illustrated).

One curious arrangement is that the wort coppers were in the basement, from there the boiled wort was pumped up to the required height before gravity did the rest. Steven's Directory of 1893 lists David and Joseph Dulley living at 20 Oxford Street, but the latter died that year. Paul Edward Dulley (b.20th December, 1862), David's son, lived at 17 Sheep Street.

In 1895, the nearby Market Harborough brewery of Eady & Dulley was registered by James Henry Dulley, in partnership with Joseph Chamberlain Eady (see Little Bowden entry).

William Dulley & Sons Ltd was registered in 1898 with capital of £100,000 and three family members on the Board. The then head of the company was David Dulley JP who had recently been defeated in the local council elections after representing Wellingborough South since 1889. An active county councillor, Chairman of the Local Board and a staunch nonconformist, deacon of the Baptist chapel, he died in 1905, aged 71. His son Paul Edward Dulley, became the Chairman and MD.

WELLINGBOROUGH (continued)

In 1918 the firm offered to sell The Dulley Baths to the town for £2,000. The council considered the offer and decided that they would need to spend a further £1,500 to repair the facilities. Despite an effort by councillor George Cox, Dulley's former Head Brewer, to convince them otherwise, the council rejected the offer.

Henry Dulley (b.1887), possibly from the High Wycombe side of the family, was the Chairman at the time of his death in 1920. Henry's death brought the end of the company. Dulleys put a proposition to NBC in July 1920, but it was turned down by the latter as being too dear and so they looked to Praeds, their neighbours and rivals.

Although the Kettering Leader for 20th August, 1920, initially uses the term amalgamation, it goes on to make clear that Praeds had taken over Dulleys. Praed's paid £82,500 for the 54 licensed premises and were in discussion about an agreed price for any plant and machinery which they were prepared to take-over. Brewing ceased almost immediately. Praeds also bought the water rights and pumping station for £1,000.

The Brewers' Gazette for 9th September, 1920, in its account of the take-over, said that brewing liquor, ie water to the general public, had been drawn from the famous Redwell medicinal spring and mentioned the pumping house on Harrowden Road close to Kilborn's Mill. From here the liquor was pumped up to a reservoir on the higher ground on Harrowden Road and thence by gravity to the brewery. The Brewers' Journal for October gave an itemised list of the plant for sale.

Dulleys were liquidated on 21st December, 1920. The official view on the closure given to the press was *"owing to deaths and other changes in the family.....with a view to closing the trust"* (Kettering Leader 27th January, 1921).

In January 1921, Messrs Pendered & Son Ltd gave further details of the sale on the premises, of brewing and bottling machinery. Not only did this include: boilers, tanks, coppers, hop backs etc, but went so far as 60 oz Georgian silver and 6 fine old Chippendale chairs. This perhaps fits with a view in the town that Praeds "asset stripped" their neighbours.

Herbert Dulley, the MD, and other family members attended the sale, which gave some indication of the relative values. For example, the Hind Hotel was sold for £14,000 to Mr AE Burrows of the Northumberland Hotel, London. However, the brewery (SP 894 677) and brewery house, the latter occupied by Bernard Archer, were sold for only £6,000 to the Progressive Bus Co. Rose Cottage, occupied by Miss Dulley, was sold for £1,300 to Mr F.W.Marriott, but in turn she bought No 18 Sheep Street for £500.

However, the Jacobean cottages, survivors of the great fire of 1738, were withdrawn at £390. Unfortunately, the *"town had not been able to acquire this property for a museum; but the town, like other people, were getting short of money"* (Kettering Leader 28th January, 1921). The baths were sold to councillor George Cox who converted the site into the Castle Works.

The old brewery was damaged during the Second World War when it was blown up by a bomb in 1942. The premises were the headquarters of the local Home Guard, although it is more likely that the Luftwaffe were really interested in the nearby American bases.

A rendering of the swan motif could be seen on the clock-tower above the old offices. This motif is preserved in the town shopping centre, unfortunately, it is now obscured by a cafe. The air-raid also led to the clock ceasing to function, although it remained as something of a local landmark.

The brewery was demolished in 1974 for the building of the new shopping centre. However, the original baths are still standing awaiting conversion to a new heritage centre for the town. The local press had carried a report that Paines were interested in buying the site for use as a brewery, but nothing came of this. Hopefully, the centre will mark Wellingborough's history as a centre for brewing, in contradiction to the view taken in the 1920s.

Leyland Brewery, *Unit 78, Lawrence Leyland Industrial Estate, Irthlingborough Road.*

After moving site in October of 1992, early in 1996 the Nene Valley brewery relocated yet again to the address above. It also merged with the Nix Wincott brewery (formerly at the Three Fyshes, Turvey, Bedfordshire) to form the new concern, which continues to brew to the recipes of both of the original businesses.

They use a five-barrel plant, with a 35 barrel a week capacity. The two ranges of are both produced under the brands of the original separate breweries. They own one tied house and supply over 20 free trade outlets

WELLINGBOROUGH (continued)

Margetts, George, *Sheep Street.*

In 1815 George Margetts occupied property previously owned by the Wilsons (see entry below), including the brew house. He is shown at the brew house in 1820 and is listed as brewing in Sheep Street in 1823.

He operated at the Sheep Street brewery until March 1827 when he put the business up for sale on 4th April. Margett's lease on the property was until Michaelmas 1834. He did not succeed in selling the brewery at the first attempt and in desperation he put it up for sale that same June without a reserve price. It seems to have been bought by a James Sloan, although there is no record of him as a brewer. Eventually it was bought by John Woolston (see Praed entry).

The brewery was described as on a scale for brewing fifteen quarters of malt, with the two maltings of wetting fifty quarters of barley a week, with granaries over them capable of containing from 1,500 to 2,000 quarters of corn, and stabling for eight horses.

A George Margetts of Billericay, Essex, still owned land in Wellingborough in 1831, and was the owner of the White Hart at Weedon Bec. In 1836, he seems to have moved to Hemingford Grey, St Ives. The Margetts family seem to have had links with Huntingdon and may have had connections with Henry Margetts who was brewing at Deddington, Oxon in 1854 (see also Peterborough).

Pettit, Peter, *Angel Lane, Silver Street.*

In 1830, Pettit is shown as a builder in Silver Street, but the Poll Book for the following year describes him as a brewer. At this time the Angel was kept by Jacob Anthony, but there is no information linking the two. In 1874, a John Pettit was a baker and beer house-keeper at 7 Herriotts Lane.

Praed, Campbell and Company (F5457), *30 Sheep Street.*

John Woolston, seems to have started out as a grocer in 1811 and by 1823 was a butcher on Silver Street. However, by 1830, William Woolston is shown at the butchers and a John Woolston is a maltster and corn factor in Hind Lane. It is possible that William and John were the sons of the earlier John. Certainly, the brewing side of the family was involved with the butchers shop property in later years.

Around 1827, a John Woolston (b.1810) took over the Margett's business, certainly it was in his possession in 1846. He was the father of Alderman Charles Joseph Keep Woolston, who seems to have taken control of the business at some stage, and who married William Dulley's daughter Mary.

Although John Woolston is shown at Market Street in 1847, thereafter his main address is shown as Sheep Street and it was on this site that a new brewery was built in 1878. In the 1851 census his address is at West End, Wellingborough and also owning the Swan Inn and land at Roade. He established a small tied estate, for example supplying William Johnson at the Wooden Walls of England Collingtree in 1853 and the Red Lion, Irchester from at least 1847.

In 1860 the estate included the Station Hotel, Wellingborough, and in 1864 he is also listed at Midland Road which is where the pub was located. The maltings at the side of the pub were rebuilt in 1901 and 1924 when trading as Messrs Woolston & Bull; perhaps, surprisingly, mainly supplying brewers elsewhere. The maltings closed in the mid-1970s and became a dried pea factory for Whitworths before being demolished in 1984, with the site finally cleared in 1997.

John Woolston died in 1878 and the family sold the brewery to the Praeds. The links between the families probably originated in financial dealings involving licensed houses. For example, in 1876 the transfer of property in Wellingborough by Francis Alfrey and William George Lovell, brewers of Newport Pagnell mentions both a William Woolston and Arthur Campbell Bulkley Praed.

Arthur Praed had increased his personal fortune by sheep farming in Australia, from where he had recently returned. The other partners were Charles Tyringham Praed MP and Herbert Bulkley Praed.

The new owners set about building up the small brewery which was hemmed into a tightly populated area of the lower town centre. New pubs were added to the tied estate such as the Green Dragon bought in 1881. Papers from 1882 show that they owned the Old Swan (site now Lloyds Bank) in Silver Street, Wellingborough. By 1896 they are also shown as having a wine and spirits outlet in Daventry. Their trademark was a unicorn's head surmounting a coronet.

WELLINGBOROUGH
(continued)

The Brewers' Journal of July 1883 carried a report that Praed's Brewery had been remodelled, with the architect E.Sharman of Wellingborough, and the engineers Oxleys of Frome. Brewing had continued during the rebuilding, although once or twice they had to mash in the open air. The work included the erection of a new 100 foot chimney shaft, the addition of spacious malt and hop stores and extension of the cask washing and storing rooms. New hot liquor backs, mash tuns and underbacks made the mash room one of the finest in England, the whole brewing operation being confined to two floors and all within site of the brewer's office.

In 1884, Arthur Praed, and Samuel Praed, were living at Chester House, Irchester, but with a London address of 16 Talbot Square, Paddington. Arthur was also a director of Stretton's Manchester Brewery of Derby (F1433 see NBC entry) when it became a limited company in 1890.

The Wellingborough business was trading well, with profits as follows:-

1894: £8,869   1895: £10,561   1896: £12,904

Praed's Wellingborough concern was incorporated on 11th November, 1896, to acquire the business at a purchase price of £185,000. The directors of the business were Arthur Praed, Herbert B.Praed, W.K.D'Arcy and Herbert Sartoris. William Knox D'Arcy, who had become a partner in 1889, was the founder of BP and had also made his fortune in Australia. The ordinary shares were held as follows:-

| Arthur Campbell Bulkley Praed | 2,499 | Herbert Bulkley Praed | 2,498 |
| William Knox D'Arcy | 2,498 | Mackworth Bulkley Praed | 2,498 |

Arthur having managed the business for some 18 years was to be retained as the Managing Director for a further 5 years. The business owned the freehold of some 80 premises - 46 full licence, 18 beer houses and 16 off-licences - and supplied 7 leasehold. They had their offices at 30 Moorgate Street, London.

Arthur's interests spread far afield in that he was one of the founding directors of the San Francisco Breweries Ltd. This was one of a great wave of UK registered holding companies floated in the 1880s and 1890s to acquire breweries across the USA from their, usually German-American, owners and which turned out almost uniformly disastrous and none of which survived Prohibition. The records held at Lloyds bank also make reference to Anglo-Vienna Beer promotion papers of 1888-90. In 1893 Arthur Praed purchased a patent for brewing with raw maize from an A.W.Billings of Brooklyn and formed a company to exploit this variation.

WELLINGBOROUGH
(continued)

Preserved in the bar of Banks' brewery reception centre at Wolverhampton is the brass plate off the foundation stone of the North Worcestershire Breweries Ltd of Stourbridge. This was laid on August 26th 1897 by the Chairman H.B.Praed esq. Family connections with the Grand Junction Canal were maintained in that Winthrop Mackworth Praed was elected Chairman in April 1888 and served as such until his death in February 1890.

Profits continued to rise, the 2nd AGM on 21 December reported them as £13,091 and further properties were bought. The purchases also included an attempt to buy into the lucrative London trade such as the Talbot, Tottenham, and the Kilmarnock, Lower Tooting; however, these consistently showed a loss and the London properties were disposed of in 1901. The general speculation of the "Brewers War" had collapsed partly as a result of Viscount Peel's Royal Commission on the industry in 1899.

Arthur Praed died very suddenly on 4th November, 1901, having attended a Board meeting in the morning. His widow Rosa Caroline Mackworth Praed (1851-1935) had become a prolific author with some thirty titles, mostly romance, to her credit. As a result of Arthur's death, Herbert B.Praed and Bulkley Campbell Praed became joint Managing Directors. In January 1911 B.C.Praed resigned from the Board and was replaced by John H.Smith of the Oundle brewery family. The following year B.C. became the Rt Hon The Earl of Cork & Orrery.

The brewing room, Campbell Praed's Brewery, 1911

Photo: BHS Photographic Archive

WELLINGBOROUGH
(continued)

Inside Campbell Praed's Brewery, 1911

Photo: BHS Photographic Archive

The bottle washing plant, Campbell Praed's Brewery, 1911

Photo: BHS Photographic Archive

The boiler room, Campbell Praed's Brewery, 1911

Photo: BHS Photographic Archive

WELLINGBOROUGH
(continued)

From the brewing room stairs, Campbell Praed's Brewery, 1911

Photo: BHS Photographic Archive

The spirit store, Campbell Praed's Brewery, 1911

Photo: BHS Photographic Archive

Mash tun No.1 Campbell Praed's Brewery, 1911

Photo: BHS Photographic Archive

WELLINGBOROUGH
(continued)

Inside Campbell Praed's Brewery in 1911

Photo: BHS Photographic Archive

The winch and the racking room, Campbell Praed's Brewery, 1911

Photo: BHS Photographic Archive

WELLINGBOROUGH
(continued)

Fermenting vats Campbell Praed's Brewery, 1911

Photo: BHS Photographic Archive

Campbell Praed's Brewery, 1911

Photo: BHS Photographic Archive

WELLINGBOROUGH (continued)

However, the Report for 18th December, 1914, was qualified by the auditor Cecil Nixon, who reported a serious deficiency of cash of some £2,703 10s 5d. This was as a result of the late secretary Mr Briggs, *"looked upon as a man quite beyond reproach"*, having manipulated the books for several years. Nevertheless, the business was also investing in new equipment such as a chilling plant from Messr Adlam of Bristol.

Unfortunately, the impact of war on trade was apparent in that December sales were 311 barrels down on the same month in 1913. The six months to March 1915 saw a fall of 1,000 barrels from 6,126 to 5,070, compared with the same period in the previous year. The government in an attempt to restrict trade had imposed dramatic increases in beer duty. In 1914, duty was 7s 9d per barrel, but by 1918 it was 50s per barrel. In addition, in early 1917 the Output of Beer (Restriction) Act limited each brewery to a quota output, effectively little more than a half their pre-war production.

In March 1916, Edwin Basil Ludlow replaced the late J.H.Smith, and also bought shares in the business. It is noticeable that the minutes of the directors meetings show a marked turn towards a financial analysis of the business with this change in personnel.

In 1917, Knox D'Arcy died and the new director was a Lt Cecil J.S.Holden, Writtle Park, Chelmsford. A new brewer, the recently demobbed Mr Sprake was appointed. His previous experience had been at Ockendens of Crawley. The local manager was Richard John Gregson. The end of the war also brought an upturn in trade, 442 barrels in June 1918 to 1403 barrels in July 1919.

In 1920 Praeds bought out their neighbours Dulleys. The take-over brought 36 licensed premises and 17 off-licenses valued in total at £84,950. This cost some £82,950 which was financed by the sale of their investments in war bonds and stock, together with a 10 year mortgage of £50,000 on the properties. The 2 Northampton pubs it seems were leased to the Abington Brewery Co.

The closure of Dulleys brought an immediate benefit in terms of increased sales:-

1919		1920
October	1,297	2,356 barrels
November	1,036	2,085

Sadly, Sir Herbert Praed, the Chairman for 20 years, did not see the benefits of the new business, dying on 21 October. His place on the Board was taken by Victor Stanley Wright, whilst Gen H.A.Jones, Arthur Praed's nephew, became the new Chairman.

The new sales allowed a dividend of 5% to be declared for the year. Some property management took place, with the sale of the Dolphin at Moulton, the Barley Mow at Watford and an off-licence in Rushden. The following year, the purchase of Dulleys was described as a satisfactory investment, but the generally poor state of trade meant that the interim dividend was passed. June sales figures comparison:-

1920		1921
Praeds	1,826	1,648
Dulleys	839	666

A further problem arose in September when an analysis of water from Dulley's well near the Dog & Duck revealed a slight organic impurity which it was hoped would "probably disappear in a short time". It was decided to carry out another analysis in 3 months, but despite its reputation, water supply continued to be a problem for the brewery for many years.

In October, Praeds were forced to reduce the price of their mineral waters because of competition. They also further rationalised their estate and deliveries by selling the Horse & Groom, Rearsby and King William IV, Holwell for £2,500 to W.E.Moore of Leicester. This allowed them to reduce their fleet of lorries from 6 to 5 in November, resulting in a driver being laid off as well as 2 men from the brewery department. Nevertheless, they looked to the future by investing £550 in a new hop back from Adlams of Bristol. Despite the water problems, Praeds decided to brew a special stout at 165/- per barrel emphasising *"we now brew the famous Dulleys Stout from the Redwell waters"*.

Nevertheless, they were still able to declare a dividend of 5%. February 1922 brought a decision that sales of Guinness and Bass should be limited as far as possible, particularly in those places where there was no competition. If competition was particularly severe, reference had to be made to the directors. The new cost-consciousness even applied to the Brewer, in that his duties should be more clearly defined and a list of them posted in the office. This included weekly returns on the cost of production, fuel etc.

In June 1922, Praeds were writing to Phipps to ask about rumours that they were offering discount to tenants and the free trade. They thanked them for their response and went on to *"ask if the understanding which was arrived at during the war, regarding the pooling of information as to beer etc. is still operating"*.

October saw the purchase, for £400, of Mr C.Cobley's mineral water business. However, November brought problems with the malt, which Mr Sprake the brewer was asked to investigate and £20,000 was written off from the Goodwill Account. Perhaps linked to this, Mr Sprake's request for a bonus was turned down because of the decline in sales and hence output, it was also noted that in the present state of the industry it would not be difficult to replace him. The following year it was decided to investigate using the Boby malt mill which they had bought from Dulleys.

In April 1923, the sales problems and competition led to prices being lowered by £1 4s per barrel and 1/- per dozen pint bottles.

However, the worst seemed to be over and in March 1924, Praeds ordered 50 new casks from Dunbar's cooperage, Millwall, and 3 months later placed an order for 100 gross dozen bottles from United Glass. In August they received compensation for the closure of the Crispin Arms in Wellingborough and the Prince of Wales at Old. In September the estate of Battles (see entry) was for sale by auction at Kettering and Praed's bought 3 pubs. This probably allowed further rationalisation of the estate as follows:-

City Arms, Peterborough	Smiths, Oundle
King's Head, Whittlesey	Smiths, Oundle
George, Shefford	Wells, Bedford

In 1925 Bulkley Campbell Mackworth Lodge Praed was living at Middlewent, Kettering and maintaining the family political interests as a county Alderman. However, he died not many years afterwards.

July 1928 saw alterations to the brewery and a new bottling store. In August John Sprake junior who had received 12 months training as an assistant brewer, presumably from his father, was appointed to a full-time position on a salary of £130 pa. However, he left in October 1929 to take a position with John Joules at Stone, despite his short time with them the Board wished him success. He was to go on to become the Head Brewer for Youngs in the 1960s. A C.R.Sprake was also at Chesham & Brackley in 1948.

The year 1929 saw the rejection of the proposed take-over of Eady & Dulley (see entry), probably because the 10 year mortgage on the Dulley properties would be due soon. However, despite all the trading problems, Praeds had been able to accumulate £55,000 in stocks and securities which could be sold to pay off the mortgage. This conservative approach to investment was to remain a part of the Board's philosophy.

April 1929 brought a move by Whitbread to persuade them to change the name of their Brown Ale, since they proposed to register "Double Brown". It seems that negotiations with Whitbread would allow Praeds to retain their own brand within a 40 mile radius, but this was unacceptable and in February 1930 they were looking to engage counsel to fight the case. In July, they sold investments to realise £47,495 to remove the Dulley mortgage and also bought the Hind Hotel for £16,000. Times were improving and Mr Sprake's salary was increased from £500 to £700 per annum. Sales were rising and a bonus of 1½% was declared in addition to the 6% dividend. However, they had lost the battle with Whitbreads and in February 1931, they informed them that they had stopped using the term "Double Brown" and were now selling "Praed's Prize Brown". Whitbread's concern may have been linked to the similarity of trade marks (see below for the Praed's advertisement as a later tongue-in-cheek response).

The rise in beer duty in the Budget led to a trade depression which caused the cancellation of the 1932 employee annual outing. On 20th May, 1932, the brewer Mr Sprake was leaving and the position was offered to Frank Holgate Smith of Ushers at a much reduced salary of £350, but with the proviso that he would get a £50 increase should beer duty be lowered. The under-brewer was Mr Murray Hutton. In November, Praeds resigned from the Institute of Brewers. Nevertheless, they managed a profit of £15,184 and declared a 6% dividend.

WELLINGBOROUGH
(continued)

Post-war advertisement taking note of the similarity with the Whitbread trade mark

Authors' collection

A shortage of bottled beer in 1932 was solved when the storekeeper admitted manipulating stocks to cover the deficit. He was dismissed and 6 other workmen who admitted receiving bottles were reprimanded and had their wages docked by 3s for six months as well as losing their beer allowance for the same period.

On 28th April, 1933, following the reductions in duty, new prices were announced:-

XXX 5°	86/- per barrel	IPA 6°	106/- per barrel
Stout 6°	106/- per barrel	Best 8°	147/- per barrel

Mr Holgate Smith got his £50, although one doubts he played a major role in persuading the Chancellor! That year, Praeds bought Eldred, Everett & Wills, of Kettering.

In 1935, General Jones had to reduce his role as Chairman of Praeds because of his commitments as a Director of Imperial Tobacco. The Ludlows still seemed to be the driving force at Wellingborough and the close links with Oundle were strengthened with the purchase of 12,000 shares in Smiths. Praeds had survived the worst of the depression and the year end output was the highest since 1924. The following year saw more purchases:-

Nelson Inn, Little Braunston £900

Elwes Arms, Great Billing	£2,750
Cat & Custard Pot, Shelton	£1,750

Throughout the thirties they had a rolling programme of putting in new fermenting vessels at the brewery. They were also bottling and selling Worthington.

The war period brought increased sales, with output hitting 2,000 barrels a month, but at a reduced gravity. For example, in 1941 the Government had requested brewers to reduce their average gravities by 5%. In 1944, sales had risen to 3,000 barrels per month, yet they were able to reduce the working week from 48 to 47 hours per week. The end of the war saw an approach to take-over Hopcraft and Norris (see Brackley) which was turned down. Post war shortages lead to Praed's advertisements which stated - *"BEER - when supplies are short don't ask for more than your share!"*

The changes at the top brought in David John Arthur Jones, son of the Chairman, as a Director in 1946. The following February, D.J.A.Jones was confirmed as the MD with a salary of £1,000.

Praeds continued to invest, with 2 new fermenting vessels in 1948 and in November 1948 a new mash tun from Mortons for £3,745, followed by a hop back for £4,491 in 1952/53. In 1948, the 52nd Annual Report showed a profit of £60,550 for the financial year ending on the previous 30th September.

David Jones' experience as a Colonel resulted in a new management approach, which in June 1948 saw a 5 Year Plan being presented to the Board. The Board agreed to introduce a new bottled brown ale at 10½d and a bottled sweet stout - Redwell - with a gravity of 1034°OG. In August, they increased the gravity of their beers.

In August 1949 the overall property of the business was revalued at £725,120, giving a surplus of £420,687, on the 1947 valuation, which was transferred to a revaluation reserve. On 29th September, 1949, the capital of the company was increased to £300,000 by the creation of 100,000 ordinary shares and 100,000 5% cumulative preference shares. This was achieved by capitalising the reserves and issuing them as a bonus to the ordinary shareholders. The ordinary shares were quoted on the stock exchange and were trading at 27s. Praeds also formed a subsidiary company the Hind Hotel (Wellingborough) Ltd to own the hotel which had been in their possession since 1930.

The Budget of 6th April, 1948, which had repealed the tax on Bonus Issue Shares, had obviously influenced the share re-organisation. The EGM of 29 September, 1949, also showed the external influences on the decision to revalue the properties since the *"ultimate objective was to obtain the best compensation in the event of nationalisation"*. The valuation of the brewery side of the business was:-

105 freehold	£607,100
1 leasehold	£10,000
42 off-licences	£35,795
Brewery etc	£66,752
Total	£719,647

Robinson and Riddey Ltd, local wine and spirit merchants in Sheep Street, were bought in April 1950, followed by F.G.Thompson (Tobacconist) Ltd and R.C.Allen, bottler, Leicester in 1951. They also acquired F.E.Ball & Son (F5454), described as manufacturing wine merchants of the Vineries, Buckwell End, Wellingborough, which they did not close until 1951, despite having their own mineral water factory in Commercial Lane since the 1930s.

BHS Archive
Birmingham Central
Library

CAMPBELL PRAED & CO. LTD.

TELEGRAMS: PRAED'S WELLINGBOROUGH 3211.
TELEPHONE NO. 3211 (3 LINES)
ALL COMMUNICATIONS TO BE ADDRESSED TO THE COMPANY

THE BREWERY,
WELLINGBOROUGH.

24th. January, 1951.

This brought meetings with Phipps' management to discuss mineral water supplies. This may also have been linked to a D.Phipps buying shares in January 1951. It was debated whether to rename the mineral water in order to help sales to Phipps and the free trade. In addition to the R.C.Allen brands, Praeds also owned the name "Archer" bought pre-war (presumably from Bernard Archer, 62 Midland Road). The Northants Brewers Association had been discussing the possibility of a tie on mineral waters for several years.

On 11th May, 1951, it was decided that, as a result of the increase in beer prices agreed by the Bedford and Northants brewers, the gravity of the IPA could be increased by 1 degree and XXX mild by 2 degrees, with a reduction in priming of the latter. Mr Hartley junior became a pupil brewer. The post-war prosperity saw a brewery outing to Southend on Sea in June. In December, the Board wrote to Phillips of Stamford requesting that they be informed of any possible sale resulting from the owner's death.

Praed's Brown Ale became known as "Prize Winning Brown" after a success in the 1952 national brewer's exhibition. Pride was reduced in strength and price from 1/9d to 1/6d per bottle. In addition, IPA was reduced from 34° to 33°, XXX from 32° to 31°, and Redwell Stout from 37° to 36°. However, they also introduced Cromwell IPA at 1043°. That year they, like many other breweries, produced a special brew for the Coronation. It is recorded that the strength of the brew was 100°, presumably a misprint for 10°. and would be sold at 2s 6d per half pint bottle.

In July of the following year, Colonel Jones at a local meeting of the LVA, expressed his view that the increased sales of bottled beer would lead to the closure of pubs, a somewhat prescient statement.

1952 Praed Price List

Bottled Beers

Praed's Pride Strong Ale (Gold Top)	1/9d
Cromwell I P A (Silver Top)	1/-
Brown Ale (Green Top)	10½d
Redwell Stout (Brown Top)	10½d
Pale Ale (Yellow Top)	9½d

Draught Ales

Bitter	1/2d
Mild	1/1d

The previous take-overs represented strengthening of the non-brewing areas which were to lead to the demise of the business. On 24th April, 1953, David Jones wrote to Phipps mentioning a " possible form of tie-up between us over mineral waters. The whole idea is still in a very embryonic stage and I have not yet mentioned it officially to my fellow directors". He invited E.C.M.Palmer to lunch at Wellingborough on 1st May.

At the time, sugar was coming off rationing and a battle for the soft drinks market was anticipated. Watney, Combe & Reid were looking to bottle Coca Cola and Whitbread was setting up bottling of shandy. Phipps had no mineral water plant of their own and Praeds/R.C.Allen were already supplying them with some 38,000 dozens from their total output of 200,000. The intent was to tie their tenants and supply them from a possible new joint company. Various sites for a new plant were considered at Wellingborough, Corby or the old West Bridge Maltings (Mannings). In September, Praeds had an approach from the manufacturers of "Kitty Kola" to introduce it into their range in anticipation of the expected sales drive from Coca Cola and Pepsi. Praeds decided to stick with their own "Unicola".

Guy Ludlow, who had been a driving force in the brewery, was attending fewer meetings as a result of illness. In August 1953 Praeds sold 9,000 of their shares in Smiths to Guy, who may have been putting his affairs in order.

On 16th December, 1953, it was announced that Phipps had made an offer to acquire a minimum of 90% of the ordinary shares at a price of £4, excluding any dividend for the previous year end. However, they had been planning the bid for some time, possibly as a result of the earlier approach regarding mineral water manufacture. On 14 September, the firm of Mason & Sons chartered accountants had suggested the nom de plume "Carter Patterson" for the analysis behind the deal.

Praeds owned 107 licensed premises and 42 off-licences. Despite a wort receiver dating from 1909 and a Billings water tank from 1892, the plant and machinery at the brewery was relatively modern.

The Board members owned large numbers of shares, but after the capital re-organisation the owner of the largest number, some 45,000 shares, was an elderly widow Mrs K.A.Skipwith. Two of the original subscribers in the business had been called Skipwith.

However, there were problems foreseen with the irredeemable debenture stock from March 1897. It was suggested that there might be possible breaches of covenant, in particular with the proposed brewery closure and conversion into a mineral water factory. There could be a possible claim by the Trustees, especially as the stock was 15% below par at the time and a wind-up value would be based on the average of the market value of the preceding two years. The Praed securities of £62,000 could be used for part repayment. Phipps had to consider, if it had to repay the whole of the debenture stock, whether it could borrow to do so or issue new redeemable debentures. Unfortunately, the approach to the Capital Issues Committee was turned down (see Phipps entry for details of financing).

WELLINGBOROUGH (continued)

On 25th March, 1954, David Jones told a packed meeting of Wellingborough licensees that his firm was amalgamating with Phipps.

"You may think that the amalgamation is a great pity in many ways. One regrets to see the death of an old family firm, which was started by a great uncle of mine, but it is something that has to be faced. Today the need is for productive effort by the most economic methods and I think the day must come when there is rationalisation...."

The newspapers regarded the bid as coming "out of the blue", since Praeds were trading at 42s to 45s and had been only 24s 6d in 1953. They closed at 75s. The press commented that Phipps' bid meant that the shareholders had trebled their money in 4 years. Not surprisingly the bid was successful, although it did result in a local Northamptonshire stockbrokers being prosecuted in 1956 with regard to fraudulent dealings in the shares. The take-over was completed by the due date of 31st March.

The brewery was to close on Tuesday 20th April, when Phipps would commence brewing and bottling with deliveries from 3rd May. Initially, it was planned to re-badge beer as Praeds and *"such plant as is suitable will be removed from Wellingborough to Northampton"*, under the direction of Mr Hipwell. Messrs Morton would dismantle the larger plant for storage at Northampton, and it was hoped that the mash tuns and hop back could be installed in the Autumn. The bottling unit was to be dismantled *"with all speed"* and installed at Northampton.

Various departments, eg. property maintenance, transport and mineral waters would remain at Wellingborough under the MD. The bottled beer site was sold. The old Brewery House, 10 Sheep Street, used as an office, would be sold, but the brewery foreman's cottage at No 11 would be retained for the caretaker.

Of the staff of 28, 16 would be retained, 9 offered alternative employment at Northampton and 3 retired. Unfortunately, the monthly allowance to staff of 1 bottle of wine, 1 bottle of spirits and 2 dozen ½ pints was to be discontinued. David Jones seems to have retained his monthly drinks allowance of £36. Of the 123 weekly paid employees, 78 would be retained at Wellingborough and 2 transferred to Northampton. C.P.T.Williams the brewer would move to Northampton as 3rd brewer.

Some of the brewing plant was advertised for sale in the small ads section of the Brewing Trade Review for April. The Brewers Guardian for May stated that although brewing would cease, the site would be used to produce mineral waters on a much larger scale. David Jones became joint MD of Phipps alongside Mr E.C.Palmer.

In 1955 it was announced that a new mineral water plant would be built for R.C.Allen at Northampton. That year saw the liquidation of the Praed subsidiary businesses, with the exception of Allens.

In February 1956 the proposed demolition of the Wellingborough brewery was announced and it had disappeared by the end of the year (SP 893 678). However, the ventilation outlets from the original Woolston brewery are said to have been used when the new Congregational Church was built on the corner of Salem Lane and are still visible from the High Street.

Sibley, John Dickens, *Silver Street.*

Listed as a grocer and brewer in 1862 prior to moving to 84 Newlands, Northampton, by 1864. Prior to this, he seems to have been a grocer and chandler. It seems likely that John Dickens Sibley (b.1817 London) who in 1847 occupied property in Market Street, owned by William Warren, was the son of James Sibley who was at the King's Arms, Market Square in 1824.

Turnall & Sanderson, *Belle Vue Brewery.*

The Brewers' Journal for 15th April, 1891, records the Belle Vue Brewery, Wellingborough, as being acquired by the partnership of Turnall and Sanderson in 1882, with Sanderson as the brewery manager.

Whilst Alfred Sanderson was a wine and spirit merchant in the Market Square, Wellingborough, his home address was Handsworth in Birmingham. Hence, since no other details of a brewery of this name in Wellingborough are available, it seem that it was more likely to have been located at Handsworth, Birmingham (F378 Holyhead Road and later F408 Brewery Street).

The Belle Vue had not been very successful from the start, the argument being that Sanderson had not devoted his whole time to it, nor brought in his full share of the capital. His counter argument was asserted that in several years profits had been made, that the losses had been occasioned partly by temporary causes, such as the unusually high price of hops in one year, by large breweries buying up public houses, which might be met by developing the private trade, and to some extent by the partnership having to expend money on the freehold premises which the plaintiff, as landlord, had covenanted to keep in repair. This ended in litigation over the dissolution of the partnership.

In 1909, A Sanderson's business at 46 Market Street was bought by Phipps for £853.

Wilson, Andrew, *Sheep Street.*

Andrew Wilson, previously a grocer and tallow chandler from around 1762, had also developed a coal business before buying the brewery of Henry Croft (see Craft above), around 1784.

"A. Wilson begs leave to acquaint not only his friends and customers but the neighbourhood in general that he has completed his brew house at Wellingborough as to be enabled to furnish both public and private houses with ale and beer of such a quality as cannot fail giving the utmost satisfaction. He further adds that it is in his power to convince publicans that he can serve them from three halfpence to twopence a gallon cheaper than they can brew ale of equal strength and real goodness...." (Northampton Mercury 11th August, 1787)

Wilson was soon producing a Porter which was brewed to a London recipe. It first was advertised in this 1790 advert:-

"My Porter is become of proper age and excellent in quality....any quantity, not less than four barrels, delivered free to any place within ten miles of this place....also a very excellent mild ale and beer, at moderate prices, either publicans or private families may depend on."

Advert placed in the Northampton Mercury of 30th March, 1793:-

"I take the liberty thus of acquainting my friends and the public, that they may in future rely on meeting with as good Porter at my brew house here as London produces, it being now brewed on the plan of one of the first Porter breweries there; and will be sold by the barrel and kilderkin at 1/-, and by the firkin at 13d, per gallon....Wanted nice lad as an apprentice to a grocer and tallow chandler enquire as above."

The last record of Andrew Wilson operating on his own is in 1798 when W.J.Pooley was the Head Brewer, and he died in 1800. In his Will, Andrew left the brewery and coal trade businesses to his sons William and Ralph. This included:-

> The Ship, West End:- tenant Francis Little
> The Mason's Arms, St John Street:- tenant John Charity
> The White Horse, Market:- tenant Josias Denny Roote
> The Rose & Crown, Sheep Street:- tenant John Andrews
> The Fountain, (previously Ship), Market:- tenant Thomas Kingston
> The Boot, Harriets Lane:- tenant William Pentelow
> The Chequers, Hargrave

There was a malting in the hands of Joseph Overall. The brewery is described as being in Sheep Street, adjoining the lane at the side of the Swan Inn. The brew house, was looked after by William, whilst Ralph looked after the two malt houses. In 1808 the King's Arms, Hargrave, tenant Thomas Kilborne, became part of the estate.

In 1811 the business was trading as W.& R.Wilson, brewers and merchants, but by 1816 they were only shown as merchants.

However, on 2nd May, 1815, William and Ralph were made bankrupt by Edward Everard & Sons of King's Lynn. This was for £6,769 10s 1d of goods supplied and interest on two sums of £2,000. This may be linked partly to the property annuities which they were incumbent to pay and possibly the competition from the Dulleys.

It seems that the brothers had not inherited their father's business acumen. They did a runner! William Luck of Overstone, who had known them for 10 years, described how they stayed at his home *"to secrete themselves from and to avoid their creditors"* (NRO ZB568).

The bankruptcy perhaps led to William's death at this time, whilst Ralph became a clerk in Farnham. The property was sold to pay the debts. Some of the property was conveyed to Thomas Sanderson for £1,320 in 1815. Part of this was occupied by John Woolston and part by George Margetts. The brew house and maltings were conveyed to John Dickins Passenham and by 1820 were being used by Margetts. The Boot and the Mason's Arms eventually became the property of Dulleys.

WEST HADDON	**Wilson, William,** *Crown Inn, High Street.*

In addition to being the ostler at the inn, Wilson was also the brewer in 1852. The pub is still trading.

WHITTLESEY	**George Hotel.**

The brew house was still intact until the late 1950s.

WILBY	**Challoner, William,** *Fox & Hounds, Homestall.*

When sold in 1810, the Fox & Hounds at "Welby", occupied by Challoner, included a brew house. Challoner's stone farm house also had its own brew house and the sale included William Manning's cottage, the out-house of which was used as a brew house.

Cox, Eliza, *George Inn, Main Road.*

On Mrs Eliza Cox leaving the George Inn in 1859, the effects for sale included a 100 gallon brewing copper, a 2 quarter mash vat with false bottom etc. The pub, which was a Phipps' house by 1885, is still trading.

WOLLASTON	**Cooke, William J,** *Nag's Head, London Road.*

In 1874, a Thomas Cook (shown as Cooke in 1862) was the victualler at the Nag's Head and a William Cook was a baker and farmer in the village. However, William J.Cooke is listed as a brewer in 1892. This was presumably at the pub, where he is listed as the tenant in 1888. However, in 1894 he is only shown as an agent for Phipps. The pub was probably rebuilt towards the end of the century and is still trading.

Hurry, John.

"Advertisement for the sale by auction at premises of Mr John Hurry maltster and brewer of a 100 gallon copper" (Northampton Herald 24 March 1849).

In 1847, John Hurry, described as a maltster, had been involved with land at Windmill field in connection with the Crick family (see entry for Alfred W.Crick).

The 1851 census shows one brewer in the village, so it is possible that Hurry had continued to brew. However, in the 1854 Directory Hurry junior is shown only as a beer retailer, maltster and registrar.

A

Abington Brewery Co, 79
Abington Brewery, The, 36
Abington Park Brewery Company, 30
Abington Park Hotel, The, 30
Adlams of Bristol, 66
Admiral Nelson, The
    Northampton, 35, 45
Albert Brewery, The, 108
Albion Brewery, 21
Albion Steam Brewery, The, 83
Albion, The, 12
Aldwinckle, Harriett, 114
Alexander Arms, The
    Kettering, 17
Alhambra Tavern and Music Hall, 49
All Saints Brewery, 73, 114
Allard, Francis W, 11
Allard, Henry, 11
Allen & Burnett, 12, 15, 30, 32, 50, 122
Allen, Francis, 118
Allen, John, 15
Allen, Phillip, 31
Allen, R C, 76, 143
Allied-Domecq, 35
Amalgamated Brewers, Stockholm, 56
Anchor Brewery, The
    Buckby Wharf, 5, 25
    Oundle, 91
Anchor Inn, The
    Higham Ferrers, 16
Anchor, The
    Nether Hayford, 25
    Oundle, 92
Andrews, John, 146
Angel Hotel, The, 46
Angel Inn, The, 13
Angel Lane Brewery, 34
Angel, The
    Geddingon, 123
    Wellingborough, 133
Anglo-Bavarian Brewery, 55
Ansell, James, 32
Ansell, Thomas, 127
Ansells Brewery, Aston, 56, 80
Anthony, Jacob, 133
Archer, Bernard, 143
Arnold Arms, The, 50
Artichoke, The
    Moulton, 29
Ashby, Edward, 33
Ashwell, Richard, 26
Atkinson Ltd, 56
Atkinson, J G, 100, 110, 111
Austin, John, 93
Aylesbury Brewery Co, 66

B

Bailey, Charles, 11
Bailey, Henry, 100
Bailey, Mary, 16
Baines, John, 100
Ball, F E & Son, 143
Ball, Mr, 7
Ball, William & Son, 114

Banks, Thomas, 33
Bantam Cock, The
    Northampton, 42, 87
Barber & Ross, 111
Barford, John, 32
Barley Mow, The
    Cosgrove, 28
    Watford, 140
Barnes, Clara Ann & Charles Eric, 2
Barnes, George, 14
Barnes, Thomas, 91
Barnett, H L, 52
Barratt, John Charles, 61, 89, 124
Bartlett, Isaac, 2
Basant, The, 107
Bass Ltd, 35, 39, 53, 65, 73, 76, 79, 140
Bates, Edward, 16
Battle Brothers, 10, 59
Batty, W & Son, 11
Beacon Place, 49
Beaconsfield Arms, The, 110
Bean & Molesworth, 21
Bear, The
    Banbury, 1
    Souldon, 2
Beardsley, Arthur Bent, 92
Bearward Street Brewhouse, 33
Beaver, William, 100
Beehive, The
    Peterborough, 108
    Stamford, 116
Beer House, The, 50
Belcher, James, 14
Bell & Oak, The
    Peterborough, 111
Bell Hotel, The
    Apsley Guise, 9
Bell Inn, The
    Brackley, 7
    Syresham, 122
Bell, Charles, 16
Bell, The
    East Farndon, 50
    Foleshill, 74
    Naseby, 29
    Syresham, 3
Belle Vue Brewery, The, 145
Belton, James, 19
Benboe, Richard, 84
Bennett, James, 33
Berridge, Joseph, 14
Bewsher, John, 100
Bicycle Tavern, The, 85
Biglands family, 110
Billing, Margaret, 59
Billingham, William, 33
Billings of Brooklyn, 134
Bird in Hand, The, 32
Black Boy and Trumpet, The, 110
Black Boy Inn, The
    Daventry, 11
Black Boy, The
    Northampton, 35
Black Moor's Head, The, 100
Black, Mr, 63
Blake, Fanny, 22
Bland, Amos, 114
Blencowe & Co, 1, 122
Blow, William, 112
Blucher's Arms, The
    Croughton, 2

Blue Anchor, The
    Kettering, 50
    Northampton, 43
Blue Bell, The
    Collyweston, 115
    Cowgate, 100, 102
    Rothwell, 114
Blue Boar, The, 86
Boat Inn, The, 118
Boddington, R S, 63
Bodger, W, 15
Bohemian Breweries, Prague, 50
Boon (e), William, 33
Boot & Slipper, The
    Northampton, 34
Boot Inn, The
    Eastcote, 28
Boot, The
    Daventry, 12, 25
    Market Deeping, 105
    Northampton, 86
    Wellingborough, 146
Boothville, The, 59
Bostock & Co, 52
Bosworth, Brian, 1
Boughton House, 1
Bourne Brewery, The, 21
Bourne, Frederick Coutts, 20
Bowerman, Mrs, 3
Boyer, Samuel, 109
Brackley & Banbury Brewery, 4
Bradford, William, 54
Brafield, Charles, 13
Brafield, Septimus, 13
Brasserie L'Union, 57
Brewer's Arms, The, 106
Brewery Tap, The
    Kings Cliffe, 21
    Peterborough, 103
Brighton Brewery, The, 5
Britannia Brewery of Stony Stratford, 47
Britannia Inn, The
    Little Brington, 86
Britannia Life Assurance Company, 46
Britannia, The
    Northampton, 85
British Standard, The, 87
Britts, George, 19
Broadmead Hotel, The, 75
Bromley, Thomas, 7
Brooker, Ernest, 33
Brown & Pank Ltd, 84
Brown, Arthur G W, 57
Brown, Frederick Bennet, 66
Brown, Horace, 54
Brown, John, 33, 34
Brown, Richard Guest, 7
Brown, William, 109
Browning, Thomas, 11
Browning, Walter Buchanan, 25
Buccleuch Arms, The
    Broughton, 10
Buccleugh Hotel, The
    Northampton, 45
    Northampton, 10
Buckle, Samuel, 100, 102
Bull & Dolphin, The, 112
Bull & Short, 126
Bull Hotel, The
    Olney, 18
    Peterborough, 109

Bull Inn, The
   Irthlingborough, 16
   Stony Stratford, 47
Bull, Francis Desvaux, 9
Bull, Fuller, 34
Bull, The
   Weedon, 127
Bull's Head, The
   Northampton, 60
   Towcester, 123
Bullen, William, 91
Bunton, William Wallis, 29
Burgess Joseph, 34
Burkitt, Thomas, 101
Burnham, Robert, 11
Burnham, William, 11
Burton Latimer WMC, 23
Buswell, William, 26
Butcher, William, 34, 44
Butcher's Arms, The, 23
Butler, George O'Connor, 34
Butler, Robert, 34
Butler's Wolverhampton Brewery, 2, 52
Butlin, Thomas, 34

C

Calcutt, Herbert Charles, 107
Cannock Brewery, The, 2
Cannon Brewery, The, 69
Cannon, Parker & Son Brewers Ltd, 128
Cannon, The, 128
Canons Ashby House, 7
Cardinall, D E, 50
Cardington Brewery, Bedfordshire, 114
Carlsberg, 34, 59, 79, 80, 82
Carpenter's Arms, The
   Peterborough, 110
Cartwright Arms, The, 1
Cartwright family, 1
Castle Ashby House, 8
Castle Brewery, The, 44
Castle Works, 132
Castle, The, 119
Cat & Custard Pot, The, 143
Cattle Market Refreshment Saloon, 33
Cattle Market Restaurant, 25
Cavalier, The
   Collyweston, 21
Cave, John, 73
Cave, Sir George, 2
Cave, William, 1, 3
Cawthorpe House, 21
Challoner, William, 147
Chamberlain, Joseph, 86
Chambers, Eleanor, 91
Chance, John, 35
Chandos Arms, The
   Winslow, 75
Chaplin, William, 88
Chapman, Edward Sibbley, 3
Chapman, James, 35
Chapman, John, 20
Chapman, Robert, 128
Chapman, Thomas, 35
Chapman, W C N, 50
Charity, John, 146
Charrington, Mr, 55
Charringtons Ltd, 55, 57, 73, 117
Charter, Charles, 129
Checkley, Thomas, 29

Cheltenham & Hereford Breweries, 6
Cheltenham Original Brewery, 70
Chequers Inn, The
   Rothersthorpe, 45
   Rothwell, 113, 118
Chequers, The
   Boongate, 106
   Grendon, 129
   Hargrave, 146
   Old, 90
   Peterborough, 105
   Wellingborough, 129
   Yaxley, 94
Cherry Tree Inn, The, 19
Cherry, Graham, 41
Chesham & Brackley Breweries Ltd, 6, 80, 141
Chetwynd, Arthur, 51
Chouler & Co, 50
Choules, Robert, 50
City Arms, The, 141
City Hotel, The
   Coventry, 50
City of London Brewery Co, 50
Clark, John, 7
Clark, Thomas, 35
Clarke, A A, 73
Clarke, John, 11
Clarke, Mr, 33
Clarke, Thomas, 29
Clarke's Brewery, 101
Clayson, James, 35
Clicker, The, 59
Clifton, John, 91
Coach & Horses, The
   Banbury, 4
   Brixworth, 7
   Daventry, 12
   Stamford, 118
   Woodford, 17, 118
Coales & Allen, 32, 60
Cobden Arms, The, 103, 104
Cobley, C, 141
Cock Inn, The
   Northampton, 42
Cock, The
   Stony Stratford, 45
Cockerill, Thomas, 26
Colegrove & Son, 22
Colledge, Robert, 35
Commercial Hotel, The
   Peterborough, 111
Compasses, The
   Milton Malsor, 26
   Silverstone, 2, 122
Cook, William, 35
Cooke, William Michael, 13
Cooke, William, J, 147
Coombs Table Waters, 76
Coombs, Thomas, 129
Coope, Jerome, 14
Cooper, Henry, 31
Cornfield, George, 84
Cornfield, Pearce, 42
Cotterell, George, 2
Coventry & Stamford Brewery, The, 48
Cox, Benjamin, 11
Cox, Eliza, 147
Cox, John, 100
Craddock, Edward C, 35
Craddock, George, 35
Crafts, William, 95, 129

Crawford & Co, 104
Cream of the Valley, The, 34
Crick family, 86, 147
Crick, Alfred W, 15, 35
Crick, Charles, 15
Cricketers Inn, The, 2
Crispin Arms, The
   Northampton, 43, 84, 86
   Wellingborough, 141
Croft, Henry, 146
Croot, Frederick James, 14
Crosby family, 3
Crosby, George, 3
Cross Keys Commercial Hotel, The, 20
Cross Keys, The
   Brackley, 3
   Northampton, 60
   Oundle, 125
Cross, Joseph, 113
Crosse & Blackwell Ltd, 127
Crow & Horse, The, 84
Crowhurst, Percy, 21
Crown & Anchor Maltings, 83
Crown & Anchor, The, 46
Crown & Boot Inn, The, 113
Crown Brewery, The, 16
Crown Hotel, The, 2
Crown Inn, The
   Brackley, 1
   Kettering, 16, 17
   Rothwell, 113, 114
   West Haddon, 147
   Whitchurch, 103
Crown, The
   Cottingham, 17
   Napton, 2
   Northampton, 84
   Oundle, 95
   Peterborough, 109
   Staverton, 25
   Towcester, 123
Cunnington, John, 19
Cunnington, William, 20
Cutlack & Co, 101, 110, 111
Cutlack & Harlock Ltd, 104
Cutlack, Charles, 102, 110
Cutlack, John Yarrow, 103
Cutlack, William, 102
Cutlers Ltd, 36

D

Dabbs, Arthur John, 114
Dadford, T, 25
Dallington Brook, The, 59
Daulby, Ann, 114
Davenports Ltd, 65
Daventry & Northants Brewery Co, 11
Daventry Electric Light & Power Co, 13
Davison and Scamell, 62
Day & Sons of St Neots, 73
Deacon, Richard, 91
Denbigh & Co, 36
Denny, Josias Roote, 146
Devenish of Weymouth, 97
Diment, Colin, 8
Dines, Joseph Allen, 13
Dixon, James, 105
Dixon, Mr, 55
Dixon, Reuben & Libbeus, 20
Dodderidge Church, 83

Dodford Brewery, The, 127
Dog & Duck, The, 140
Dolphin Hotel, The, 99
Dolphin Inn, The, 85
Dolphin, The
   Moulton, 140
   Northampton, 35, 44
Door, William, 16
Dorman Pope & Co, 15, 34, 36
Dorman, George, 36, 65
Dorman, Thomas, 68
Dorman, Thomas Phipps, 36, 62
Dorr, Herbert H, 36
Douglas, Mrs Mary Ann, 39
Drage, Alexander, 122
Draper's Arms, The, 60
Duck's Nest, The, 102
Dudley, James, 105
Duke of Clarence, The
   Northampton, 42
Duke of Edinburgh, The, 38
Duke of York, The, 36
Dukes Arms, The
   Kettering, 19
Dulley and Whitworth, 129
Dulley, Herbert, 24, 132
Dulley, James, 24, 130
Dulley, W & Sons, 54, 129
Dun Cow, The
   Daventry, 11
Dunckley, Sarah, 26
Dunkley, Edward Thomas, 40
Dunkley, Sarah, 44
Duquesnoy, Pierre, 57
Durham Ox, The, 39
Durham, James & Sons, 33, 40
Durrans & Beardsley, 92
Durrans, Paul, 91
Duttons of Blackburn, 55, 57
Dychurch Lane Brewery, 33

E

Eady & Dulley, 23, 54, 64, 83, 131
Eady family, 46
Eady, J Toller, 24
Eady, Joseph Chamberlain, 23, 83, 86
Eady, Kenneth, 24
Eagle & Child, The, 89
Eagle Brewery, The, 19, 21
Eagle Tavern, The
   Kings Cliffe, 19, 21
Earl of Pomfret, The, 90
Earl, M A, 40
East, W.J. & Co, 26, 28, 33, 52
Eastgate, The, 50, 105
Eayrs, George, 125
Edme, 55
Edmunds, Francis, 40
Edmunds, William, 40
Edwards, William, 13
Edwards, William Brown, 114
Elephant & Castle, The, 106
Elgood & Harrison, 105
Elgood & Sons, 105
Elliott, Edmund, 8
Ellis, Thomas, 91
Elliss, George Henry, 21
Elwes Arms, The, 143
Elworthy, John & Co, 16
Elworthy, William & Co, 17

Elworthys of Kettering, 55
Emerton, John, 122
English, Alan Ernest, 58
English, Robert, 105
Everard & Sons, 146
Everitt, Robert, 103
Exeter's Arms, The
   St Martins, 114
Eyres of King's Lynn, 112

F

Falcon Inn, The, 14, 42
Falcon, The
   Cowgate, 100
Fane, William Henry, 20
Farmer, Bevershaw, 3
Feast, Robert, 105
Fighting Cocks, The, 100
Firtree, The, 90
Fisher, George, 106
Fitzgerald Arms, The, 29
Fitzhugh, J T, 13
Fitzwilliam Arms, The
   Peterborough, 109
Fitzwilliam's Arms, The, 110
Fleece Commercial Inn, The, 29, 33, 61
Fleece, The
   Peterborough, 110
Flying Horse, The
   Crick, 87
   Northampton, 88
Folly, The, 39
Foot & Hamper, 106
Foote, Edwin & Co, 106
Forget Not, The, 33
Fountain, The
   Northampton, 94
   Wellingborough, 146
Fox & Hounds, The
   Daventry, 12
   Deanshanger, 13
   Pitsford, 112
   Wilby, 147
Fox Inn, The
   Farthinghoe, 14
   Market Harborough, 23
Fox, The
   Old, 90
Freeman, Henry, 106
Freeman, Richard, 41
Freeman, Robert, 41
Friary, Holroyd & Co, Guildford, 46
Frog Island Brewery, 41
Frost, Samuel, 7
Frost, Thomas, 42
Frost, William, 12
Fulda, Silvester, 103
Fulford, Joseph, 15

G

Gardener's Arms, The
   Northampton, 48
Gardner, James, 42
Gardner, William, 12
Garibaldi Hotel, The, 37
Garibaldi, The, 34
Garner, William, 109

Garton Hill & Co, 69
Gauge, Samuel, 7
Geeston Tap, The, 20
Gent, William, 10
George & Dragon, The, 122
George Hotel, The
   Stamford, 118
   Whittlesey, 147
George Inn, The
   Roade, 126
   Wilby, 147
George, James Henry, 21
George, John, 16
George, The
   Ashley, 1
   Kettering, 11, 17
   Maidwell, 22
   Shefford, 141
Gibson, Christopher, 42
Gibson, H, 106
Gibson, Isaac, 8
Gibson, J, 8
Gibson, William, 42
Gilchrist, Ian, 58
Gladstone Arms, The, 103
Globe Hotel, The, 128
Goat, The
   Northampton, 46
Goddard, Christopher, 11
Golden Ball, The, 20
Golden Fleece, The, 112
Golden Lion, The
   Kettering, 16, 50
   Peterborough, 100
   Wellingborough, 129
Goldsmith Inn, The, 86
Goodman, Feast, 106
Goodman, James, 42
Goodman, John, 42
Goodwood, William, 8
Gorman, Mr, 6
Gotch & Sons, 113
Gotch, T.H. & J.D., 113
Grand Junction Canal, 135
Grand Union Canal, 51
Grand Union, The, 11
Grant, Arthur, 115
Gray, G T S, 18
Gray, John, 88
Gray, Parker, 86
Green Dragon, The
   Market Harborough, 23
   Northampton, 42
   Wellingborough, 133
Green Man, The
   Hanslope, 15
   Oundle, 91
Greens of Luton, 117
Greyhound Inn, The
   Buckby Wharf, 25
   Milton Malsor, 26, 28, 89
Greyhound, The
   Brackley, 1, 2
   Eye, 14
Grose, Thomas, 24
Grove, Henry, 11, 24
Guignol, Joseph Jules, 33
Gurdon-Rebow, H J, 50
Gurney, George, 112
Gurney, John, 47, 112

H

Hagger & Jope, 31
Hagger, Thomas, 30
Half Moon, The
    Grendon, 28
    Northampton, 34
    Oundle, 95, 98
Hall, Cutlack and Harlock Ltd, 105
Hallamshire Vinegar Co Ltd, 2
Halls of Ely, 105
Halls of Oxford, 2, 49
Halls' St Giles Brewery, Oxford, 52
Hanch Hall, 49
Hand, Mr, 23
Hare & Hounds, The
    Northampton, 8, 42
Harlock of Ely, 102
Harper, William, 114
Harris family, 12
Harris, Francis, 36
Harris, Henry, 25
Harris, John, 42
Harris, Thomas, 12, 42
Harris, William, 25
Harrison family, 102
Harrison, Vincent, 42
Harroll, Samuel, 1
Harrow, The
    Braunston, 12, 25
Harrows, The, 3
Hatton Arms, The
    Gretton, 33
Hay, Will, 7
Haycock, The, 125
Haynes, G, 88
Healy & Maddox, 106
Heavermann, John, 12, 23
Heneage, Simon, 81
Heppenstall, Christopher, 21
Herbert, John, 40
Heron, Mr, 55, 82
Heron, Robert, 57
Hesketh, Lord, 39, 75, 124
Higgins brewery, 123
Higgins, Charles, 123
Higgins, John, 49
Higgins, William, 47, 48, 123
Hill, C C, 106
Hill, Cicyly, 40
Hill, George, 109
Hill, James, 106
Hill, Thomas, 106
Hilliam, John, 106
Hilltop Brewery, The, 127
Hind Hotel (Wellingborough) Ltd, 143
Hind Inn, The, 60
Hind, The, 43
Hipwell & Co, 18, 73
Hipwell family, 19, 50, 63, 73, 78, 80, 145
Hipwell, Richard, 7
Hobbs, William, 42
Hogan & Co, 25
Holes of Newark, 26, 55
Hollowell, Samuel, 12
Hollowell, William, 13
Holts Brewery, 63
Homan, T, 42
Home Brewery, The, 104, 111
Home Butler Ltd, 24, 56

Hook Norton Brewery, 2
Hop House Brewery, 42
Hopcraft & Norris, 2, 3, 25, 57, 74, 88, 143
Hopcraft, Alfred, 3
Hopcraft, Barnet John, 3
Hopcraft, Edward, 6
Hope Brewery, The
    Irthlingborough, 16
    Milton Malsor, 26
Hopper, Thomas, 43
Horse & Groom, The
    Burton Latimer, 10
    Northampton, 10, 60
    Rearsby, 140
Horse & Hounds, The, 90
Horse & Jockey, The
    Boongate, 110
    Peterborough, 110
Horse Market Tavern, The, 37
Horseshoe Inn, The
    Weedon, 125
Horseshoe, The
    Nash, 9
    Oundle, 91, 98
Horspool, Mrs Mary, 43
House & Stones, 111
House, G F, 111
House, John, 111
Howard, Laomi, 34
Howes, John, 125
Hull Brewery, 50
Hunt & Co, 110
Hunt, Edmunds of Banbury, 29, 73, 80
Hunt, George & Henry Robert, 114
Hunting, Frederick, 14
Huntsman, The
    Peterborough, 104
Hurry, John, 147

I

Ind Coope, 6, 31, 59, 65, 76, 79, 80
Ives, Zebulon, 43

J

Jackson, Edward, 109
James & James, 84
James, Herbert Eli, 43
Jeffrey, Christopher, 110
Jeffrey, William, 83
Jervis, Thomas, 49
Jesson, William Ward, 114
Johnson & Mason, 74
Johnson of Melton Mowbray, 109
Johnson, John, 19, 101
Johnson, William, 133
Jones, David, 81, 143
Jones, John, 43
Jones, Thomas, 22
Jope & Jope, 31

K

Keep Brothers, 49
Kenna, Frank, 23
Kent, Charles, 40

Ketton & Kings Cliffe Brewery Co, 20
Kilmarnock, The, 135
Kinder, Arthur & Co, 17
King George beer house, 110
King, Stephen, 43
King, William, 107
King's Arms, The
    Hargrave, 146
    Kettering, 94
    Thrapston, 118
    Weldon, 128
King's Brewery & Stores, 119
King's Head, The
    Kettering, 17
    Mayorhold, 43
    Northampton, 88
    Peterborough, 100
    Syresham, 2, 59, 122
    Wadenhoe, 115
    Whittlesey, 141
    Wilbarston, 17
Kings Cliffe Brewery, 20
Kingston, Thomas, 107, 146
Kinnell, Mr, 32
Knight, William Douglas, 8
Knightley Arms, The, 35
Konow, Charles, 33

L

Labour in Vain, The
    Mounts, 35
Lacons of Great Yarmouth, 80
Lamb Inn, The
    Stoke Goldington, 9
Lamb, Henry, 10
Lamb, The
    Bedford, 130
Lamb, William Henry, 63
Lamplighter, The
    Northampton, 88
Langham, Sir James, 10
Langton & Sons, 69
Langton, James, 2
Lankester & Wells, 55, 58
Lascelles Hall Brewery, 92
Law, John, 43
Lazenby, John William, 107
Leeson, Robert, 44
Leics & Rutland Brewers Assoc, 70
Leigh, T, 118
Leopard, The, 10
Leyland Brewery, 132
Liddington family, 23
Liddingtons of Rugby, 12, 23
Lilley, James, 26
Linnell, James, 84
Linnell, Sarah, 122
Linnell, William, 10, 44
Linnett, William, 44
Linthwaite, George, 9
Lion & Lamb, The
    Daventry, 12
    Northampton, 30
Lion Brewery, The
    Northampton, 15, 30, 50, 88
    Peterborough, 110
Litchborough Brewery, 12, 22
Little Bell Inn, The, 42
Little, Francis, 146
Littler, Bruce, 41

Longdon Hall, 51
Lord Nelson, The
   Stanion, 17, 118
Lord Palmerston, The
   Northampton, 88
Low, James, 19
Lucas of Leamington, 12, 54, 56, 74
Lucas, W, 130
Ludlow family, 98
Ludlow, Edwin Basil, 96, 140
Lumbertub, The, 59
Lyster, Gilbert, 42

M

Mackesons of Hythe, 68
MacLeod, Charles Campbell, 15, 21
Maddocks, John Frederick, 109
Magpie, The, 62
Major-Lucas, Edward, 25, 42, 52, 87
Malden, Aubrey, C.E., 107
Malt & Hop Brewery, The, 20, 21
Manchester Brewery Co Ltd, 50, 51
Mann, Crossman & Paulin, 58, 81
Manning, John, 44
Manning, T E, 70
Manning, Thomas, 44, 62
Manning, Thomas & Co, 13, 17, 41, 44, 87
MAnning, Thomas & Co, 74
Manning, William, 44, 147
Mansion House Brewery, 109
Mansion House, The, 110
Margetts, George, 133
Margetts, Henry, 133
Marine Brewery, London, 2
Marks, William, 26
Marquis of Granby, The
   Peterborough, 104
Marriott, James & Sons, 49, 115
Marriott, Miss Maria, 114
Marshall Brothers, 73
Marshall, William, 15
Marston Inn, The, 3
Marston, Thompson & Evershed, 18, 70
Martin, Edward Victor, 108
Martin, Henry & Co, 36
Mason's Arms, The
   Finedon, 14
   Peterborough, 100
   Twywell, 17, 118
   Wellingborough, 146
May, John, 123
Mayo, Mrs Harriet, 123
Mays, Thomas, 108
McGee, Bill, 6
McKee, Charles Frederick, 91, 92
McMullen, Herbert, 127
Meads, Edward, 123
Melbourne Arms, The
   Duston, 12, 13, 59
Melbourns of Stamford, 80, 117
Melton Arms, The
   Kettering, 11, 17
Merivale, Ian, 8
Merivales Ales Ltd, 8
Mermaid, The, 91
Messenger, William, 12
Midland Brewery, The, 8
Miller, Noel William, 57
Milner, A L, 46

Milton Arms, The, 94
Minards, William, 26
Minerva Brewery, 15
Moffat, Graham, 7
Molineux Ground, 51
Molineux Hotel, 51
Monk & Minstrel, The, 10
Montgomery & Harris, 25, 125
Montgomery, F & W, 25, 125
Montgomery, Francis, 25, 90
Montgomery, Joseph, 25
Montgomery, T, 67
Moore, Robert, 46
Morgan & Eady, 73
Morland Brewery Co, 57
Morley, Julia, 20
Morley, Samuel, 20
Morrells of Oxford, 52
Mowbray & Co of Grantham, 59, 115
Muddeman, William, 46
Murphy, C, 52

N

Nag's Head, The
   Northampton, 44, 90
   Peterborough, 105
   Wollaston, 147
Nash Brothers, 6
National Trust, 106
Neal, John, 8
Neill, George, 46
Nelson Inn, The, 142
Nene Valley Brewery, 15, 132
New Brewery, The, 9
New Dolphin, The, 112
New Inn, The
   Byfield, 7
   Rothwell, 113
   Shotteswell, 2
New Street Brewery, The, 12
New Zealand Breweries, 57
Newby, Mary Ann, 61
Newland Brewery, The, 46
Nix Wincott Brewery, 132
Nolan Inns, 26
Norris & Co Wandsworth, 4
Norris, Jimmy, 4
Norris, John, 125
Norris, Walter, 4
North Worcestershire Breweries Ltd, 135
North, Thomas, 12
Northampton Brewery Co, 2, 5, 8, 16, 22, 24, 29, 32, 47, 69, 76, 82
Northampton Castle, 44
Northampton Town Football Club, 52, 69
Northampton Union Bank, 28, 84
Northants & Leicester Clubs Brewery, 15
Northants Brewers Association, 4, 59, 96, 114, 143
Nunnely & Aggas, 23
Nunnely, Joseph, 23

O

Oak Brewery, Wisbech, 39
Oak, The
   Boongate, 101

   Easton, 13
   Northampton, 38
Oakham Ales, 108
Offilers of Derby, 80
Old Bakehouse, The, 37
Old Black Horse, The
   Cold Ashby, 8
Old Black Lion, The, 84
Old Crown Maltings, 73
Old Crown, The
   Barby, 12
   Market Harborough, 23
Old Friar, The, 118
Old Hind, The, 93
Old Mill Brewery Ltd, 7
Old Millstone, The, 44
Old Plough, The, 50
Old Red Lion, The, 10
Old Swan, The, 133
Old White Horse, The, 19
Oldrey, Robert Blatchford, 44
Osborn & Parker, 91
Osborn, Francis, 59, 61, 88
Osborn, George, 30, 48
Osborn, Peregrin Crosby, 60
Ostrich, The, 111
Oundle Commercial Bank, 95
Oundle School, 95
Oundle Union Brewery, 91, 93
Overall, Joseph, 146
Overstone Arms, The
   Northampton, 34

P

Packhorse, The, 101
Page, Alan, 50, 52
Page, Sidney John & Co, 109
Page, William B, 60
Paines of St Neots, 80, 81, 132
Painters, The, 101
Palmer, E C Manning, 46, 59, 81, 144
Palmer, Judith, 109
Palmerston Brewery, The, 107
Papillon Hall, 21
Papillon, Godfrey Keppel, 21
Parker, John, 60
Parker, Thomas, 16
Paul Pry, The, 100
Payne, Whitmill, 43
Peach Family, 60
Peach, James, 42
Peach, Joseph, 47
Peacock Inn, The
   Towcester, 125
Peacock, The
   Daventry, 11
   Long Buckby, 112
   Market Harborough, 23
   Northampton, 59
   Welford, 63, 128
Pedestrian Tavern, The
   Northampton, 48
Pentelow, William, 146
Percival, Thomas, 109
Perkins family, 42
Perkins, James, 7
Perrin, James, 36
Perry, John, 49, 86
Perry, Pickering Phipps, 41, 49
Peterborough Brewery, The, 109

Pettit, Peter, 133
Pheasant, The, 86
Phillips & Marriott & Co, 49, 54, 115
Phillips & Son (Coventry & Stamford), 115
Phillips & Sons, Newport, 49
Phillips & Sons, Oxford, 2, 49
Phillips Brothers, 48, 62
Phillips Stamford Brewery, 48, 58, 115
Phillips, Edward, 48
Phillips, Joseph III, 115
Phillips, Patrick Edward, 117
Phillips, Thomas, 2
Phillips, William George, 47
Phipps & Co, 2, 5, 6, 7, 8, 11, 13, 14, 15, 16, 17, 23, 33, 34, 35, 39, 47, 54, 59, 84, 98, 109, 112, 118, 123, 124, 127, 141, 145, 146
Phipps (Northampton and Towcester) Breweries, 61
Phipps Northampton Brewery Co, 78
Phipps, Edward, 63, 64, 86
Phipps, Pickering, 34, 45, 61, 123
Phipps, Richard, 33, 61
Phipps, Richard & Thomas, 41
Phipps, Samuel, 118
Phipps, Thomas, 26, 36, 61, 63, 65, 124
Phoenix Brewery, The
    Bedford, 49
    Northampton, 47
    Peterborough, 101
Phoenix, The, 89
Pickering, Elizabeth, 123
Pilgrim Inn, The
    Coventry, 48
Plackett, Richard, 83
Plasterer's Arms, The, 109
Plough Hotel, The
    Northampton, 50
Plough, The
    Brackley, 3
    Nassington, 115
    Northampton, 42
    Shutlanger, 39
    Towcester, 39, 123
Plumber's Arms, The
    Brackley, 2
    Northampton, 34, 60, 94
Plume of Feathers, The
    Lower Weedon, 127
    Oxford, 52
Pomfret Arms, The
    Northampton, 25, 89
    Towcester, 39
Pooley, W J, 146
Pope, C J, 36
Pope, William of Biggleswade, 36
Poplars House, 113
Praed, Campbell & Co, 6, 18, 54, 76, 97, 114, 117, 133
Pratt & Whitmell, 12
Pratt, John, 7, 15
Prince Albert, The
    Peterborough, 104
Prince of Wales, The
    Cranford, 10
    Finedon, 14
    Staple Claydon, 9
    Woodford, 10
Prince Regent, The, 12
Progressive Bus Co, 132
Pure Ice & Cold Storage Co, 88

Pyle, John, 108

Q

Queen's Arms, The
    Northampton, 42
Queen's Head, The
    Astcote, 28
    Northampton, 35, 64, 76
    Weedon, 127

R

Race Horse Inn, The, 34
Ragsdell, Nelly, 91
Railway, The
    Irthlingborough, 16
Ram Hotel, The
    Northampton, 17, 60
Rappitt, Alfred, 14
Ratliffe & Jeffrey Ltd, 29, 46, 64, 82, 83
Ratliffe, Thomas, 64
Ratliffe, William, 115
Raven, R O, 36
RCH Brewery, 8
Red Barrel, 81
Red Earl, The, 59
Red Lion, The
    Aldwinckle, 119
    Aynho, 1
    Brackley, 1
    Brixworth, 7
    Cranford, 10
    Eye, 13
    Great Creaton, 85
    Irchester, 133
    Isham, 10
    King's Sutton, 22
    Northampton, 35, 89
    Olney, 16
    Oundle, 94, 95
    Peterborough, 100
    Towcester, 123
    Warmington, 92
    Wisbech, 106
Redhead, Lucy, 109
Redwell Springs, 131
Reeve, Ralph Cure, 11
Reindeer, The
    Brackley, 1, 3
    Potterspury, 59, 112
Revis, Thomas, 128
Rhodes, William, 1
Rice & Co of London, 63
Richardson, John, 48
Richardson, Joseph, 90
Ridleys of Chelmsford, 117
Rifle Butts, The, 28
Rifle, The, 35
Ringrose, Thomas, 60
Rippin, Thomas, 123
Rising Sun, The, 45
Roberts, Thomas Valentine, 84
Robin Hood & Little John, The, 112
Robins, John, 84
Robinson & Riddey Ltd, 143
Rockingham Ales, 1
Roddis, John, 84
Rofe, Gabriel, 109

Rogers Engineers Ltd, 127
Rose & Co, 17
Rose & Crown, The
    Daventry, 11
    Peterborough, 110
    Rushden, 17
    Titchmarsh, 123
    Wellingborough, 146
    Wilbarston, 114, 128
Rose, William jun, 16
Round House, The, 17, 119
Rowell Brewery, The, 113
Royal Crown Brewery, The, 119
Royal Oak, The
    Collingtree, 28
    Cranford, 10
    Drayton, 11
    Eastfield, 106
    Great Glen, 28
    Little Addington, 10
    Northampton, 36
Rudd, William Hilliam, 109
Rudyard, Mr, 63
Rutland Brewery, 69
Rutter & Co, 66, 79
Ryde, Jacob, 11
Rye, Thomas, 16

S

Salt & Co, 42, 69
San Francisco Breweries Ltd, 134
Sanders, Ben, 84
Sanderson, Alfred, 145
Sandes, Ben, 84
Saracen's Head, The, 39, 123
Sargent, James, 15
Sargent, Thomas, 84
Saxby, Mr, 57
Scamell & Colyer, 49
Scarboro family, 16
Scattergood, Arthur, 2
Scattergood, William, 2
Scoley, Thomas, 109
Scott, Frederick W, 1
Sealy & Wilde, 20
Seamark, Thomas, 10
Seckham, Bassett Thorne, 50
Seckham, Samuel Lipscomb, 48
Seton & Co, 70
Seward, A G, 69
Seward, George, 69
Seward, Mr, 69
Sewell, George, 109
Sewell, Thomas, 109
Shaw, Thomas, 85
Shearsby, John, 85
Shelton, Martin, 85
Shelton, Sarah, 85
Shelton, Thomas, 85
Sheppard & King, 125
Shillingfords of Bicester, 2
Ship, The
    Mercer's Row, 34
    Northampton, 44
    Peterborough, 100
    Wellingborough, 146
Shortland, Mirzala, 19
Shoulder of Mutton, The
    Crick, 25, 30
Sibley, John Dickens, 47, 145

Sigard, Monsieur, 56
Simonds of Reading, 49, 80
Simpson & Collingwood, 109
Simpson, John, 118
Simpson, John Dauntecy, 109
Simpson, Mewburn & Miller, 109
Six Bells, The
   Bicester, 2
   Sulgrave, 1, 2
Slater's Arms, The
   Collyweston, 21
Slator, Henry, 110
Sloan, James, 133
Smart, Mrs Sarah, 85
Smith & Company Ltd, 95
Smith & Ridsdales Bank, 95
Smith & Son, 23, 125, 126
Smith & Tibbits, 95
Smith, Ann, 101
Smith, C, 45
Smith, Elizabeth, 127
Smith, Frank Holgate, 141
Smith, George
   Daventry, 12
   Weedon, 127
Smith, J T & W, 23
Smith, Jack, 96
Smith, John, 16, 23, 95, 98, 110, 123, 125, 127
Smith, John of Tadcaster Ltd, 98
Smith, Michael, 97
Smith, Mr, 91
Smith, Thomas, 16
Smith, William, 103, 110, 126, 127
Smith's Bank, 95
Smiths of Oundle, 21, 57, 94
Soames & Company, 21, 26
Soames, G M, 5, 25, 88
Soames, Robert, 26
Soames, W & S, A, 26
Southams, 55, 58
Spade & Shovel, The, 13, 14
Speechley, Edward, 110
Spiers, George, 1
Spinney Hill Hotel, The, 56
Sportsman, The, 109
Sportsman's Arms, The, 33
Sprake, C R, 6, 141
Sprake, John jun, 141
Sprake, Mr, 24, 140, 141
Spread Eagle Brewery, The, 33, 40
Spread Eagle, The
   Northampton, 40, 43
   Peterborough, 100
Spriggs, Charles, 110
Square Pond, The, 110
Squire, William & Co, 110
Stag's Head, The
   Great Doddington, 13
   Northampton, 43, 75
Stanley Arms, The, 106
Star Brewery, Canterbury, 50
Star Inn, The, 14
Star, The
   Boonfield, 106
   Peterborough, 110
Station Hotel, The
   Castle Ashby, 8
   Rushden, 8
   Wellingborough, 133
Steam Brewery, The
   Kettering, 17

Steam Engine, The, 107
Steels, Thomas John, 13
Steward & Patteson, 21, 75, 105
Stimson Bros, 76
Stockburn, Henry Lenton, 60
Stockburn, John Turner, 10
Stones, Thomas, 111
Strettons Brewery, 134
Strong, Elijah, 73
Stuchberry of Buckingham, 3, 122
Summers & Barnes, 91
Sun Brewery, The, 130
Sun, The
   Broughton, 7
   Daventry, 12
   Northampton, 84
Sunnyside, The, 59
Sutton, James, 43
Swallow, Joshua, 111
Swan & Helmet, The, 86
Swan Brewery, The, 129
Swan Inn, The
   Desborough, 13
   Kibworth Beauchamp, 23
   Wellingborough, 133
Swan, The
   Braybrooke, 7
   Holcote, 50
   Northampton, 35, 84
   Oundle, 99
   Woodnewton, 115
Swann, Christopher, 99
Swansea Old Brewery, The, 96
Sykes, Ernest William, 85

T

Tadcaster Brewery Co, 51
Tailby, William, 13
Talbot Hotel (Oundle) Co Ltd, 98
Talbot Hotel, The
   Stilton, 102
Talbot, The
   Gretton, 115
   Kettering, 17
   Northampton, 84
   Oundle, 91
   Potterspury, 112
   Tottenham, 135
Tamplin & Sons, Brighton, 50
Tansley, R, 88
Taylor, Edward, 7
Taylor, Thomas, 85
Taylor, Walker Ltd, 6, 80
Tebbut, Frederick, 17, 118
Thompson, Fred, 7
Thompson, Joseph, 85
Thompson, Samuel, 86
Thompson, William, 20
Thorne, George Edward, 91
Thornton, Robert, 7
Thorpe End Brewery, The, 69
Threadgold, William, 86
Three Cocks Inn, The, 17
Three Cranes, The, 17
Three Crowns, The, 94
Three Cups, The, 2
Three Fyshes, The, 132
Three Horse Shoes, The, 23
Three Horseshoes, The, 92
Three Lasts, The, 95

Three Potts, The
   Northampton, 60, 89
Three Tuns, The
   Broughton, 10
   Oundle, 91, 95, 98
   Peterborough, 106
Tibbits, Richard, 96
Tipler, W F, 64
Tom Thumb beer house, 47
Tomblin Brothers, 90
Tomblin, Charles Stafford, 90
Townsend, Henry Milnes, 111
Trasler, George, 86
Tresham, E and Company, 86
Trueman, Thomas, 115
Trusler, Thomas, 86
Turk's Head, The, 91
Turnall & Sanderson, 145
Turnell, L, 52
Two Brewers, The, 15

U

Underwood, John, 112
Underwood, Richard, 100
Unicorn Inn, The, 93
Unicorn, The, 31
Urquhart, Bill, 12, 22

V

Vernon family, 123
Victoria Brewery, The, 25, 86
Victoria, The, 104
Vine Inn, The, 76
Vine, The, 111
Viscount Chetwynd of Bearhaven, 51
Vivaq, 104

W

Wade, John, 14
Wade, Thomas, 128
Wagon & Horses, The
   Northampton, 61, 86
   Peterborough, 101
Waite, Thomas, 103
Walker & Soames, 5, 12, 25, 86, 125
Walker, Claud Wyborn Gordon, 21
Walker, Gerald, 25
Walker, Guy Phipps, 82
Walker, James Hubert Phipps, 75
Walker, John James, 63
Walker, Louis Edward, 66
Warden Brewery, The, 8
Warner, John, 19
Warner, Thomas, 14
Warren, Daniel, 8
Warren, J, 7
Warwick House, The, 12
Warwick, John, 112
Warwicks & Richardsons, 98, 111
Washington, Francis, 111
Watkins, W J, 54, 55, 58, 78
Watling Well, The, 125
Watney Mann, 81
Watney, Combe Reid, 22, 35, 69, 78, 144

Watney's Stag Brewery, 73
Watson, Joseph, 128
Watson, Mary, 113
Watson, Thomas, 113
Watts & Sons, 111
Watts, Charles Hills, 44
Webb, John, 111
Webster, Daniel, 128
Weedon Bec, 125
Weetabix, 57
Weldon & Son, 107
Weldon Brewery, The, 128
Wellingborough Brick & Tile Co, 130
Wellington Arms, The, 40
Wells & Winch, 107
Wells of Bedford, 6, 19, 30, 39, 80, 81, 114
Wells, Kingston, 125
West, James, 16
West, Joseph, 88
West, Septimus, 16
Westone, The, 59
Wharfinger's Arms, The, 57
Wheat Sheaf, The, 31
Wheatsheaf, The
  Banbury, 3
  Eastfield, 101
  Peterborough, 110
  Towcester, 39
  Weedon, 25, 126
Wheelwright's Arms, The, 109
Whincup, Francis, 20
Whincup, Henry, 118
Whitbread & Co Ltd, 54, 141, 144
White & Co, 52
White family, 123
White Hart, The
  Kettering, 59
  Peterborough, 110

Thrapston, 122
White Hills, The, 56
White Horse Inn, The
  Higham Ferrers, 16
  Northampton, 101
  Peterborough, 101
  Towcester, 123
White Horse, The
  Croughton, 2
  Northampton, 40
  Old, 91
  Silverstone, 56
  Wellingborough, 146
White Lion Brewery, 102
White Lion, The, 84
  Brackley, 1
  Peterborough, 110
White, Catherine, 112
White, Eleanor, 88
White, Joseph, 22
Whitehead, Henry, 15
Whitehead, Mr, 51
Whitehead, William, 15
Whitmy family, 34
Whitney, Thomas, 88
Whittle, George, 14
Whittle, James, 14, 112
Whittle, John, 14
Whitworth, James, 129
Wickes, William, 88
Wignall, George, 1
Wilfords of Coventry, 51
Willis, William, 19
Willson, Hanson & Fascutt, 61, 89
Willson, John, 88
Wilson, Andrew, 146
Wilson, Joseph, 89
Wilson, Nathan, 26, 89
Wilson, Thomas, 19

Wilson, Thomas Tupney, 14
Wilson, W & R, 146
Wilson, William, 147
Winchilsea, Lord, 128
Windmill, The
  Kings Cliffe, 20
  Orton Waterville, 101
  Peterborough, 109
Wold Brewery, The, 90
Wolverhampton Wanderers FC, 51
Wood Brothers, 12
Wood, Hanbury, Rhodes & Jackson, 56
Wooden Walls of England, The, 133
Woodford, John, 90
Woodward, Allen, 13
Woodwards, 118
Woolley, Valentine, 47
Woolpack Inn, The
  Little Weldon, 95
Woolpack, The, 60
  Peterborough, 106
Woolston & Bull, 133
Woolston, Charles Eustace, 24
Woolston, John, 133
Wootton & Son, 2
Wootton Hall, 49
World Upside Down, The, 28
Wright, Edwin, 90
Wright, John, 13

Y

Yates & Jackson, 1
Yates family, 1
Yorke Charles & Thomas, 93
Youil Brothers, 86, 112
Youil, Edwin, 112

The Authors

Mike Brown

Brian Willmott

After a career in the RAF, Mike now devotes most of his time to researching the brewing industry. Despite some 10 years in the county, his allegiance to Robbie's best bitter and the "County" might give some indication of his roots. His desire to complete a photographic record of brewing sites goes back to having walked past Charlie Creese's brewery to get to school every day. He only found out what the buildings had been after they had been demolished for yet another supermarket.

Brian was born in the pre-expanded Northampton. His early interest in history was encouraged by his parents - for which he is grateful. History, however, did not play any part in his University career. This project started out as an article in a local CAMRA beer guide which he was editing. It developed into a series of articles published in "The Local". Other beer related scribblings have appeared in the local press. He maintains an active interest in real beer which he considers to be a consuming passion. Married with one daughter he still lives in Northampton.

THE BREWERY HISTORY SOCIETY

The Brewery History Society was founded in April 1972 to bring together people with a common interest in the history of brewing, to stimulate research and to encourage the interchange of information. To this end members receive a quarterly Journal - Brewery History - which contains articles about brewers and breweries from as early a date as possible as well as more up-to-date news of mergers, take-overs and new small breweries.

Meetings are held in different parts of the country at which members can get together for a chat and a pint or two and occasional visits to breweries are arranged.

The Society has an Archivist whose responsibility it is to safeguard the books and research material acquired by the Society. He will endeavour to answer specific enquiries from both members and the general public, or will pass them on to the appropriate County Archivist. These are volunteers who take responsibility for correlating research within their own area whilst liaising with the Archivist. A Photographic Collection is maintained to which members are encouraged to donate copies of their own photographs. Copies of photographs in the collection may be purchased. The Society also maintains a Book Shop which holds a large stock of new and second-hand books on beer and brewing.

Upon joining, new members will receive a copy of the Journal, membership card, a list of fellow members and their interests, a copy of the Rules and Constitution and current Book Shop list.

Further details may be obtained from:-
THE MEMBERSHIP SECRETARY
Brewery History Society
Manor Side East
Mill Lane
Byfleet, Weybridge
Surrey KT14 7RS

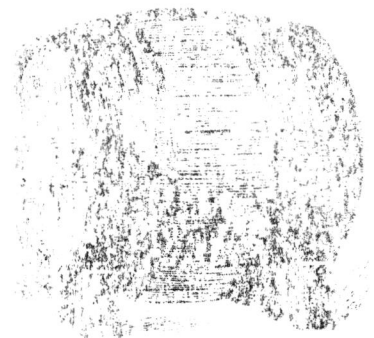

Also published by the Brewery History Society

A CENTURY OF BRITISH BREWERS 1890 to 1990
A directory listing, county by county, compiled by Norman Barber
ISBN 1-873966-04-0 - A4 Paperback

SOUTH YORKSHIRE STINGO
A DIRECTORY OF SOUTH YORKSHIRE BREWERS,
by David Lloyd Parry
ISBN 1-873966-05-9 - A4 Paperback

JUSTLY CELEBRATED ALES
A DIRECTORY OF NORFOLK BREWERS,
by Andrew P Davison
ISBN 1-873966-01-6 - A4 Paperback

WESTERHAM ALES
A BRIEF HISTORY OF THE BLACK EAGLE BREWERY, WESTERHAM,
by Peter Moynihan and K R Goodley
ISBN 1-873966-00-8 - A5 Paperback

For more information on these and other brewing related publications please write to:

The Sales Manager
Brewery History Society,
Long High Top
Heptonstall
Hebden Bridge
West Yorkshire HX7 7PF